ECONOMIC POLICY

for

A FREE SOCIETY

ECONOMIC POLICY
for
A FREE SOCIETY

By

HENRY C. SIMONS

THE UNIVERSITY OF CHICAGO PRESS

CHICAGO & LONDON

THE UNIVERSITY OF CHICAGO PRESS, CHICAGO 60637
The University of Chicago Press, Ltd., London

Copyright 1948 by The University of Chicago. All rights reserved. Published 1948. Seventh Impression 1973. Printed in the United States of America

International Standard Book Number: 0–226–75891–5

Library of Congress Catalog Card Number: 47–7075

Prefatory Note

THE essays included in this volume constitute the major writings of the late Professor Henry C. Simons except for his work on taxation. In this field there are his book on *Personal Income Taxation* and a manuscript on federal tax reform which is to be published during the coming year. A bibliography of his writings will be found on pages 313–16.

Except for "A Political Credo," the essays in this volume have all been published before, mainly in professional journals. Simons' work has not as yet received the attention it merits either in semipopular discussions of public policy or among professional economists. The former is not surprising. Although Simons was passionately interested in practical affairs, he was not a popular writer, believing as he did that short-run issues are resolved almost before they are discussed. He addressed himself to members of the economics profession in the belief that the first task of economists is to arrive at a "consensus of opinion" as the only possible method of influencing both short-run and long-run public policy. The failure of professional economists to appreciate his true worth may in part be due to the fact that he was not a writer of books. It is hoped that this collection of his essays in combination with his work on taxation will facilitate an examination of his work as a whole and contribute to a wider appreciation of his remarkable achievement.

Professor Simons occupied a unique position in American economics. Through his writings and more especially through his teaching at the University of Chicago, he was slowly establishing himself as the head of a "school." Just as Lord Keynes provided a respectable foundation for the adherents of collectivism, so Simons was providing a respectable foundation for the older faith of freedom and equality. The most descriptive title for his work is still that of his best-known essay—*A Positive Program for Laissez Faire*. The last part of this title at once identifies him as a disciple of the great nineteenth-century tradition, while the first part separates him from the horde of reactionaries who mistakenly assume that this tradition is wholly negative. There may once have been substantial merit in the notion that the free-market system would steadily gain in strength if only it were freed of widespread state interference. By 1934 it became evident that a combination of the negative attitude, which permitted the proliferation of monopoly power, and promiscuous political interference, which strengthened such power, threatened "disintegration and collapse" of the economic organization. And only the "wisest measures by the state" could restore and maintain a free-market system.

This essay, which was first published in 1934, is indeed a remarkable performance both for its broad outline of the positive measures required and for its prophetic insight into the shape of things as they were then developing. "The precious measure of political and economic freedom which has been won through centuries may soon be lost irreparably; and it falls properly to economists, as custodians of the great liberal tradition out of which their discipline arose, to point the escape from the chaos of political and economic thought which warns of what impends." With this essay Simons found his work which thereafter consisted of an ever more powerful defense of the direct relationship between the "precious measure of political and economic freedom" and the decentralization of power inherent in a free-market system and an elaboration of the program requisite for survival and proper functioning of such a system.

All of Simons' essays have a single point of departure. They differ only in the emphasis which is placed on one or another feature of the total arrangements he contemplated. It is this emphasis which has been used as the basis of grouping the essays in this volume. The first six essays contain the more general statements of his position; in the next four, the emphasis is on monetary-fiscal and financial arrangements; in the last three, the emphasis is on commercial policy.

In both his critical and his constructive work monetary-fiscal arrangements played a decisive role, and it is in this field that Simons' great originality is most in evidence. His continuous preoccupation with monetary-fiscal policy derives in large measure from the importance he attached to monetary uncertainty as an explanation of variations in aggregate output and employment. Two other circumstances were also important. The failure of the state to discharge its responsibility for regulating the supply of money constituted the outstanding example of the disastrous consequences of the philosophy of negativism we inherited from the nineteenth century. The attempt of the state to discharge its responsibility through discretionary authorities—central banks—constituted the first departure from the basic faith of liberals in the rule of law.

In the work of Henry Simons we find a combination of talents which is rare indeed. He was a first-rate economic theorist, he had an original mind, and he developed a distinguished literary style. He had a high standard of excellence, higher for his own work than for that of others. He was continuously in search of arrangements which would inhibit publication while fostering discussion. He had no illusions about the great obstacles to the re-creation of a free-market society, but he held that it was "immoral" to accept as inevitable what is itself immoral. It was his contention that in a democracy the professional economists must hope that serious discussion will gradually and ultimately enlighten public policy and in the meanwhile will perpetuate the faith in discussion. We have to believe that the additional work which Henry Simons would have accomplished will ultimately be done by others. And yet this is but small comfort for the personal loss of those of us he befriended.   AARON DIRECTOR

Contents

I

*Introduction: A Political Credo**

THE other essays of this volume deal mainly with special problems of economic policy. Inviting readers' attention to such discussion, one may offer at the start a candid statement of the more general or ancillary persuasions which inform that discussion and in awareness of which the reader may, whether with agreement or dissent, best understand it.

A good Introduction would expound a coherent scheme of practical ethics, a political-economic philosophy, or, if you please, a clear-cut ideological position. Limitations of space and of competence, however, permit only rather naked display of fragmentary ideas and opinions. I hope that they are fragments of one intelligible general position and that they do consistently inform or underlie the argument of the other essays.

The underlying position may be characterized as severely libertarian or, in the English-Continental sense, liberal. The intellectual tradition is intended to be that of Adam Smith, Herrmann, Thünen, Mill, Menger, Brentano, Sidgwick, Marshall, Fetter, and Knight, and of Locke, Hume, Bentham, Humboldt, Tocqueville, Burckhardt, Acton, Dicey, Barker, and Hayek.

The distinctive feature of this tradition is emphasis upon liberty as both a requisite and a measure of progress. Its liberty or freedom, of course, comprises or implies justice, equality, and other aspectual qualities of the "good society."

* [This essay was written in the early part of 1945 in an endeavor to formulate specifically the political predispositions implicit in his work. Subsequently the University of Chicago Press suggested the publication of a collection of essays such as is now being made available, and Professor Simons adapted the essay as an Introduction for it.]

Its society, however, is no mere aggregate of reified aspects but a living, functioning organization or "organism"; and its good society is no static conception but is essentially social process whose goodness is progress—and progress not only in terms of prevailing criteria but also in the criteria themselves. Liberalism is thus largely pragmatic as regards the articulation or particularization of its values; but its ethics, if largely pragmatic, also gives special place to liberty (and nearly co-ordinate place to equality) as a "relatively absolute absolute."

Liberalism involves a theory of history or of human progress; and it offers a generalized prescription or working hypothesis for policy—in terms of both what and how. Its claims, however, may well be limited to certain societies or cultures, if not to certain latitudes or climates. It may offer clues to why societies become progressive; but proponents need claim only a limited relevance or applicability. It purports only to tell something of how progress has occurred and of how it may be sustained in advanced nations. How unfree societies may start toward freedom; how the accumulation of knowledge may be made to prevail against the intrenchment of superstition; how economic progress may be made to prevail against inordinate birth rates—these are social problems for which Western liberalism offers no clear or simple answers, only dubious conjectures and earnest hopes. It would serve mankind mainly by sustaining progress in areas already blessed with forward momentum (i.e., in western European civilization and its outposts)—which is perhaps the largest possible contribution to progress elsewhere. Despotisms of superstition may be dissipated by external contacts; despotisms of authorities may be mitigated or disciplined by the slow osmosis of moral-political ideas and standards; and despotisms of hopelessness may be relaxed by adventitious bursts of prosperity which check population increase instead of accelerating it. An optimistic view of our own civilization thus becomes, in long perspective, an optimistic view of the whole world.

THE "INVISIBLE HAND"

Liberalism is an optimistic view of man and society. It surveys recent centuries and calls them mainly good, each better than the one before, each achieving greatly and bequeathing enlarged potentialities. Modern history testifies to the virtues of liberty; it shows man acquiring freedom and, in the process, acquiring ever larger capacity for freedom. Two frightful, global wars may now undermine our faith; but they doubtless loom overlarge to a contemporary view and well may mark the beginnings of modern world organization. They may eventually be viewed as the death struggle of aggressive, self-centered nationalism, whose growth in turn marked the demise of a despotic church and of feudal, aristocratic government.

Liberalism implicitly postulates some "invisible hand"—as does any optimistic view of man's fate or potentialities. Its beneficent force may be identified as social process in a free society. The libertarian policy prescription calls essentially for planning to sustain freedom. It argues that, if advanced nations can remain substantially free, other goods will be added unto them and gradually unto other peoples. It demands that every policy problem be examined as, in part, a problem of sustaining the vital, creative processes of a free society and that all proposals to sacrifice freedom on behalf of other ends (notably, security) be examined under a presumption of error.

POLITICAL VERSUS VOLUNTARY ASSOCIATION

A free society must be organized largely through voluntary associations. Freedom to associate or to dissociate, to belong or not to belong, especially in economic activities, is an essential liberty—and will remain so, short of the millennial "economy of abundance." Man will continue indefinitely to be occupied, even in the richest nations, mainly in "making a living"; and his other liberties are unlikely to be or to remain larger than the liberty he enjoys in such central activity.

Freedom of association, of course, implies also coercive association, that is, strong government and an elaborate, stable, confining structure of law. Liberals exalt the "rule of the law" and hold that, as the antithesis of the rule of men or authority, it is attainable only within an economy of (largely) voluntary association.

Freedom to belong or not to belong also implies multitudes of similar associations among which one may choose and move, as worker, as investor, as customer, etc. Likewise it implies effective freedom to initiate new associations, that is, free enterprise. Economics properly stresses competition among organizations as a means to proper resource allocation and combination and to commutative justice. But effective competition is also requisite to real freedom of association—and to real power dispersion. All monopolies, and all very large organizations of sellers (or buyers), are impairment of that freedom and, unless transitory or unsubstantial, must tend to be governmentalized, not only because they involve exploitation (departure from commutative justice) and diseconomies, but also because adequately strong government cannot tolerate usurpation of its coercive powers.

At the bottom of any structure of voluntary associations, of course, is the family. Perhaps the hardest problems of libertarian policy concern the division of responsibilities between the family and the government. Liberal ideals include equality of opportunity—or steadily diminishing inequality. This and other purposes doubtless require governmental assumption of responsibilities once largely or exclusively those of families, notably as regards the health and education of children, and, also, substantial restriction on family accumulation of wealth. In either case, limitation on the freedom of families is involved; and hard questions arise of how and how rapidly egalitarian measures may be pursued without undermining the structure of voluntary associations at its foundation.

COMMUTATIVE AND DISTRIBUTIVE JUSTICE

The norm in all voluntary economic association is commutative justice. Such justice connotes exchange of equal values, as measured objectively by organized markets. It is an obvious or "natural" basis of co-operation among strangers or persons not members of the same "primary" groups, and especially among communities, enterprises, and nations. It dictates that each shall receive according as he (or it) contributes to organized, co-operative, joint production or, in technical economic language, according to the productivity of his property, capital, or capacity (including personal capacity).

Commutative justice simply takes for granted an existing distribution of capital, among persons, families, communities, regions, and nations. Large-scale organization, and supranational organization especially, must start from a status quo. All participants will, generally speaking, be far better off with co-operative production, division of labor, and exchange. A few, to be sure, may prosper by altering the distribution of existing possessions, that is, by theft, robbery, or war. But every violent or arbitrary redistribution impedes or disrupts the elaborate, co-operative production on which all depend; and no large group anywhere can possibly gain enough from redistributing wealth to compensate for its probable income losses from the consequent disorganization of production. Economic co-operation, like supranational organization, must largely accept possessions as facts.

A free society must be organized, not wholly but basically or primarily, around voluntary, free exchange of goods and services. The alternative is no large organization at all. A little understanding of interregional trade suggests, moreover, that supranational organization is nearly impossible save among areas, communities, or nations in which substantially free exchange prevails.

To stress commutative justice is not to ignore distributive justice, or the real problem of inequality, but merely to urge that two problems be distinguished in analysis, discussion, and action. It is a virtue of a free-exchange society that it invites separation of these problems. But it also involves and permits progressive mitigation of inequality; indeed, it affords the largest possibilities of substantial equality. However, our primary problem is production. The common man or average family has a far greater stake in the size of our aggregate income than in any possible redistribution of income. Large and efficient production requires close approximation to the norm of commutative justice. Achieving or approaching that instrumental end, we may and properly do sharply modify the distributional results of free exchange and, in the long view, may further modify them almost indefinitely. What is important, for libertarians, is that we preserve the basic processes of free exchange and that egalitarian measures be superimposed on those processes, effecting redistribution afterward and not in the immediate course of production and commercial transactions.[1]

Commutative justice assures no one a livelihood. It is almost entirely superseded within families or primary groups and is radically modified in all societies, especially free-exchange societies, by private charity and governmental outlays at the bottom and, notably, by taxation at the top. Even extreme collectivism, by the way, must sharply distinguish, if only for purposes of planning and accounting, between payments for services and mere transfers of income. Moreover, the best mitigation of inequality will involve progressive equalization of personal or family contributions to the social income, not increasing disparity between contributions and receipts. The good society is not one that achieves substantial or increasing equality by extensive redistribution or manipulation of incomes but one that enjoys such equality on the basis of commutative justice. Sound meliorative measures must yield not mere leveling of incomes but leveling accretions of capacity, capital, and possessed power.

Equality of opportunity is an ideal that free societies should constantly pursue, even at much cost in terms of other ends. Freedom without power, like power without freedom, has no substance or meaning. The practical problem of freedom now is one of dispersing or redistributing power among organizations. Inequality, on the other hand, is overwhelmingly a problem of investment in human capacity, that is, in health, education, and skills; it can hardly be scratched by possible re-distributions of wealth.[2]

Freedom and equality convey, among libertarians, similar and complementary meanings. Both imply responsible individuals or families, the rule of law, and great dispersion of power. An equality imposed from above, or by remote authority, is a negation not only of freedom but of equality as well. Progress connotes ever enlarged human capacity for responsible freedom. Such capacity is power; and its future enlargement must mean mass accumulation of the private capital in, mainly, personal capacities. Save as the bride of liberty, equality is pale and deadly dull, if not revolting. But the ultimate liberty obviously is that of men equal in power.

DISCUSSION AND CONSENSUS

An essential ingredient of good social process is organized, free discussion. The virtues of freedom in the pursuit of scientific truth are obvious and undisputed. It is now unthinkable that any question of physics or biology should be answered by appeal to force, to political authority, or to soothsayers or that any scientist should seek to establish a thesis by deliberate fraud. The modern test of truth is simply voluntary rational consensus, and the moral standards of scientific discussion or controversy are a priceless human achievement. These standards tend to elevate all discussion, to discipline all controversy, and to subordinate mere persuasion to co-operative discovery of the best answers, in matters of morals as well as in natural science.

If the social process of free discussion is essential to the progress of scientific knowledge, it is even more obviously essential to moral progress; and, to repeat, truth-seeking is itself a matter of moral standards. The good, progressive moral order must rest on intelligent consensus and on much the same kind of free, critical discussion as is involved in scientific inquiry. A moral order imposed by force or fraud, by authorities, or by threats of punishment in this world or the next is a contradiction in terms. Moral individual conduct is meaningful only within a range of responsible freedom; and social morality is, like truth, a matter of voluntary consensus. The libertarian recognizes no test of moral truth or moral wisdom save such consensus. Society is always right—provided it is the right kind of society. The social processes of a free society are, if not infallible, the only reliable means to moral truth and the best means to security under law.

DEMOCRACY AS GOVERNMENT BY DISCUSSION

Democracy, as viewed by libertarians, is basically a process of government by free, intelligent discussion. It is a means for promoting discussion of obtrusive social problems and for achieving continuous improvement of the moral order through experimental action-out-of-discussion. Such a process implies an elaborate structure of political institutions and conventions, including constitutions, legislatures, executives or ministries, courts, and parties. It implies an inclusive electorate, if not universal adult suffrage, and moral, intelligent electors—although qualitative selection for suffrage, with universal eligibility to qualify, should not be hastily ruled out. It also implies, at best, a continuing process of relevant discussion and inquiry among professional truth-seekers or academic problem-solvers, who, though scrupulously detached from active politics and from factional affiliations, subtly and unobtrusively guide or arbitrate political debate by their own discussions. Effective discussion presupposes an elaborate division of labor—between agitators and dispassionate students, between debaters and inquirers, between specialists and philosophers, between political tacticians and statesmen; and, at the highest levels, it presupposes hierarchies of competence, based on the standards of many intellectual disciplines, with groups shifting from the status of arbiter-authorities to that of laymen as different problems arise for discussion.

The democratic process rests proximately upon representative, deliberative assemblies. It contemplates agitation, discussion of problems, proposals for dealing with them, examination of such proposals, continuous compromise and revision of bills, and eventual enactments of legislation. At best, such final enactments will mainly not involve close votes or sharp dissent; discussion and compromise should usually eventuate in substantial legislative consensus. Occasionally, however, there will be "agreements to disagree" which afford the proper issues at general elections, especially under two-party systems of an organized "government" or ministry and a similarly organized "opposition" or alternative "government."

With good government, the discussion of problems is more important than the action to which it immediately leads. It tends to define areas of large agreement (if only by neglecting or ignoring) as well as of small disagreement and thus to enlarge or to deepen that consensus which is the moral basis of order. All legislative acts are provisional, experimental changes in the moral code, subject to repeal or to progressive modification. They may rest initially on mere majorities and thus remain controversial, in which case compromise will probably continue on the basis of experience until the legislation really becomes law, that is, until dissent from the majority decree is dissipated and mature consensus realized. Acts, like bills, are primarily discussion projects, focusing controversy upon important problems and inducing continuous redefinition or rearticulation of what is beyond serious dispute.

CONTINUITY AS REQUISITE TO DEMOCRATIC PROCESS

Sound democracy must continuously reaffirm faith in its own processes. There must be implicit agreement to preserve the process of action through deliberative discussion and continued compromise. This means agreement to proceed slowly and to avoid radical, irreversible experiments. In this respect, democracy is inherently conservative, as our radicals lament. It can try short cuts but only by abdication, that is, only by imposing discontinuity, which is the negation of its process.

Democracy is properly conservative in guarding liberty and in protecting itself against zealous power-seekers, megalomaniacs, and fools. In highly undemocratic societies revolution may permit movement toward freedom or displacement of worse authorities by better ones. Given a functioning democratic process, however, revolution means abandonment of government by discussion in favor of authorities, claiming a mandate for "temporary" dictatorship. It means grand innovations consolidated without benefit of compromise or of experimental gradualism. No really democratic government of the day, however large its electoral or legislative majority, may grossly impair the prerogatives of future governments; no legislature may closely bind future legislatures to continue particular innovations, to disregard experience, to avoid compromise, or to ignore strong persisting dissent; and no dominant faction may properly act in a way that requires revolution to undo its acts. Given substantial political freedom, there are no worthy institutional changes which preclude gradual, tentative, experimental measures—and, in any case, no "leaders" who may be trusted either to conceive or to execute schemes that involve prompt burning of bridges back. To believe otherwise is to trust grand revelations instead of tedious experiment and to trust men, cults, or mobs instead of society and free societal process.

Radical, imaginative societal constructs, as construct goals of slow, orderly changes, are invaluable for informing discussion of immediate policy problems. Everyone should try to judge particular measures in terms of the kinds of total systems toward which they lead. Radical factional differences in the long-term objectives that inform current proposals may jeopardize democracy. But, adhering to gradualist measures, a nation may sustain large consensus in its step-by-step actions, in spite of sharp ideological controversy; and sharp ideological differences may themselves be effectively compromised and gradually disintrenched in the process. (The conflict between socialists and libertarians, in a good future, will afford a striking case in point.) Democratic action, however, must never defy or impugn dissent; it must not run far ahead of general, fundamental consensus or squander opportunities for reconciling opposition; it must recognize its basic task as ever that of re-creating and enlarging moral consensus among free men.

Strong, organized opposition is of the essence of responsible government—and its most fragile element. It may be lost in the too-strong government of the one-party system or, along with properly strong government, in the multiplication of parties and factions. The golden mean between these evil extremes is again a matter of underlying consensus, between "government" and "opposition" and, in only slightly larger measure, within each organization. In these circumstances agreements to disagree are powerful weapons on both sides; and the pressure for tolerant, salutary compromise is then effective. Elections may then be contested in terms of discrete, discussable issues; debate may be disciplined by intellectual standards; and controversy may involve genuine political education. Factions may contest without seeking or desiring to destroy one another; the "government" and the "opposition" may change places without serious discontinuity and without much shift of power; and the community as voters may be required to answer only questions which men can and must be trusted to answer, namely, along what lines particular, tentative, *experimental* changes in laws or institutions shall proceed. Such millennial conditions have never prevailed and doubtless will never be closely approached. But they have in fact always been approached wherever democracy functioned well; they may always be brought nearer by closer observance of the proper rules of democratic process; and continued departure from such conditions can only impair or destroy such freedom as men have won.

LIBERALISM AND FEDERALISM

Traditional liberalism commends constitutional federalism. It calls for a political structure in which organization becomes looser and more flexible, and functions narrower and more negative, as one moves from local bodies to counties, to provinces or states, to the central, national government, and on to supranational or world government. Its good state is instrumental, subordinate to society, and so constructed as to minimize the dangers of power concentration, that is, the danger that governmental power may be usurped by armies, factions, or majorities and used to dominate society rather than to implement free societal process and social-moral development.

Good political structure should be closely similar to the informal organization or federation of large societies, cultures, or civilizations. The range and kind of governmental activities and legislation at different levels should reflect the different range and kind of consensus, attained or attainable. As one moves from primary groups through small to large communities and on to inclusive society, the range of moral consensus becomes narrower and its content at once more fundamental or abstract and more vague or ambiguous. Government in a free society must, at different levels, adapt itself to the existing hierarchy of moral consensus and try to build, or to facilitate society's building, a strong, bottom-heavy moral structure.

CENTRAL VERSUS LOCAL GOVERNMENTS

Individualism and collectivism are usually discussed largely in terms of political (coercive) versus voluntary (free) association and of governmental-monopolistic versus private-competitive organizations. The range of aggregate governmental activities, however, is hardly more important, as a policy problem, than their distribution between small and large, local and central, governments. Extensive local socialization need not be incompatible with, or very dangerous to, a free society. Local bodies are themselves largely voluntary associations; people have much freedom to choose and to move among them; they are substantially competitive and, even if permitted to do so, rarely could much restrain trade. The libertarian argument against "too much government," consequently, relates mainly to national governments, not to provincial or local units—and to great powers rather than to small nations.

Democratic process is an invention of local bodies. It has been extended upward and may be extended gradually toward world organization. In any case, modern democracy rests upon free, responsible local government and will never be stronger than this foundation. Free, responsible local bodies correspond, in the political system, to free, responsible individuals or families and voluntary associations in the good society. A people wisely conserving its liberties will seek ever to enlarge the range and degree of local freedom and responsibility. In so doing, it may sacrifice possible proximate achievements. Doing specific good things by centralization will always be alluring. It may always seem easier to impose "progress" on localities than to wait for them to effect it for themselves—provided one is not solicitous about the basis or sources of progress. A community imposing good local government from above may seem to get ahead rapidly for a time. Likewise, a community may temporarily raise its economic scale of life by living up its capital. And the analogy seems closely in point. Progress to which local freedom, responsibility, and experimentation have pointed the way may be accelerated for a time and effected more uniformly by the short cut of central action. But such short-cutting tends to impair or to use up the roots of progress in order to obtain a briefly luxuriant bloom.

The inefficiency and corruption of local government are recognized evils—which make us unduly complacent or enthusiastic about centralization. It is generally supposed that almost any function will be more efficiently and more honestly discharged by a larger unit of government. So, we readily accept increase of central responsibility, through supervision or outright transfer of functions or both. As regards corruption, the prevailing view is simply wrong—unless one sticks to a narrow, legalistic definition. Our federal government (I venture) is far more corrupt in its best years than municipal government at its worst, if one judges by the proportion of outlays (activities) which serve the common interest as against the proportion spent in vote-buying, that is, in serving special interests against the common interest. Municipal machines at worst divert a modest tribute; their graft and patronage are small fractions of the value of public services actually rendered. Our national government typically spends freely on behalf of organized, logrolling minorities, tossing in some general welfare outlays for good measure. For decades the subsidies appropriated in the form of protective tariffs probably amounted to more than the total of all other federal outlays, including silver subsidies.[3]

The notion that large governmental units are more efficient than small ones is equally wrong but hard to attack, because efficiency is far more ambiguous or deceptive in meaning than is corruption. Large administrative units may seem more efficient than small ones, if only because they contain so many people employed to increase efficiency rather than to produce substantive services. But administrative efficiency in government, at best, is a false god and a dangerously static good. Large governments, like giant business corporations, may effectively mobilize existing technology, realizing fully its current potentialities. In a shortsighted view they are instruments of progress; but they lack the creative powers of a multiplicity of competitive smaller units. They are, to repeat, at best only means for "forcing" the plant—for enriching the present at the expense of the future. The French genius for *administration* would appear to have been purchased dearly in terms of capacity for *government*. Free government is always worth some cost in terms of "good" or efficient government.[4]

The political agnostic or specialized reformer would transfer control or responsibility upward whenever proximate gains seemed thus attainable. Libertarians would counsel a bolder scheme of improving local government by enlarging local freedom and removing the props of central control—and they would join in recommending central measures for facilitating proper discharge of local responsibilities.

CENTRAL GOVERNMENT FUNCTIONS: WAR

The most obvious central function is that of external defense. In the ultimate federalism this function disappears, and only at or near this limit can libertarian democracy be securely attained. Total war, actual or imminent, demands extreme centralization, that is, a unitary, military, collectivist state which is the antithesis of a free society. It involves moral, economic, and governmental mobilization in which all freedom may be subordinated to one overriding, concrete purpose. And such mobilization is hard to undo after the emergency is past, for it brings its own other "emergencies" and invites retention for all manner of worthy purposes. The emotional experience of war and the impressive achievements of mobilization leave us ill prepared for the prosaic processes of a free society and for renewed faith in any "invisible hand."

Fortunately, however, even the demands of external defense are ambivalent. If wars are frequent, victories will probably accrue to those who remain mobilized. Otherwise, planning for peace may also be the best planning for war. If there are vital, creative forces to be released by demobilization—by return to a free society—the nation may thereby gain enough strength to compensate handsomely for the risks involved. Victories may consistently accrue to those who bet on peace; and progress toward world order may continue secularly in spite of disastrous retrogressions.

This a libertarian must believe, for war is the great threat to his kind of society. There is simply no democratic answer to the problem of external defense, save indefinite extension of federalism, first, into a predominantly powerful supranational federation, and then gradually into inclusive world organization of all nations capable of responsible participation. Here the important next steps must be taken in the field of commercial policies; and the next conspicuous institutional innovation will be an international court with compulsory jurisdiction, albeit only among some Western democracies at the start. Libertarian democracy can survive without world order but not without secular movement toward such order.

OTHER CENTRAL FUNCTIONS

The basic function of central government is to sustain domestic peace. Internal order is prerequisite to external defense and, of course, is the essence of world federation. The good central government will represent a monopoly of violence; it must sustain that monopoly against both its constituent political units and all extra-governmental bodies. It must promote all kinds of peaceful intercourse, intellectual and commercial. It must articulate the prevailing moral consensus and promote enlargement of that consensus by organized, free discussion and legislative-judicial experimentation.

Two more definite central government functions are stressed by libertarians: first, the maintenance of free trade and, second, the provision of a stable currency. The central government, retaining its monopoly of violence, must either itself conduct trade or prevent any other organization from exercising effective control. A federation which is not at least a customs union is hardly a federation. The central government must deny to its constituent units the power to engage in economic warfare among themselves. It must prevent them from arbitrarily restraining commerce or from blocking national economic integration. It must systematically prevent, destroy, or control all artificial private monopoly, that is, all extra-governmental organizations with power to restrain trade. Such organizations are not merely an economic evil; they are also an impairment or usurpation of the state monopoly of coercion and, to repeat, of individual freedom of association.

Stabilization of the currency is a function implicit in federal monopoly of currency issue and in federal fiscal powers. Legal-tender money, stable in value, is almost indispensable to orderly internal commerce and to economic development. Monetary stabilization, moreover, affords an invaluable guide for fiscal policy and a salutary, quasi-constitutional rule limiting the abuse of fiscal powers by particular legislatures or governing factions. Its obvious virtue is that of requiring "governments" to pay for the political blessings of expenditure with appropriately heavy taxation.[5]

SERVICE FUNCTIONS AND THE RULE OF LAW

Beyond these specifications it is difficult to indicate concretely a proper distribution of powers or functions among grades or levels of government. Two general prescriptions, however, may be suggested, although they are largely reducible one to the other.

First, the service functions or community-housekeeping activities of government should be concentrated at the bottom of the scale and not ordinarily or permanently intruded at the upper levels. Larger units may properly do all manner of things to facilitate local discharge of service responsibilities. They may conduct research, formulate standards, publicize relevant information, offer training for local personnel, and even contribute funds, provided that assistance is not (long?) combined with positive, direct control and that local responsibility remains essentially unimpaired. This means, in terms of one obtrusive issue, that all grants of funds from above should be (tend to become) bloc grants and largely unconditional. Grants should involve a minimum of central control and should not (permanently) be made for special purposes. Moreover, all federal grants should be made to and through the states, even when intended for local bodies—and, again, unconditionally.

These prescriptions require, to be sure, some qualifications. Disciplinary action against communities is occasionally admissible, as against criminals or irresponsible persons. But such intervention must be confined to extreme cases of persistent departure from moderate, accepted standards. Moreover, conditional and special-purpose grants, even with substantial control from above, may sometimes be defensible as temporary subsidies to particular local experimentation, provided they are clearly recognized as temporary expedients and as deliberate aberrations from an accepted general policy. The same may perhaps be said, more cautiously, of more extreme measures of centralization.

Second, the older strictures about the rule of law should be interpreted more and more severely as one moves up through the governmental hierarchy. Extensive delegations of power to executive or administrative officers should be largely confined to local bodies. At higher levels such delegations of legislative discretion should be severely economized and, when invoked, should be regarded as a temporary or transitional expedient. National government should be government by law, by legislative rules, and by legislation which follows clear, announced rules of policy. A national legislature should bind administration by closely confining rules, enforcible by an independent judiciary; and it should, at least as "government" and "opposition," also bind itself by confining rules of policy (platforms) which preclude sheer opportunism or tactical nose-following.

This prescription largely repeats the first prescription about service functions but is perhaps more fundamental. Local government, as a service-rendering agency, must be largely a government of men. Legislation and administration are almost indistinguishable; and responsible administration, closely confined by legislative rules, is unthinkable in education, health, police, fire protection, and other local utilities. Local government is largely a collection of business or service enterprises that must be run as such. The proper function of state, and especially federal, governments, on the other hand, is largely not that of providing services but that of providing the framework within which business, local-public and private, may effectively be conducted. This framework may, of course, include a vast amount of services, provided they are not final services but services rendered primarily to enterprises.

THE RULE OF LAW AND GOVERNMENT BY DISCUSSION

If such prescriptions are followed, government by discussion and consensus is facilitated and strengthened thereby. At higher levels, and especially at the highest level, political discussion should be focused on clear-cut, general rules of law and policy. It is such discussion that feeds the growth and diffusion of the basic moral consensus. Only from slow action out of such discussion may a nation build solidly and progressively the principles and working rules which afford political security and economic stability. Only by adherence to the rule of law and to announced rules of policy may a people have strong government without granting inordinate, arbitrary power to ruling parties, factions, or majorities of the moment. Only thus may it assure the use of governmental power in the common interest or avoid the degradation of government by logrolling, patronage-seeking, special-interest groups. Only thus may freedom be protected against large-government power and, to repeat, large-scale discussion focused on questions that can be fruitfully discussed or usefully settled by discussion.

The alternative is "plebicitary democracy," the antithesis of libertarian government. Elections then merely choose among leaders or factions. Campaigns are mere contests for power—slogan-mongering, promising everything to all minorities save the scapegoats, absurd eulogies and vilifications. Platforms are unprincipled in themselves and binding, if at all, only during the campaign. Parties are simply organizations for promising and dispensing patronage, standing for nothing but unlimited prerogative of tactical opportunism, either as "government" or as "opposition" (if any). Such, at all events, is the meaning of government by men as the antithesis of government by law and policy rules.

These prescriptions in terms of service functions (concentrated at the bottom) and the rule of law (severely adhered to at the top) are, like federalism itself, designed to assure minimal dispersion or decentralization of power. Executive-administrative discretion in large governments is an ominous thing—as is *ad hoc* legislation on behalf of particular areas, industries, producers, or pressure groups. Constitutional rules, enforced by courts, are one means for limiting the exercise of power implicit in central government. But constitutional provisions are no stronger than the moral consensus that they articulate. At best, they can only check abuse of power until moral pressure is mobilized; and their check must become ineffective if often overtly used.

Protective tariffs and silver subsidies are instructive cases in point. They fall outside any seriously discussable rule of policy. If any party proposed to subsidize uniformly all domestic production, all domestic enterprises, it would only expose itself to ridicule. If anyone undertook to formulate rules which are or should be implicit in a system of highly differential subsidies, that is, rules determining how the differentials are or should be fixed, he would soon abandon the undertaking. Here, then, are dispensations which follow no rule or principle whatever and, consequently, can continuously be manipulated as patronage or vote-buying and fixed by the procedures of log-rolling. Moreover, since there is no rule of policy, there is no issue to discuss or to debate usefully and no possibility of intelligent electoral decision or significant consensus. Campaign discussion, like legislation, stresses the special interests of each community or producer group; and the basic policy problem is obfuscated and ignored. The virtue of bad rules as against no rules, by the way, is evident in the case of agricultural subsidies. The "parity principle," if not very confining, is amenable to discussion—which leaves farm subsidies in a much weaker political position than the analogous worse subsidies of our tariff. The parity principle is inherently ridiculous; people can see what it would mean if generalized, that is, applied to all commodities; but protective tariffs are strongly intrenched simply because they involve no principle whatever and admit of discussion not as a policy but only as an unintelligible mass of expedients.[6]

FEDERALISM AND INTERNATIONAL ORGANIZATION

A great virtue of extreme federalism or decentralization in great nations is that it facilitates their extension toward world organization or their easy absorption into still larger federations. If central governments were, as they should be, largely repositories of unexercised powers, held simply to prevent their exercise by constituent units or extra-governmental organizations, then supranational organization would be easy if not almost gratuitous. Indeed, such great-nation decentralization or deorganization is both end and means of international organization.

War is a collectivizing process, and large-scale collectivism is inherently warlike. If not militarist by national tradition, highly centralized states must become so, by the very necessities in sustaining at home an inordinate, "unnatural" power concentration, by the threat of their governmental mobilization as felt by other nations, and by their almost inevitable transformation of commercial intercourse into organized economic warfare among great economic-political blocs. There can be no real peace or solid world order in a world of a few great, centralized powers.

To count on early breakup of Russia or the United States is fantastic, desirable as it would be for the world in both cases. But it is not fantastic to contemplate steady decentralization within both these nations. One may be slightly encouraged by several facts. The third world power is, at the top level, almost the ideal federation, so decentralized that the central government can hardly be said to exist. Its major constituent, to be sure, has recently been rushing into extreme centralization; but this Continentalizing of Great Britain may be a passing aberration and might be rapidly undone in an orderly, prosperous world. The Dominions have also been moving the same way; but there would seem to be great obstacles, constitutional and other, to rapid or extreme centralization in Canada or Australia. Second, the tradition or memory of federalism is still honored in the United States, and the substance may still be resurrected. Third, Russia, having fulfilled the great purpose of its new centralization, namely, erasure of disgraceful defeat and destruction of German power, may consolidate its domestic achievements by rapid, orderly decentralization. It has already made grand gestures toward constitutional democracy and democratic federalism. With all skepticism about their immediate significance, one may recognize these formal commitments as evidence of genuine aspirations and of national purposes which, with an orderly world outside, might steadily be realized.

DECENTRALIZATION AND PEACE

Collectivism is a name for an extreme form of governmental centralization or power concentration. To the student of society, it must seem wholly unnatural and utterly unstable. It may serve useful purposes for a time; but it is not itself a viable social or political order. Its order is synthetic and fragile; its order is imposed from above, while real social order is a growth or building-upward. A highly centralized world government is nearly unthinkable—save as a hysterical imputation of evil purpose in an enemy power. It could be the imposition only of a predominant, militarized nation and, in the modern world, would be the most precarious basis of peace—if it is not the antithesis of peace—in any discerning apprehension of meanings.

If order were not merely a quality or aspect of a substantial, functioning society, if it could be reified, synthesized, and poured on the world like manna or DDT, the application would surely induce (mean?) rapid, radical decentralization and deorganization of power among men. Centralization is a product of disorder. In advanced societies it is retrogression, induced by disasters. The obvious case is, of course, war or prospect of war, when everyone naturally looks to the largest available organization and demands mobilized concentration of power—which assures the war if it is still only a fear. But the economic disasters of depression and deflation work the same way. Indeed, it may reasonably be said that economic disaster was the crucial proximate cause of World War II— that it caused a governmental mobilization, or reversal of the gradual demobilization from World War I, and that this in turn precipitated the conflict.

To recognize that an orderly world would be highly decentralized (if only by definition) is to see something of how durable peace may wisely be sought. If we can apprehend fragments or aspects of an organized world, we apprehend something of how the firm substance may gradually be realized.

"POWER ALWAYS CORRUPTS"

Traditional liberalism, to repeat, is an optimistic faith in the potentialities of free men and free societal process. By vulgar repute, however, it is a narrow, negative, and pessimistic doctrine perhaps by association with "the dismal science." The charge of pessimism is valid as regards "Malthusian" societies, notably India. Moreover, all positive or optimistic prescriptions necessarily have their negative corollaries. And one of these, while implicit above, may properly be stressed in passing.

A cardinal tenet of libertarians is that no one may be trusted with much power—no leader, no faction, no party, no "class," no majority, no government, no church, no corporation, no trade association, no labor union, no grange, no professional association, no university, no large organization of any kind. They must forever repeat with Lord Acton: "Power always corrupts"—and not merely those who exercise it but those subject to it and the whole society. The only good power is that of law based on overwhelming voluntary consensus of free men and built and rebuilt by gradual experimentation, organized discussion, and tolerant compromise. They do not deny that concentrated power may occasionally serve human progress as a temporary or transitional expedient. They do deny its uses in advanced nations, save in the gravest military emergencies and then only until the peak of crisis has been passed—and any libertarian who cries wolf easily or frequently is automatically disqualified.

LIBERALISM AND COMMERCIAL POLICY

Liberalism is also notorious for its uncompromising opposition to governmental restraint or manipulation of foreign trade. This "negative" aspect of liberalism, that is, its categorical free-trade prescription, perhaps merits a few remarks in connection with world problems.

The main content of centralization in the modern world has been control of foreign trade. It was this aspect of mercantilism that Adam Smith mainly attacked; and this same aspect of government remains, or has again become, the proper first concern of libertarians. Commercial policy is not only the hard core of bad national centralization; it is also the necessary basis or prerequisite of bad centralization in other manifestations. Bad central planning begins historically in commercial policy and, in all major aspects, involves or requires arbitrary restrictions on foreign trade. Free foreign trade would largely frustrate all major enterprises in economic centralization or in direct federal control of relative prices, wages, or production. To specify that central economic planning or regulation should proceed with a framework of free external trade is to suggest perhaps the most useful distinction between good and bad "planning." To achieve free trade would be to realize, directly and indirectly, most of the decentralization that libertarians propose.

Nationalism, as imposition of internal free trade, is a means to prosperity and peace. As imposed control of trade, external and then internal, it is mobilization for war, which immediately jeopardizes world order and, in the longer view, also undermines the moral basis of internal peace.

The proximate future of libertarian democracy depends crucially on the future of commercial policy, especially in the United States. This country cannot long have free internal trade without free or much freer trade across its borders; and, be that as it may, this country cannot maintain a libertarian political-economic system as an isolated island surrounded by increasingly antithetical systems. On the other hand, its power is adequate to re-establish a libertarian trend among its friends and neighbors; and, so re-established, libertarian democracy may then resume its gradual, peaceful "conquest" of the world.

Recent decades have witnessed a steady resurgence of protectionism, culminating during the great depression in disastrous economic warfare. The subtle, substantial international organization implicit in mutual self-denying ordinances, under the rule of equal treatment or nondiscrimination, was suddenly swept away in an orgy of bilateralism, quota restrictions, clearing agreements, and exchange control. Blame for this disaster may be placed largely on the United States—on its stupid tariff legislation, on its impardonable devaluation, and primarily on its failure, as custodian of the dominant or world currency, to prevent a long and deep deflation. Whosesoever the blame for what is past, this country alone can lead the world back to decent commercial policies.

We may negotiate all manner of nobly vague resolutions and paper organizations of sovereign great powers. Much ultimate good may come from such beginnings. But the substance of supranational order will in the near future be achieved, if at all, largely in the field of commercial relations. Here organization, though subtle and obscure, is a matter of almost continuous, daily national actions; it grows or is cut away with every political decision, legislative and administrative, affecting world trade and finance. Thus commercial policies become more or less discriminatory, more or less restrictive, more or less collectivist, more or less informed by narrow national or bloc interests in relative power; and thus commercial intercourse becomes more or less subject to arbitrary controls, more or less governmental, and less or more free.

Whether such changes cause or reflect changes in the degree

of international organization and stability is mainly a question of intellectual fashions among contemplators of "first causes" —a question of what abstractions or aspectual qualities are commonly hypostatized, of whether one set of "causes" is prevailingly translated into another or conversely. The prospect is that world commercial, productional, financial organization will mainly lead the way, or manifest the basic direction of change, during the next decade. Major national issues in commercial policy seem certain to obtrude themselves; momentous decisions are likely to be made; and these decisions will either fill or empty the synthetic forms of political structure.

Free trade is an essential feature of stable federation. Real international organization, removing sovereign national prerogatives of trade manipulation, must come slowly out of discussion, experiment, and compromise. The proximate means toward abolition of the prerogatives is gradual abandonment of the practices, under the venturesome leadership of the nation which is at once most influential, best able to risk the venture and likely to gain most by its success.

International organization must be pursued opportunistically on every front which offers opportunity for substantial institutional growth. Beyond the immediate problems of the enemy nations and a political *modus vivendi* lie the persistent problems of economic instability and commercial warfare. Toward progressive mitigation of economic nationalism, blocism, and commercial separatism, America might offer almost irresistible leadership. We should dismantle our tariff. We should assure the world a dollar currency highly stable in purchasing power and enlist co-operation in its stabilization. We should eschew all preferential treatment of our exports in our colonies and dependencies. We should abandon "tied" foreign lending, save possibly as loans are tied to reduction of trade barriers and discrimination in the borrowing nations. Along these lines, we might lead wisely toward an ordered world and toward a Western world economy compatible with libertarian political-economic institutions in the United States.

Such bold investment of our national power offers fabulous returns to us and to the world.

PRIVATE PROPERTY

It seems necessary here to say something about "private property" because of its conspicuous place in ideological controversy. "The institution of property" is a kind of shorthand notation for an infinitely complicated political-economic system and, indeed, for almost any possible alternative system. Meaning both nothing and everything, it naturally is the subject of much loose talk and impassioned rhetoric, among both stupid reactionaries and romantic radicals. To say that liberal democracy rests on private property is almost pure tautology. To discuss policy problems of "property" would be to discuss almost all economic-policy problems of our society. Only a few discursive remarks on the subject are here in order.

Private property in the instruments of production is an institutional device both for dispersing power and for securing effective organization of production. The only simple property system is that of a slave society with a single slaveowner— which, significantly, is the limiting case of despotism and of monopoly. Departure from such a system is a fair measure of human progress. The libertarian good society lies at an opposite extreme, in the maximum dispersion of property compatible with effective production or, as process, in progressive reconciliation of conflicts between equality and efficiency. Such process involves increasing dispersion both of wealth among persons or families and of proximate productional control among enterprises or firms.

Basic to liberty are property rights in labor or personal capacities. The abolitions of slavery and serfdom are the great steps toward freedom—and, by the way, are striking reconciliations of apparent conflict between productional and distributional considerations. Property in one's own services, however, is a secure, substantial right only where there are many possible buyers. It thus implies private property in other resources and freedom of independent sellers of labor to choose and to move among autonomous, independent organizations or firms.[7] It also implies a distinctively modern institutional achievement, namely, the separation or dissociation of the economic and the political—a political order that sustains formal rights and a largely separate economic order that gives them substance. Otherwise, freedom to contract for one's services is merely an anomalous, synthetic, administrative construct, resting on "platforms" or on "administrative law," that is, freedom to contract with a single buyer or to choose among the offers of a single ultimate authority.

It is advisable, for most practical purposes, to avoid or to minimize categorical distinction between "inalienable" or "personal" capital and "external" property—to regard all property rights as integral aspects of personal capacity. Both kinds of property are the result of investment; both are largely inherited and hence are bound up with the family; both are largely acquired by luck; and each is subject to deliberate transfer from parents to children and transmutable into the other for that purpose. There is no obvious tendency, at any particular income level, toward excessive relative investment in either kind of property; and it certainly is doubtful whether any social gain would result if the more fortunate families endowed their children with access to political power instead of with "material" property. It is no accident that income taxes represent the substantial modern institutional achievement among taxes; that property taxes serve a narrow special purpose unrelated to personal inequality; and that inheritance taxes should remain inelegant, inequitable, ineffective, and chock-full of ineradicable anomalies.

A society based on free, responsible individuals or families must involve extensive rights of property. The economic responsibilities of families are an essential price of their freedom and, like the inseparable moral responsibilities, are necessary to moral development. Family property, in the occidental sense of the primary family, moreover, is largely the basis of preventive checks on population and of the effort to increase personal capacity from generation to generation, that is, to raise a few children hopefully and well or to sacrifice numbers to quality in family reproduction.

Private property is practically indispensable, if only as an administrative device, in modern large-scale organization of production. This organization is national and supranational; it requires wide delegation or dispersion of managerial control, and freedom and opportunity responsibly to initiate new undertaking. Responsible control of managerial units or firms implies property against which responsibility may be enforced; and responsibility for costs implies rights to revenues, especially if there is to be venturesome enterprise and progress.

LIBERTARIAN SOCIALISM

Modern socialism has been deeply sobered by the first meager efforts to become something more than a negative, revolutionary movement. Its intellectuals have finally begun to face the task of drafting positive proposals and an intelligible platform for action beyond the revolution. Their positive prescriptions are usefully and paradoxically epitomized in the name "decentralized socialism."

A revolutionary movement is naturally sobered by the possibility of acquiring power without revolution. Socialists have largely ceased to be revolutionary, and socialism has thus almost ceased to be a distinctive ideology. In a world obviously plagued by excessive nationalism, it must speak cautiously about the extreme nationalism of its own centralization, about the military implications of its governmental mobilization, and especially about its implications for international commercial policy. It is senseless to talk about world socialism and almost senseless to talk about order among national state socialisms. Socialists are thus in an awful dilemma, being deeply internationalist in sentiment and irredeemably nationalist in their economic program—just as they must be at once syndicalist in tactics and antisyndicalist in strategy or principle.

Socialism, of necessity, has been deeply corrupted by liberalism and conversely, for they have been contemporaries in a world of free discussion and have been catalyzed by the same evils and guided by much the same aspirations. Indeed, it is now hard to see how socialists and libertarians can long sustain substantial intellectual differences, save by avoiding all discussion.

Modern socialism is avowedly concerned mainly about inequalities of wealth (and power?) and about industrial monopoly—both major concerns of libertarians. Inequality, in the sense of too much at the top, is admittedly a matter of taxation; but taxation presents no issues which need divide socialists from libertarians—if socialist interest in the subject or its problems ever becomes substantial and informed. On monopoly problems there is at least a tactical difference: socialists talk much about enterprise monopolies; libertarians talk much about both enterprise monopolies and labor monopolies. Real difference appears only in the respective policy prescriptions for "basic industries." Socialists would "cure" monopoly problems by extending, consolidating, and "politicalizing" monopolies, that is, by abolishing competition in areas where it is relatively "impure." Libertarians would directly regulate or governmentalize only a small group of intractable "natural monopolies," leaving them largely to local bodies, and then seek, by innumerable policy devices, partly direct but mainly indirect, to render competition more and more effective everywhere else.

When socialists begin to talk about decentralization, however, even this difference promises to become empty and nominal. "Decentralized socialism" has perhaps great merit as vicarious, intellectual experimentation. It may be fruitful of insights to ask what government should do if a basic industry, paralyzed by administrative disorganization, were simply dropped in its lap. The first step, of course, would be to impose organization from above, perhaps by putting the army quartermasters in charge. Vicarious experimentation, intelligently pursued, probably would lead to a financial-administrative organization in which the administrative units, if autonomous enterprises, would be numerous enough to assure effective competition. Properly decentralized in administration, a socialized industry would probably be completely ripe for alienation; indeed, alienation would be necessary to implement the administrative decentralization. Wise central control would surely come to rely more and more on competition among numerous, similar administrative units, if only to set standards. The administrative devices necessary to sustain such competition would probably transform the central authority gradually from a proprietor to a bondholder or prior claimant. At this stage the public administrative units would become private enterprises, but with the worst possible financial structures. The next obvious step would be to liquidate the government's fixed claims from the proceeds of common-stock issues—and thus to reduce the government debt.

"Decentralized socialism" may thus be regarded as a very roundabout kind of antitrust policy—and as a stimulating approach to both economic and political theory. As social experimentation, however, it is not likely to be well conducted unless it is purely vicarious. Socialist rules regarding outputs, prices, wages, and marginal cost could hardly be implemented against the inevitable pressure-group demands; no governing faction could be expected to eschew the enormous available patronage; and the desirable administrative decentralization would be blocked by central appetites for power and jobs.[8] At best, however, the experiment would turn out to be not one of abolishing private property but one of contriving new property arrangements. If, out of such vicarious experiment, one is able better to apprehend the good property arrangements, one may attain a sound directional sense for actual experimentation and see more clearly the promising routes from here and now. The more intelligently socialists plan for decentralization, the more does socialism fall into line with an orderly, gradual, libertarian process of dispersing property and of continuous, experimental development in the institution of property itself.

PROGRESS AND SECURITY OF PROPERTY

As in the case of the democratic political process, the importance of continuity in property arrangements can hardly be overstressed. Property must be secure[9] in advanced nations, if production is to sustain living standards and if real social wealth is to be conserved or accumulated. Insecurity of property means diversion of production toward precious metals and jewels, that is, high valuation of assets that permit of concealment and can be securely possessed at the price of serviceless possession. Security of property means production of highly useful things, especially improved instruments of production. In the one case, property means withdrawal of resources from socially useful production and accumulation of assets in socially useless forms; in the other, property releases resources from merely protecting possession and promotes their accumulation in forms which augment both currently useful output and the progressive accumulation of capacity.

Economic progress requires that property be secure. Otherwise, those who hold it—governments, organizations, or individuals—must or will use property (and personal capacity) largely to protect property. Such use may involve either the concealment of oriental hoarding or the gross social abuse of property in rivalrous military organization. A telling objection to collectivism is that it locates property where it is least secure and aggravates total insecurity thereby. Its extreme national centralization, if only by threatening other nations, aggravates world insecurity and, in turn, commends external threats as indispensable to domestic order. An unnatural concentration of property affords, at best, only momentary, relative external security, at the cost of greater insecurity for everyone outside; and its only real protection against either the *coup d'état* or divisive civil war is unremitting fear of external attack.

Security of property, moreover, implies a flexible institution of property and persistent, progressive resolution of problems as they obtrude themselves into the democratic discussion process. Radical movements may impair economic organization and disturb economic processes by their direct threat to security of property; on the other hand, they may mainly serve merely to keep us properly busy with the small, manageable problems which are the grist of the democratic mill. Whether radicalism is excessive or inadequate at any period is not for contemporaries to judge with confidence. Whatever the balance of benefits and costs, however, the main cost now lies in the diversion of intellectual and political talents away from urgent small problems and the dull business of particularist discussion, compromise, legislation, and experimentation. Radicals jeopardize the security of property less by attacking the institution than by neglecting it. There is nothing more insidious than the notion that big, rapid changes are easier or more fruitful than small, slow changes; it leads to talk without action, to action without talk, and perhaps to collapse of democracy under a mass of accumulated, neglected routine business. The way to multiply big problems is to neglect small ones. There is nothing seriously wrong with our institution of property or our institutional system save our proclivity to waste time in attacking or defending it and to neglect proper tasks of changing it continuously by wise collective experimentation.

DEMOCRACY VERSUS SYNDICALISM

Effective competition is indispensable for adequate dispersion of power within industries and functional groups. The antithesis of a competitive economy is not socialism but syndicalism. It is, to repeat, one of the deep anomalies of socialism that its political strength derives mainly from highly syndicalist labor organizations. Syndicalist organization is equally incompatible with democratic socialism and libertarian democracy and, indeed, inherently incompatible with order. It bars both concentration and dispersion of power.

All monopoly or bargaining power implies special privilege to limit production, to restrict entry into industries or occupations, and thereby to levy tribute upon the whole community. As an actual present evil, it involves a concentration of power that has little relation to the concentration of personal wealth.

In one aspect it is a matter of uncontrolled corporate imperialism and giant enterprise aggregations. The profligate dispensation of privileges under incorporation laws may have accelerated the industrialization of America. Existing corporation laws may have been somewhat appropriate to an agricultural nation bent on rapid change. They may, by their extravagances, have accelerated progress. But they are surely ill designed to sustain progress or tolerable operation of the economy they promoted. Turned loose with inordinate powers, corporations have vastly overorganized most industries. Having perhaps benefited briefly by corporate organization, America might now be better off if the corporate form had never been invented or never made available to private enterprise.

A heritage of excessive centralization may be a necessary or reasonable price to pay for rapid maturing of new industries and new technology—and the same may be true of some desirable new governmental functions or services. In any case, America should face now an urgent task of deorganizing industry and deconcentrating industrial control. Some direct dismantling of corporate empires seems indispensable. The main concern of policy, however, should be that of facilitating new enterprise and multiplication of moderate-sized firms. There are grave productional diseconomies in giant enterprises; but these are compensated by larger artificial, private "economies" which wise public policy may and should cut away. Notable are the "economies" of national advertising and vast sales organizations (a problem of consumer education, consumer-goods standards, and technical information), of differential access to technical knowledge[10] (patent-pooling and research), and differential access to new capital funds (inordinate centralization of securities markets). All these merely private advantages of great, monopolistic size present challenges which can be met. Reasonable access to markets, to technology, and to capital funds, on the part of new and moderate-sized firms, would mean an end of serious enterprise monopoly.

Industrial monopolies are not yet a serious evil. Their organization is largely superficial; their powers, with rare exceptions, are very limited and precariously held; they tend to fall apart, though too slowly, in spite of policy. Their menace remains largely potential and complementary. In a community bent on preserving libertarian democracy, enterprise monopolies, standing alone, would be diagnosed as a simple skin disease and easily remedied.

The hard monopoly problem is labor organization. Here are monopolies, actual and imminent, with really great power, economic, political, and military. Once grown large, they cannot easily be taken apart like enterprise aggregations. Like corporations and up to about the same size or scale, unions have real social uses—which may outweigh abuses. But their size potentials and their appetites for power exceed even those of business corporations. Organized like armies rather than like businesses, and encountering no productional diseconomies of size because they produce nothing, they tend to absorb all competitors and to use power zealously and overtly while any eligible workers remain outside. Their size tendencies, moreover, are almost unamenable to the check of law or governmental policy. There would appear to be no stable or attainable happy mean. Strong labor organizations either die aborning or grow into intolerable monopolies. Moreover, labor monopolies and enterprise monopolies are ominously complementary; each tends to foster and to strengthen the other, fighting together to maximize joint exactions from the public while also fighting each other over division of the spoils.[11]

Libertarians can offer no specific for the affliction of labor monopoly. They may propose to deal intelligently with other problems, in the hope that this one may somehow be mitigated or rendered less intractable by progress on other fronts.

An awful question here, as in the case of tariffs and other producer subsidies, is the capacity of democracy to protect the common interest or general welfare against organized minorities. Labor organization presents the hardest of the tests which democracy must meet. It can hardly meet this severest test unless it improves its record in dealing with other minorities as beneficiaries of promiscuous vote-buying and as usurpers of the coercion which all private restraint of trade involves. The old easy tests were matters of obvious corruption—government buying off groups with votes to sell. The hard test ahead involves all this plus a contest for power with organizations whose capacity for violence and coercion rivals that of the state itself. Under modern division of labor, any one of many large organizations of workers can stop or seriously disrupt the whole production process; such coercive power, resting fundamentally on violence, is an abuse (indeed, a negation) of freedom of association, which freedom must be limited by prohibition of monopoly as well as by prohibition of private armies. Here is the perennial problem of pressure groups developing into threat of civil war—the state monopoly of violence so impaired that no remedy compatible with democratic government is readily available.

INEQUALITY AND SYNDICALISM

The modern problem of inequality largely and progressively ceases to be a problem of ordinary property or personal wealth. Already it is overwhelmingly a problem of acquired status within organizations—parties, factions, civil service, giant corporations, labor unions, and farm organizations—and of differential access to high salaries and power. Only deorganization of extra-governmental, functional "states," along with decentralization of government, offers solution for such inequality. Otherwise, our society must offer superlative rewards of power and income to those few whose task it is to hold together organizations that should not exist—and that draw its ablest or most aggressive citizens into essentially antisocial activities. Libertarian society, with its multitude of small organizations, offers a field for millions of leaders and the prospect of moderate power differences among officials within organizations. It places a premium on personal qualities and skills which are, at worst, not grossly unbecoming to men and may properly be cultivated in the good society. It protects men from the corruption of great power by dispersing power, by avoiding large organizations outside government, and by limiting severely the exercise of power by large governmental units. In government the power of men may be limited by constitutional-conventional rules; outside, the power of men within organizations may be limited by keeping organizations loose or small. The best single device, in business organization, is to limit the power of officials by keeping their organizations under the severe discipline of competition. Moreover, wars apart, the need for exercise of central-government power varies progressively with the size and power of extra-governmental organizations. Extreme federalism becomes easiest when there are no strong extra-governmental "states."

PROSPECTIVE CHANGES IN "PROPERTY"

Libertarian policy contemplates a scheme of property law which is both stable and flexible and which, even with prompt excision of archaic elements, becomes more and more complex. There is, and always will be, obvious need for substantial changes. Our progressive personal taxes remain needlessly crude, full of loopholes, and inequitable among persons in similar real circumstances. They can easily be made more equitable, more effective in curtailing inequality of income and opportunity, and at the same time less injurious to desirable incentives. There is need for new arrangements regarding property in fugacious materials, notably oil; for reconsideration of property rights in knowledge, technology, and names; for wise experiments with laws concerning farm tenancy and urban housing; etc.

The time is more than ripe for undoing most of the complexity in property that modern corporations, and finance corporations especially, have imposed. In the good society private property would consist almost exclusively of claims against government (money and consols), unincumbered titles to tangible assets, and homogeneous equities in enterprises— together with the inevitable minimum of accounts in process of (quick) collection and of interpersonal debts. Interest-bearing government debt should be issued, if at all, only in consol form, should rise only during grave war emergencies, and should be retired rapidly thereafter. Net returns from personal wealth normally should accrue only to owners of tangible assets and to pure proprietors, partners, and common shareholders in riskful enterprises.

The problem here, to repeat, is mainly one of corporation finance, of corporate issue powers, and of financial corporations, notably banks. The recent trend in business finance has turned sharply and surely in the right direction and largely in spite of governmental policy. The policy task is thus a fairly simple one, first, of getting out of the way (e.g., by tax reform) and, second, of guiding and accelerating a trend already well established. The goal, while wisely attainable only by gradualist measures, is fairly clear: an economy where the securities of private corporations consist exclusively of common stocks, where financial corporations exist only as pure investment trusts (highly localized as to both portfolios and shareholders), and where only pure investment-trust corporations are permitted to own securities of other corporations.

Libertarian policy also calls for a currency of stable purchasing power, that is, for firm, conventional rules of fiscal policy calculated to prevent aberrations of inflation or deflation. No advanced nation has ever had a good monetary system or the financial structure and institutions necessary to stable employment and orderly economic progress. Only with firm monetary stabilization and minimal monetary uncertainty can the best potentialities of the libertarian political-economic system be released; and, incidentally, stabilization of our currency is perhaps the largest single contribution America can make to the progress of international organization. Here, however, as in the paragraph just above, we touch fiscal problems which are the central subject of other chapters.

II

A Positive Program for Laissez Faire
Some Proposals for a Liberal
*Economic Policy**

THIS is frankly a propagandist tract—a defense of the thesis that traditional liberalism offers, at once, the best escape from the moral confusion of current political and economic thought and the best basis or rationale for a program of economic reconstruction. This view has been widely ridiculed of late, by Communists and Fascists, by most of our "liberal" reformers and politically ambitious intellectuals. Old-fashioned liberals, and the more orthodox economists especially, have responded meagerly to the attack; only their position is inadequately represented in the welter of current controversy. Consequently, one is impelled to try, humbly but uncompromisingly, to state that position and to indicate specifically how economic reconstruction might be achieved along lines dictated by a faith in liberty.

There is in America no important disagreement as to the proper objectives of economic policy—larger real income, greater regularity of production and employment, reduction of inequality, preservation of democratic institutions. The real issues have to do merely with means, not with ends (or intentions); but the future of our civilization hangs in balance as these issues are decided; and those whom the recent crisis has brought to positions of political and intellectual leadership seem to lack insight as to the nature of our economic ills or the effects of their own prescriptions.

* This essay was published as "Public Policy Pamphlet," No. 15, ed. Harry D. Gideonse (Chicago: University of Chicago Press, 1934).

We have witnessed abroad the culmination of movements from constitutional government to dictatorships, from freedom back to authority. This spectacle, for most of us, is revolting; and the experience, something to be avoided at all costs. Yet, faced with the same problems, we adopt measures and accept political slogans which call explicitly for an "American compromise," that is to say, for more authority and less freedom here and now. Thus do we justify and rationalize a policy and accelerating movement in a direction which we overwhelmingly disapprove.

The real enemies of liberty in this country are the naïve advocates of managed economy or national planning; but with them we must agree on one vital point, namely, that there is now imperative need for a sound, positive program of economic legislation. Our economic organization is perilously near to disintegration and collapse. In earlier periods it could be expected to become increasingly strong if only protected from undue political interference. Now, however, it has reached a condition where it can be saved only through adoption of the wisest measures by the state. Modern democracy arose under conditions which made only negligible demands for intelligence in economic legislation; it remains soon to be seen whether democracy can survive when those demands are very great.

It is the main purpose of this tract to criticize current policies, simply by defining the main elements of a vitally different program. Part I undertakes to present the minimum of general analysis or diagnosis which seems essential for exposition of the program and specific proposals presented in Part II.

I

Much significance has been, and should be, attached to the simultaneous development of capitalism and democracy. Indeed, it seems clear that *none of the precious "freedoms" which our generation has inherited can be extended, or even maintained, apart from an essential freedom of enterprise—apart from a genuine "division of labor" between competitive and political controls.* The existence (and preservation) of a competitive situation in private industry makes possible a minimizing of the responsibilities of the sovereign state. It frees the state from the obligation of adjudicating endless, bitter disputes among persons as participants in different industries and among owners of different kinds of productive services. In a word, it makes possible a political policy of laissez faire.

This policy and the correlative political philosophy, nineteenth-century liberalism, have been subjected latterly to gross misrepresentation and to shallow satirical jibes in the "new economics." The representation of laissez faire as a merely do-nothing policy is unfortunate and misleading. It is an obvious responsibility of the state under this policy to maintain the kind of legal and institutional framework within which competition can function effectively as an agency of control. The policy, therefore, should be defined positively, as one under which the state seeks to establish and maintain such conditions that it may avoid the necessity of regulating "the heart of the contract"—that is to say, the necessity of regulating relative prices. Thus, the state is charged, under this "division of labor," with heavy responsibilities and large "control" functions: the maintenance of competitive conditions in industry; the control of the currency (of the quantity and value of the effective money); the definition of the institution of property (especially with reference to fiscal practices)—not to mention the many social welfare activities.

The great errors of economic policy in the past century may be defined—and many of our present difficulties explained—in terms of excessive political interference with relative prices, and in terms of disastrous neglect of the positive responsibilities of government under a free-enterprise system. Our governments have tinkered interminably with relative prices (witness the tariff). On the other hand, they have never really tried to maintain effectively competitive conditions in industry (witness the "rule of reason" and the absurd grants of powers to corporations). They have evaded—when they have not abused —their responsibility of controlling the currency (witness the growth of private banks which provide, and potentially can destroy, all but a small percentage of our total effective circulating media). Moreover, they have scarcely recognized the obligation, or the opportunities, of mitigating inequality through appropriate fiscal practices—that is to say, through appropriate definition of the institution of property. Consequently, the so-called failure of capitalism (of the free-enterprise system, of competition) may reasonably be interpreted as primarily a failure of the political state in the discharge of its minimum responsibilities under capitalism. This view may suggest reasons for skepticism with reference to currently popular schemes for curing our ills.

It seems clear, at all events, that there is an intimate connection between freedom of enterprise and freedom of discussion and that political liberty can survive only within an effectively competitive economic system. Thus, *the great enemy of democracy is monopoly, in all its forms:* gigantic corporations, trade associations and other agencies for price control, trade-unions —or, in general, organization and concentration of power within functional classes. Effectively organized functional groups possess tremendous power for exploiting the community at large and even for sabotaging the system. The existence of competition within such groups, on the other hand, serves to protect the community as a whole and to give an essential flexibility to the economy. The disappearance of competition would almost assure the wrecking of the system in the economic struggle of organized minorities; on the political side, it would present a hopeless dilemma. If the organized economic groups were left to exercise their monopoly powers without political restraint, the result would be a usurpation of sovereignty by these groups—and, perhaps, a domination of the state by them. On the other hand, if the state undertakes to tolerate (instead of destroying) such organizations and to regulate their regulations, it will have assumed tasks and responsibilities incompatible with its enduring in a democratic form.

Thus, for one who prizes political liberty, there can be no sanguine view as to where the proliferation of organization leads. If the state undertakes, under popular government (or perhaps under any other form), to substitute its control for competition in the determination of relative prices and relative wages, the situation must soon become chaotic. Congressional meddling with relative prices through tariff legislation has never hurt us severely, for we have had within our tariff walls an enormous free-trade area. The legislative history of the American tariff, however, does suggest most clearly the probable outcome of an experiment in the political manipulation of the whole structure of internal prices. That our political system could endure either the economic effects of such control or its consequences for political morality is at least highly improbable.

If popular government did for a time achieve that infinitely wise and effective control which would be necessary merely to prevent economic collapse, the system could not survive. Political determination of relative prices, of relative returns from investment in different industries, and of relative wages in different occupations implies settlement by peaceful negotiation of conflicts too bitter and too irreconcilable for deliberate adjudication and compromise. The petty warfare of competition within groups can be kept on such a level that it protects and actually promotes the general welfare. The warfare among organized economic groups, on the other hand, is unlikely to be more controllable or less destructive than warfare among nations. Indeed, democratic governments would have hardly so good a chance of arbitrating these conflicts tolerably as have the League of Nations and the World Court in their field.

Suppression of the competitive struggle within economic groups, and their organization into collective fighting units, will create conditions such that only ruthless dictatorship can maintain the degree of order necessary to survival of the population in an economy of intricate division of labor. Under these circumstances the distribution of power among nations is likely, by the way, to be altered drastically in favor of those people best disciplined to submission and least contaminated with dangerous notions about the rights of man. In the Western world the price of short-run security under such political arrangements is likely to be greater insecurity in the long run; for Western peoples will probably insist on changing dictators occasionally, even at the expense of catastrophic upheavals, disintegration of national units, and progressive political and economic separatism.

It seems nowise fantastic, indeed, to suggest that present developments point toward a historic era which will bear close resemblance at many points to the early Middle Ages. With the disappearance of the vestiges of free trade among nations will come intensification of imperialism and increasingly bitter and irreconcilable conflicts of interest internationally. With the disappearance of free trade within national areas will come endless, destructive conflict among organized economic groups —which should suffice, without assistance from international wars, for the destruction of Western civilization and its institutional heritage.

Thus, the increasing organization of interest groups (monopoly) and the resurgence of mercantilism ("planning")[1] promise an end of elaborate economic organization (of extensive division of labor, nationally and internationally), and an end of political freedom as well. If the situation is not yet hopeless because of the technical difficulties of turning back (and I refuse to believe it is), one finds abundant reason for despair in the fact that our sophisticated generation seems simply not to care. It has become unfashionable to reveal affection for democracy, and the meager curiosity about the future of our institutions leads only to the publication of our cheapest romantic literature in the guise of economics.

Competition and laissez faire have not brought us to heaven. The severe depression, regarded as resulting from competition *instead of from the lack of it,* naturally produces an impairment of our affection for the system. But the widespread disposition to deprecate our institutional heritage seems explicable only in terms of general unwillingness and inability to consider seriously what the actual alternatives are—where new roads lead—or, whatever their destination, how much human suffering must be endured on the way. Few people are now interested in assessing the opportunities for remodeling the old system without destroying its foundations. Worst of all, perhaps, is the popular disposition to accept from zealous "uplifters" devices for salvaging our institutions which are, in fact, the most effective means for undermining them irreparably.

Let us consider now what circumstances are most inimical, within the old system, to production of a large social income (to economic efficiency). The effective functioning of our economic organization requires full utilization of existing resources, including labor, use of the best available technical methods, and, less obviously, economical allocation of resources among available, alternative uses. This latter aspect of the problem may well be emphasized here.

Any judgment of efficiency implies a standard or scale of values—merely physical efficiency is an absurd conception. For economic analysis, such a scale of values is available in the market values (prices) of commodities. These market values, being the result of competitive purchase by persons free to utilize purchasing power as they please, may be accepted as measuring roughly the relative importance (for the community) of physical units of different things. To be sure, these prices are the result of free disposition of purchasing power by individuals of widely different income circumstances. But the problems of efficiency and of inequality may usefully be separated for purposes of discussion—and properly, if one accepts the view that the appropriate measures for improving efficiency and for mitigating inequality are, within fairly wide limits, distinct and independent.

Efficient utilization of resources implies an allocation such that units of every kind of productive service make equally important (valuable) contributions to the social product in all the different uses among which they are transferable. Such allocation will be approximated if, by virtue of highly competitive conditions, resources move freely from less productive (remunerative) to more productive employments. It is an essential object of monopoly, on the other hand, to maintain an area of abnormally high yield (productivity) and to prevent such influx of resources as would bring the monopolized industry down to the common level. Any effectively organized group may be relied upon to use to this end the power which organization brings.

Monopoly thus means the exclusion of available resources for uses which, on the market-value standard, are more important, and, therefore, means diversion of resources to less important uses. Every organized group, whether of employers or of workers, possesses great power, both for exploiting consumers and for injuring other groups of producers to whose industries resources are diverted by virtue of the monopoly restrictions.

Such characterization fits best the case of the strongest and most nearly complete monopolies. For the more typical, partial monopolies (the organization basis for which the National Recovery Act has sought to establish everywhere), the situation is somewhat different and possibly worse from the viewpoint of the community at large. The looser forms of organization for price maintenance and output control (cartels, trade associations), while able to enforce output limitation upon existing firms, are seldom able to restrict the growth of investment (to control the number and size of firms); nor does their position permit them to withhold output quotas from newcomers in the industry. Such arrangements lead to gross wastage of investment as well as to exploitation of consumers. New firms, attracted by the high returns resulting from price maintenance, will construct plants; and they will be drawn into the organization and given their appropriate quotas (presumably on the basis of "capacity"). This means reduction in the quotas of other firms and increasingly meager utilization of plant capacity throughout the industry. Finally, producers within the organization may obtain, in spite of the price maintenance, no higher return on investment than prevails in competitive fields. But consumers will be paying heavily, in higher prices, for the policies of the organization; and the industry will end up with much smaller production, in spite of much larger total investment, than would have obtained under competitive conditions. In technical language equilibrium under the cartel or trade-association form of monopoly means equality between average cost and price, in spite of enormous discrepancy between marginal cost and price. This, in general terms, describes the goal toward which "planners" unwittingly direct us.

The situation is strikingly similar with respect to trade-union monopoly, which usually involves a similarly partial monopoly power. The main device of trade-union strategy is the maintenance of the standard rate of pay, through collective bargaining. The raising of rates of wages in a particular field above the competitive level, by whatever methods of coercion, serves to diminish the volume of employment available within that field—inducing economy of such labor by substitution (of machinery and of other labor) and relative contraction of the industries requiring such labor. If the organization admits newcomers freely and rations employment, the occupation may continue to grow in numbers, or fail to decline, in spite of decline in the total amount of employment available—the increased rate of pay more than offsetting, for a time, the reduction in employment available per man. As with the trade association, numbers may increase until the members are no better off than they would have been without any organization at all.

Yet product prices in the industries concerned will be higher; and a large part of the community's labor resources will be wasted—a situation which roughly describes, except for the denouement, recent conditions in coal-mining in the Midwest. If the union can prevent entrance into the trade, if the older members are given full employment before newcomers are employed at all, or if the demand for this kind of labor is highly elastic, the effects of the wage control in this particular field will manifest themselves largely in diversion of labor into less important *and less remunerative* occupations. In any case, the diseconomies for the community are sufficiently evident.

The gains from monopoly organization in general are likely, of course, to accrue predominantly to the strong and to be derived at the expense of the weak. Among producers, organization is least expensive and most easily achieved, as well as most effective, within groups whose members are unusually large and prosperous at the outset. Among workers, the bias is not less striking. The most highly skilled and most highly remunerated trades are the trades where organization is least difficult and where the fighting strength of groups once organized is greatest. Little evidence, inductive or analytic, can be conjured up to support the popular conception of trade-unionism as a device for raising incomes at the bottom of the scale. Its possibilities lie mainly in the improvement of the position of labor's aristocracy[2]—and largely at the expense of labor generally. Here as elsewhere the gains from monopoly are exploitative. The restriction of employment in the more remunerative occupations injures other laborers, both as consumers and as sellers of services rendered more abundant in other areas by the restriction.

Another major factor in the inefficient allocation of resources is to be found in government regulation and interference. Tariff legislation is again the main case in point, for the protective tariff is essentially a device for forcing resources from uses of higher to uses of lower productivity. Moreover, there are good reasons for believing that political controls will generally work out in this way. Government interference with relative prices is in the nature of arbitration of conflicts of interest between minority producer groups and consumers (the whole community); and such interference inevitably involves decisions which have regard primarily for the interests of the minorities. Producers are, from a political point of view, organized, articulate groups; and it is in the nature of the political process to conciliate such groups. Anyone may detect the notorious economic fallacies, and thus see the dictates of sound policy, if he will look at every issue from the viewpoint of consumers; but no politician can be expected to do this, or to act on his conclusions if he does, except in a world where legislators are motivated primarily by the desire to be retired at the next election. People as consumers are unorganized and inarticulate, and, representing merely the interests of the community as a whole, they always will be. This fact, perhaps, suggests the decisive argument for laissez faire and against "planning" of the now popular sort.

While the tariff is the example par excellence of how the political process works in the control of relative prices, our experience with regulation of the so-called "natural monopolies" is also instructive. With the railroads, the abuse of private monopoly power led finally to real control over the prices of services. We have developed in the Interstate Commerce Commission an unusually competent and scrupulous public body. Even here, however, the preposterous system of relative charges (freight classification), and the disastrous rigidity of freight rates during the depression, testify eloquently to the shortcomings of the regulation expedient; the intrenched position of the railway brotherhoods indicates clearly how governments reconcile the interests of small, organized groups and those of the community at large. In the field of local utilities a half-century of effort at regulation yields up a heritage of results, a cursory inspection of which should suffice to dampen anyone's enthusiasm for a system of private monopoly with superimposed government regulation.

Public regulation of private monopoly would seem to be, at best, an anomalous arrangement, tolerable only as a temporary expedient. Halfhearted, sporadic, principle-less regulation is a misfortune for all concerned; and systematic regulation, on the basis of any definite and adequate principle, would leave private ownership almost without a significant function or responsibility to discharge. Analysis of the problem, and examination of experience to date, would seem to indicate the wisdom of abandoning the existing scheme of things with respect to the railroads and utilities, rather than of extending the system to include other industries as well. Political control of utility charges is imperative, to be sure, for competition simply cannot function effectively as an agency of control. We may endure regulation for a time, on the dubious assumption that governments are more nearly competent to regulate than to operate. *In general, however, the state should face the necessity of actually taking over, owning, and managing directly, both the railroads and the utilities, and all other industries in which it is impossible to maintain effectively competitive conditions.* For industries other than the utilities, there still remains a real alternative to socialization, namely, the establishment and preservation of competition as the regulative agency.

Turning now to questions of justice, of equitable distribution, we may suggest that equitable distribution is at least as important with respect to power as with reference to economic goods or income; also, that the cause of justice, perhaps in both directions, would be better served if well-intentioned reformers would reflect seriously on what their schemes imply with respect to the distribution of power. Surely there is something unlovely, to modern as against medieval minds, about marked inequality of either kind. A substantial measure of inequality may be unavoidable or essential for motivation; but it should be recognized as evil and tolerated only so far as the dictates of expediency are clear.

If we dislike extreme inequality of power, it is appropriate to view with especial misgivings the extension of political (and monopoly) control over relative prices and incomes. Either socialization or the mongrel system of "national planning" implies and requires extreme concentration of political power, under essentially undemocratic institutions. A system of democratic socialism is admittedly an attractive ideal; but, for the significant future, such a system is merely a romantic dream. On the other hand, it seems unlikely that any planners or controllers, with the peculiar talents requisite for obtaining dictatorial power, would be able to make decisions wise enough to keep an elaborate economic organization from falling apart. Even if one regards that prospect as not unpromising, the implied division of power between controllers and controllees would seem an intolerable price for increased efficiency.

An important factor in existing inequality, both of income and of power, is the gigantic corporation. We may recognize, in the almost unlimited grants of powers to corporate bodies, one of the greatest sins of governments against the free-enterprise system. There is simply no excuse, except with respect to a narrow and specialized class of enterprises, for allowing corporations to hold stock in other corporations—and no reasonable excuse (the utilities apart) for hundred-million-dollar corporations, no matter what form their property may take. Even if the much-advertised economies of gigantic financial combinations were real, sound policy would wisely sacrifice these economies to preservation of more economic freedom and equality.

Another cardinal sin of government against the free-enterprise system is manifest in the kind of institution of property which the state has inflicted upon that system. It has lain within the powers of the political state, in defining rights of property and inheritance, to prevent the extreme inequality which now obtains; and the appropriate changes might still be effected without seriously impairing the efficiency of the system. In a practical sense, there is not much now wrong with the institution of property except our arrangements with respect to taxation. Instead of collecting their required revenues in such manner as to diminish the concentration of wealth and income, governments have relied on the whole upon systems of levies which actually aggravated inequality. Until recently (and the situation is not strikingly different now) governments have financed their activities largely by conglomerations of miscellaneous exactions which have drawn funds predominantly from the bottom of the income scale. Modern fiscal arrangements, like those of medieval barons, must be explained largely in terms of efforts to grab funds wherever they could be reached with least difficulty—to levy upon trade wherever tribute could most easily be exacted—and with almost no regard for consequences in terms of either economic efficiency or personal justice.[3]

The problem of stabilization, of maintaining reasonably full employment of resources, calls for emphasis mainly upon two factors, one of which again is monopoly. If all prices moved up and down with substantial uniformity, changes in the general level of prices would have only unimportant effects upon the volume of production or employment. A major factor in the cycle phenomenon is the quite unequal flexibility of different sets of prices and, more explicitly, the stickiness of prices which, for the bulk of industry, determine out-of-pocket operating (marginal) costs. This stickiness of prices reflects, first, competition-restraining organization and, second, a widespread disposition to sacrifice volume to price—which is the characteristic exercise of monopoly power. Decisively important in the total situation is the exceeding inflexibility of wages—the explanation of which would require attention to many factors, of which effective labor organization is but one. To some extent it reflects merely a subtle sort of defensive cooperation among workers to protect themselves in a market which is often only nominally competitive on the employers' side. To some extent it involves employer deference to an attitude of the public, which condemns wage-cutting and yet accepts wholesale discharge of employees as unavoidable and unreprehensible. More interesting than the stickiness of wages, if not more important, is the price policy in depression of those basic industries which have long since disciplined themselves along lines now widely approved, against "unfair"(!) competition. Equally significant, or more so, is the depression behavior of railroad rates and the charges in other public utilities subject to government regulation, especially freight rates. At all events, the existence of extreme inflexibility in large areas of the price structure is one of the primary factors in the phenomenon of severe depression. This inflexibility increases the economic loss and human misery accompanying a given deflation, and it causes deflation itself to proceed much farther than it otherwise would.

The major responsibility for the severity of industrial fluctuations, however, falls directly upon the state. Tolerable functioning of a free-enterprise system presupposes effective performance of a fundamental function of government, namely, regulation of the circulating medium (money). We should characterize as insane a governmental policy of alternately expanding rapidly and contracting precipitously the quantity of paper currency in circulation—as a malevolent dictator easily could do, first issuing currency to cover fiscal deficits, and then retiring currency from surplus revenues. Yet that is essentially the kind of monetary policy which actually obtains, by virtue of usurpation by private institutions (deposit banks) of the basic state function of providing the medium of circulation (and of private "cash" reserves). It is no exaggeration to say that the major proximate factor in the present crisis is commercial banking. This is not to say that private bankers are to blame for our plight; they have only played the game (and not so unfairly, on the whole) under the preposterous rules laid down by governments—rules which mean evasion or repudiation by governments of one of their crucial responsibilities. Everywhere one hears assertions of the failure of competitive controls, of the chaos of unplanned economy, when the chaos arises from reliance by the state upon competitive controls in a field (currency) where they cannot possibly work. Laissez faire, to repeat, implies a division of tasks between competitive and political controls; and the failure of the system, if it has failed, is properly to be regarded as a result of failure of the state, especially with respect to money, to do its part.

We have reached a situation where private-bank credit represents all but a small fraction of our total effective circulating medium. This gives us an economy in which significant disturbances of equilibrium set in motion forces which operate grossly to aggravate, rather than to correct, the initial maladjustments. When for any reason business earnings become abnormally favorable, bank credit expands, driving sensitive product prices farther out of line with sticky, insensitive costs; earnings become more favorable; credit expands farther and more rapidly; and so on and on, until costs finally do catch up, or until some speculative flurry happens to reverse the initial maladjustment. When earnings prospects are unpromising, credit contracts and earnings become still smaller and more unpromising. In an economy where costs (especially wages, freight rates, and monopoly prices in basic industries) are extremely inflexible downward, the deflation might continue indefinitely (until everyone was unemployed) if governments did not intervene (inflate) to save the banks or to mitigate human suffering.

Thus, the state has forced the free-enterprise system, almost from the beginning, to live with a monetary system as bad as could well be devised. If, as seems possible, both capitalism and democracy are soon to be swept away forever by a resurgence of mercantilism (by the efforts of persons who know not whither they lead), then to commercial banking will belong the uncertain glory of having precipitated the transition to a new era. Such is likely to be the case, even if our institutions survive this time the attentions of their misguided, if well-meaning, guardians. Capitalism seems to retain remarkable vitality; but it can hardly survive the political rigors of another depression; and banking, with the able assistance of monopoly, seems certain to give us both bigger and better depressions hereafter—unless the state does reassume and discharge with some wisdom its responsibility for controlling the circulating medium.

II

We shall now try to define, for present conditions, the main features of a genuinely liberal program, in the traditional sense of liberalism. Such a program, if it could be realized politically, would suffice to permit tolerable functioning of a free-enterprise system and to prevent (or postpone) revolutionary change in our whole institutional framework. The time has come (some will say it has already passed) for close co-operation between those interested in making capitalism a better system and those of less liberal persuasion who merely dislike revolutions. Consequently, we hope that the proposals described below may receive consideration, both from liberals who are not naïvely romantic and from conservatives who are not stupidly reactionary.

The proposals, of necessity, are rather drastic. A liberal-conservative movement must now resist and overcome long-established, cumulative trends; it must set itself against the forces of history. We are drifting rapidly toward political and economic chaos. Consequently, a political movement which is conservative in its objectives must be radical in terms of its means. Those who hope for dictatorship, whether under proletarian or Fascist symbols, may rather fittingly refer to us as the impractical visionaries. It is they who may now complacently embrace the faith that what is going to be is good, merely because it so obviously is going to be—in spite of us. The cause of economic liberalism and political democracy faces distinctly unfavorable odds and, therefore, requires above all a strategy boldly and intelligently conceived.

The main elements in a sound liberal program may be defined in terms of five proposals or objectives (in a descending scale of relative importance):

I. Elimination of private monopoly in all its forms
   1. Through drastic measures for establishing and maintaining effectively competitive conditions in all industries where competition can function as a regulative agency (as a means for insuring effective utilization of resources and for preventing exploitation), *and*
   2. Through gradual transition to direct government ownership and operation in the case of all industries where competition cannot be made to function effectively as an agency of control

II. Establishment of more definite and adequate "rules of the game" with respect to money, through
   1. Abolition of private deposit banking on the basis of fractional reserves[4]
   2. Establishment of a completely homogeneous, national circulating medium, *and*
   3. Creation of a system under which a federal monetary authority has a direct and inescapable responsibility for controlling (not with broad discretionary powers, but under simple, definite rules laid down in legislation) the quantity (or, through quantity, the value) of effective money

III. Drastic change in our whole tax system, with regard primarily for the effects of taxation upon the distribution of wealth and income

IV. Gradual withdrawal of the enormous differential subsidies implicit in our present tariff system

V. Limitation upon the squandering of our resources in advertising and selling activities

The case for a liberal-conservative policy must stand or fall on the first proposal, abolition of private monopoly; for it is the *sine qua non* of any such policy. Reasonable differences of opinion may appear as to methods; but there can be no intelligent dispute, among liberals and conservatives, as to the objective.

This proposal contemplates deliberate avoidance of the regulation expedient—or, if you please, adherence to the kind of regulation which works only through the preservation of competitive controls. It implies that every industry should be either effectively competitive or socialized and that governments should plan definitely on socialization of the railroads and utilities and of every other industry where competitive conditions cannot be preserved. On the other hand, it should be a main objective of policy to prevent the development, in the case of other industries, of conditions which would necessitate political control of prices, or socialization. It must suffice here merely to sketch some of the requisite measures.

There must be outright dismantling of our gigantic corporations and persistent prosecution of producers who organize, by whatever methods, for price maintenance or output limitation. There must be explicit and unqualified repudiation of the so-called "rule of reason." Legislation must prohibit, and administration effectively prevent, the acquisition by any private firm, or group of firms, of substantial monopoly power, regardless of how reasonably that power may appear to be exercised. The Federal Trade Commission must become perhaps the most powerful of our governmental agencies; and the highest standards must be maintained, both in the appointment of its members and in the recruiting of its large technical staff. In short, restraint of trade must be treated as a major crime and prosecuted unremittingly by a vigilant administrative body.

As a main feature of the program, *there must be a complete "new deal" with respect to the private corporation.* As many writers have pointed out, the corporation is simply running away with our economic (and political) system—by virtue merely of an absurd carelessness and extravagance on the part of the states in granting powers to these legal creatures. The following proposals, while tentative in detail and obviously inadequate in scope, will suggest the kind of reform which seems imperative:

I. Transfer to the federal government of the exclusive power to charter ordinary, private corporations, and subsequent annulment of all charters granted by the states
II. Enactment of federal incorporation laws, including among others the following provisions:
   1. That no corporation which engages in the manufacture or merchan-

dising of commodities or services shall own any securities of any other such corporation

2. Limitation upon the total amount of property which any single corporation may own

   a) A general limitation for all corporations, *and*

   b) A limitation designed to preclude the existence in any industry of a single company large enough to dominate that industry—the principle being stated in legislation, the actual maxima for different industries to be fixed by the Federal Trade Commission[5]

3. That corporations may issue securities only in a small number of simple forms prescribed by law and that no single corporation may employ more than two (or three) of the different forms

4. Incorporation of investment corporations under separate laws, designed to preclude their becoming holding companies or agencies of monopoly control—with limitations on their total property, on percentage holdings or securities of any single operating company, and on total investment in any single industry (again under the immediate control of the Federal Trade Commission)

5. That investment corporations shall hold stock in operating companies without voting rights, and shall be prohibited from exercising influence over such companies with respect to management

6. That no person shall serve as an officer in any two corporations in the same line of business and that no officer of an investment corporation shall serve as an officer of any operating company

7. That corporate earnings shall be taxed to shareholders in such manner as to prevent evasion of personal income tax with respect to undistributed earnings (see below, pp. 66–68)

The corporation is a socially useful device for organizing the ownership and control in operating companies of size sufficient to obtain the real economies of large-scale production under unified management. It should not be made available, however, for financial consolidation of operating enterprises which are (or which, without serious loss of efficiency, might be) essentially independent as to production management. Horizontal combinations should be prohibited, and vertical combinations (integration) should be permitted only so far as clearly compatible with the maintenance of real competition. Few of our gigantic corporations can be defended on the ground that their present size is necessary to reasonably full exploitation of production economies: their existence is to be explained in terms of opportunities for promoter profits, personal ambitions of industrial and financial "Napoleons," and advantages of monopoly power. We should look toward a situation in which the size of ownership units in every industry is limited by the minimum size of operating plant requisite to efficient, but highly specialized, production—and even more narrowly limited, if ever necessary to the maintenance of freedom of enterprise.

Only a special class of investment corporations should be permitted to hold stock in other corporations; and their powers should be circumscribed narrowly, in order to assure that they confine themselves to performing the important and legitimate functions of the investment trust. These corporations should be merely passive investors, protecting their own stockholders by diversification rather than by exercising control over operating companies; and full precautions should be taken against their becoming, in effect, holding companies or devices of producer organization.

All corporations should be held to a Spartan simplicity in their capital structures. There should be the sharpest distinction between owners and creditors; and, where this distinction becomes impaired through financial adversity, reorganization should be compulsory and immediate. It would seem wise, indeed, to require the maintenance of a predominant residual equity and to limit narrowly (say to 20 per cent) the percentage of contractual obligations to total assets.

The establishment and preservation of effective competition throughout the labor market is a difficult and forbidding task. Given real competition among employers, one might wisely advocate application to labor organizations of the general prohibitions upon restraint of trade. If trade-unions could somehow be prevented from indulging in restrictive monopolistic practices, they might become invaluable institutions. They might then assume their proper role as agencies for making labor articulate politically, for preventing arbitrary and oppressive treatment of individual workers, for rendering special services to their members, and for promoting consumer co-operation with respect to both commodities and the various forms of social insurance. Such policy, however, may seem politically fantastic. The community regards unions as representing the interests of labor generally rather than as agencies for exploitation within the ranks of labor. Even the weaker groups who largely bear the brunt of such exploitation co-operate with their organized brethren and applaud their conquests.

The best one may hope, perhaps, is that labor monopolies, if not fostered and supported by the state, will cease to grow and even decline in power. Developments of recent years afford some grounds for this hope. Moreover, if genuinely competitive conditions were established among employers, and if we had an efficient system of public employment exchanges, labor monopoly would probably have to face a more hostile public opinion. Full publicity, through the employment exchanges, as to the numbers of qualified workers unable to obtain employment in various trades would create some pressure, in normal times, against unreasonable wage demands. Greater stabilization of production and employment, under a sound system of money and credit, should eliminate the boom periods in which organization proliferates and also minimize the need for pressure to overcome the lag of wage rates when costs of living are rising.

One scarcely need remark that the establishment of good public employment exchanges is immensely important, on other grounds, for the strengthening and improving of our economic system.

The proposal for abandonment of the regulation expedient in the case of the railroads and utilities requires little comment here. We can worry along with existing arrangements, to be sure, for a considerable time. It seems imperative, however, that we recognize the inherent limitations of these arrangements and plan toward gradual change. Mere recognition of the ultimate difficulties should help to dissuade us from extending needlessly the range of regulation.

Much can be said for early socialization of the railroads, if only for the training of governments in the discharge of such functions, and for the light which experience would throw upon the expediency of extending gradually the scope of public ownership. The feasibility of public ownership and operation of the other utilities will vary from locality to locality, according to the efficiency of public administration and the level of political morality. A good case can be made for extensive experimentation, however, if only because the present system of regulation is failing so completely.

The proposals with reference to banking and currency arise out of the conviction that extreme fluctuations of production and employment may be prevented by rather simple (if drastic) measures with respect to money and credit. The proposals may be defined tentatively in terms of the following measures:

1. Outright federal ownership of the Federal Reserve banks.
2. Annulment of all existing bank charters (as of a date, say, two years in the future), and enactment of new federal legislation providing for complete separation, between different classes of corporations, of the deposit and lending functions of existing deposit banks.
3. Legislation requiring that all institutions which maintain deposit liabilities and/or provide checking facilities (or any substitute therefor) shall maintain reserves of 100 per cent in cash and deposits with the Federal Reserve banks.
4. Provision during the transition period for gradual displacement of private-bank credit as circulating medium by credit of the Federal Reserve banks.

   (This implies enormous increase in the investments and in the demand obligations of the Reserve banks—i.e., long continued open-market purchases which would serve to inject the substitute credit medium and also to facilitate gradual liquidation of the investments of existing deposit banks. At the end of the transition, the Reserve banks should find themselves in possession of investments amounting to a substantial portion of the federal debt—or, perhaps, in possession of the greater part of the debt itself—thus eliminating the burden of the debt, to that extent, without taxation and without inflation.)

5. Displacement by notes and deposits of the Reserve banks of all other forms of currency in circulation, thus giving us a completely homogeneous national circulating medium.

   (This implies permanent retirement of all United States notes ["green-backs"], all silver dollars and silver certificates, all gold coin and gold certificates, and all national bank notes. Subsidiary silver might be re-tained [though it might better be replaced by coins of a cheaper and more durable metal]. Monetary gold would be held exclusively by the Reserve banks, in the form of bars, and utilized only for settlement of international balances.)

6. Prescription in legislation of an explicit, simple rule or principle of mone-tary policy, and establishment of an appointive, administrative body ("National Monetary Authority"), charged with carrying out the pre-scribed rule, and vested with no discretionary powers as regards funda-mental policy.

7. Abolition of reserve requirements against notes and deposits of the Re-serve banks, and broad grants of powers to the "National Monetary Authority" for performance of its strictly administrative function.

   (The foregoing measures contemplate an economy in which the rules of the game as to money are definite, intelligible, and inflexible. They are intended to avoid both the "rulelessness" of the present system and the establishment of any system based on discretionary management. "Managed currency," without fixed rules of management, appeals to me as among the most dangerous forms of "planning." To establish, as part of a free-enterprise economy, a monetary authority with power to alter vitally and arbitrarily the position of parties to financial contracts would seem fantastic.)

There will be wide differences of opinion as to what the specific rule of monetary policy within such a system should be, but this is not the place to discuss the relative merits of different possible rules. Two observations, however, may be submitted dogmatically: (1) that the adoption of one among the several definite and unambiguous rules proposed by com-petent students is more important than the choice among them and (2) that rigid stabilization of exchange rates on other (gold-standard) countries is totally inadequate and undesir-able as a rule of national currency policy. The various rules which merit consideration differ with respect to the amount of change in the quantity of circulating medium proposed. At one extreme is the rule of fixing the quantity (M) or the total turnover (MV); at the other is the rule of stabilizing some index of commodity prices. The former contemplates ultimately a policy of balancing federal expenditures and federal tax revenues; the latter would require continuous financing of expenditures (or retirement of outstanding debt) to some extent by mere issue of currency. It is important to consider how different possible rules would operate, given the basic inflexibilities in the price structure; but it is equally important that the rule be chosen with regard for the political possibilities of securing adherence to it over long periods without substantial modification. (The rule must be such that strong sentiments against "tinkering with the currency" can be regimented around it.)

The proposals with reference to banking contemplate displacement of existing deposit banks by at least two distinct types of institutions. First, there would be deposit banks which, maintaining 100 per cent reserves, simply could not fail, so far as depositors were concerned, and could not create or destroy effective money. These institutions would accept deposits just as warehouses accept goods. Their income would be derived exclusively from service charges—perhaps merely from moderate charges for the transfer of funds by check or draft. Given generous co-operation on the part of the Reserve banks, the deposit banks should be able to offer their facilities at quite reasonable cost to their customers. Incidentally, a good case could be made for extending the facilities of the postal savings system for the provision of something like checking accounts.

A second type of institution, substantially in the form of the investment trust, would perform the lending functions of existing banks. Such companies would obtain funds for lending by sale of their own stock; and their ability to make loans would be limited by the amount of funds so obtained. Various types of agencies, for bringing together would-be borrowers and lenders, would of course appear. In a word, short-term lending would be managed in much the same way as long-term lending; and the creation and destruction of effective circulating medium by private institutions would be impossible.[6]

These banking proposals define means for eliminating the perverse elasticity of credit which obtains under a system of private, commercial banking and for restoring to the central government complete control over the quantity of effective money and its value. The success of such measures, to repeat, requires the adoption of sound rules of monetary and fiscal policy, effective administration under those rules, and a high degree of stability in the rules themselves. But no monetary system, however perfectly conceived and administered, can make a free-enterprise system function effectively in the absence of reasonable flexibility in the price structure—that is, in the absence of effective price competition among enterprisers and among owners of productive services.[7]

Our proposal with reference to taxation is based on the view (1) that reduction of inequality is per se immensely important; (2) that progressive taxation is both an effective means and, within the existing framework of institutions, the only effective means to that end; (3) that, in a world of competitive, invidious consumption, the gains at the bottom of the income scale can be realized without significant loss to persons of large income, so long as their rank in the income scale is unchanged; and (4) that drastic reduction of inequality through taxation is attainable without much loss of efficiency in the system and without much impairing the attractiveness of the economic game.[8]

Taxation must affect the income distribution, whether we will it so or not. Actually, it has operated to increase inequality, except for a slight opposite effect at the upper extremes of the income scale. The proposal here is simply that tax systems be ordered in such a way as to diminish income differences all along the line and that the funds which governments require be obtained through a system of levies which is actually progressive throughout the income scale.

Such a policy requires the establishment of the personal income tax as the predominant element in our whole fiscal system and the rescue of inheritance taxation from its miserable failure. The following measures may be suggested as among the important steps in this direction:

1. Elimination of all exemptions of income by kind, establishment of the tax as a purely personal levy, and clear recognition in the law that the tax is a tax upon persons according to their incomes, not a tax upon income as such.

   a) Abolition of "tax-exempt securities" and inclusion of all interest and salary items in the calculation of taxable income, whether such items are received from governmental bodies or from private persons.

   b) Elimination of all special treatment for "capital gains" (and for "capital losses"), but with introduction of rebates under a simplified averaging system, to avoid undue penalty on persons of widely fluctuating annual incomes.

   (For example, rebates might be made every five years to persons whose actual tax payments had exceeded by more than 5 per cent what their total tax payments would have been if their taxable income each year had been their average income for the period.)[9]

   c) Levy upon estates under the income tax with respect to all "unrealized" appreciation of investment assets—i.e., levy of income tax upon the estate just as though the decedent had sold all his property at the time of his death at the appraised value as of that date.

   (This would eliminate, except for nonrational behavior, the unfortunate, but exaggerated, effects during booms of taxes upon capital gains. There is now a strong incentive for elderly people to hold on to appreciated investments, merely because the appreciation may be realized without becoming subject to taxation as income *as soon as the owner dies*. This is the rational explanation of why stocks remain in big strongboxes during stock-market booms—instead of being peddled out to the lower middle class! By such arrangement, moreover, we might eliminate the worst practical fault of income calculation according to the "realization criterion"—i.e., according to the anomalous, but practically useful, rule that "unrealized income is not income until it is realized through sale.")[10]

   d) Effective provision against evasion of personal income tax by stockholders with respect to the undistributed earnings of corporations.

(The objective here should be that of taxing shareholders in corporations in exactly the same manner as members of partnerships. This is, perhaps, altogether impractical under existing conditions; but, given the "new deal" proposed above with respect to corporation law, it would be feasible.)

  e) Provision for inclusion, in the calculation of taxable personal income, of the net use value of all real estate used by the owner for consumption purposes (residence, etc.).

(The unhappy omission of this item is peculiar to income taxes in America. Such income-in-kind must be accounted for if the income tax is to be equitable among individuals. For the best solution, we might well follow the Australian practice of measuring this item of income by taking a fixed percentage [say 5 per cent] of the capital value of the property. This would eliminate the complications of depreciation and maintenance allowances. It would be an enormous improvement over existing arrangements, even if this item of income were measured merely on the basis of existing local assessments of real property.)

2. Treatment of all inheritances, bequests, and (large) gifts *inter vivos* as personal income of the recipient for the year in which received.

(This, a cardinal feature among these proposals, is conceived as the only practicable method of securing effective application of the principle of inheritance taxation—i.e., for successfully avoiding evasion through distribution of property prior to death. Its adoption should be accompanied by repeal of existing inheritance taxes; a case could be made for retention of moderate estate taxes.)

3. Reservation of estate, inheritance, and personal income taxes for levy exclusively by the federal government, but with provision for generous sharing of revenues with the states.

(One may suggest, tentatively, the return of 50 per cent of the revenues to the states, on the basis of collections—i.e., on the basis of the residence of the individual taxpayers. Herein lies, perhaps, the only real opportunity for eliminating antiquated and regressive elements in our state and local tax systems.)

4. Drastic alteration in the rate structure of the personal income tax, with more rapid progression, and above all with the introduction of really substantial levies upon the so-called middle- and lower-income brackets.

(Something may be said for retaining the present exemptions, but in the "vanishing" form—i.e., with the exemptions expressed in terms of amounts of tax, instead of in terms of amounts of income. A good case can be made for requiring every income receiver to file a return and perhaps to pay a small fee. With present exemptions, we should have an initial rate [normal tax] of at least 20 per cent, and the rates should rise

rapidly to at least the present maximum. Whether the rates should be
higher in the upper brackets than at present is of minor importance from
a revenue point of view. If these heavy levies on middle-class incomes seem
objectionable, one should remember that the alternative is the retention,
as a major element in the system, of the drastically regressive levies on
commodities of wide and general consumption. The really important
question, as I see it, is whether government revenues shall be derived
largely from the middle class or pumped largely out of the bottom of the
income scale by excise levies.)

These proposals look toward arrangements whereby something like 10 per cent of the whole national income would pass,
via personal income taxation, into the hands of government.
They contemplate abolition of all excises on commodities of
wide and general consumption and ultimately of the innumerable miscellaneous levies which have no justification in
terms of broad considerations of policy. Levies like the gasoline taxes might well be retained indefinitely—being eminently
defensible as charges for special services of government to a
class (or to a form of consumption) which does not merit
subsidy. Taxes upon real property also might properly be re-
tained without diminution of long-established rates. These
levies are largely in the nature of fixed charges, representing
an established equity of the state in real property. Such property has long been bought and sold subject to the prospect of
continued taxation; to reduce the levies would involve a large
gift by the community (through increase in capital value) to
persons who happened to be in possession at the time.

On the expenditure side, we may look forward confidently
to continued augmenting of the "free income" of the masses, in
the form of commodities and services made available by government, either without charge or with considerable modification of prevailing price controls. There are remarkable opportunities for extending the range of socialized consumption
(medical services, recreation, education, music, drama, etc.)
and, especially, for extending the range of social welfare activities. The prospects in these directions, however, must remain somewhat unattractive so long as the expenditures in-

volvcd must be covered by the kind of taxes on which we have relied in the past—that is, so long as what the government gives to the masses with one hand is largely taken away with the other.

Opposition to tariffs is, of course, a cardinal element in the liberal creed. Our tariff system is essentially a system of subsidies financed by means of commodity taxes. The precisely equivalent system of explicit subsidies and taxes would surely look like a monstrosity to every reasonable person—with subsidy expenditures exceeding all other federal expenditures and with an enormous burden of highly regressive excise levies. Two arguments especially may be urged against our tariff: (1) if we are to have enormous subsidies, they ought not to be borne by consumers in proportion to their consumption; and (2) there is something absurd about wholesale subsidizing of particular industries by the government. An "equitable" subsidy system, whereby every producer group both shares and contributes uniformly, is, of course, merely ludicrous. Tariff subsidies, to be sure, can never be uniform, being available only to producer groups whose products might otherwise be imported; but that only raises the question of why public subsidies should be confined to such groups (and the question of why the inevitable burdens should be inflicted upon producers for export).

Thus, our tariffs serve both to reduce substantially the total of our real national income and to increase markedly the degree of income inequality. But two other points may be especially emphasized here.

In the first place, drastic tariff reduction is an important and perhaps indispensable element in a program for eliminating private monopoly and restoring reasonable flexibility in the price structure. There are technical difficulties, in the case of some industries, in establishing adequately competitive conditions merely within national boundaries. With a high tariff wall, it might be necessary, in order to assure real competition, to enforce an otherwise undesirable smallness of firms which would be quite unnecessary with freedom of importation. Though we do have strong international cartels, the fact remains that it is much more difficult to enforce price maintenance on an international scale. Moreover, it is difficult to imagine a thoroughgoing political program which undertook to introduce competition and flexibility internally, while freezing the economy against competition from abroad.

The second point has to do with the general argument against public regulation of prices in private industry and its consequences for political morality and the future of democracy. A nation which wishes to preserve democratic institutions cannot afford to allow its legislatures to become engaged on a large scale in the promiscuous distribution of special subsidies and special favors. Once this occurs, there is no protecting the interests of the community at large, and, what is more important, there is no protecting the political institutions themselves. Tariff legislation is politically the first step in the degeneration of popular government into the warfare of each group against all. Its significance for political morality is, moreover, quite patent. Against the tariff, all other forms of "patronage" and "pork-barrel legislation" seem of minor importance.

The way to reduce the tariff is simply to reduce it. There is, to be sure, a decisive case in favor of gradualness. One must recognize legitimate vested interests in even the most objectionable subsidies. An ideal program would call for a continued scaling-down of duties, with the announced objective of getting rid of them all, over, say, a ten-year period.[11] If some reciprocal reductions can be obtained from other nations, well and good. But let us understand that, given an independent national currency administered according to sound rules, the gains to this country from reduction of its tariff are nowise conditional upon reduction of tariff duties abroad.

The fifth proposal must be dealt with briefly here and left somewhat unprecise. It is a commonplace that our vaunted efficiency in production is dissipated extravagantly in the wastes of merchandising. This economic system is one which offers rewards, both to those who direct resources into industries where the indirect pecuniary demand is greatest and to those who divert pecuniary demand to commodities which they happen to be producing. Profits may be obtained either by producing what consumers want or by making consumers want what one is actually producing. The possibility of profitably utilizing resources to manipulate demand is, perhaps, the greatest source of diseconomy under the existing system. If present tendencies continue, we may soon reach a situation where most of our resources are utilized in persuading people to buy one thing rather than another, and only a minor fraction is actually employed in creating things to be bought.

Firms must spend enormous sums on advertising, if only to counteract the expenditures of competitors; and, finally, all of them may end up with about the same volume of business as if none had advertised at all. Moreover, every producer must bribe merchants into pushing his product, by providing fantastic "mark-ups," merely because other producers are doing the same thing. Consumers must be prohibited access to wholesale markets and prices, in order to protect the "racket" of retailers whose co-operation the individual producer requires; and there follows inevitably the absurd proliferation of small retail establishments which spring up to exact on small volumes of trade the large percentage tribute which existing arrangements allow to those who can classify as dealers rather than as consumers. There appears to be no significant limit, along these lines, to the potential accumulation of economic waste; for every producer must at least keep up to the pace which others set.

In these practices of merchandising, moreover, one finds an outstanding incentive to combination and producer organization. Firms acting co-operatively may spare themselves the expense of competitive selling activities; and organization permits of profitable joint enterprise in building up demand for their common product, at the expense of other industries. Thus, organization of competing firms tends to change the form of advertising rather than necessarily to reduce the total of such outlays; selling activities become competitive among industries instead of merely within industries; the battle of advertising becomes a battle between organized groups, instead of between competing producers of similar commodities. While organization has little or nothing to offer by way of merchandising economies for the community, it has much to offer to the individual participants. Besides, advertising intrenches monopoly by setting up a financial barrier to the competition of new and small firms. Consequently, an appropriate remodeling of the system with respect to merchandising would do more than free wasted resources for useful employment; it might remove one of the main factors working to destroy real competition in industry.

The reform of merchandising offers immense economic rewards; but, unlike the other proposals, it is not immediately indispensable for survival of our economic and political system. Moreover, there is prospect of substantial and continued improvement in merchandising, even in the absence of any deliberate political action to that end. The unfortunately wide differentiation between wholesale and retail prices, and the sharp separation between wholesale and retail markets, may be regarded as a vestigial remainder of the mercantilist system (as a colossal system of restraint upon trade) which has only recently begun to be undermined. The growth of mail-order houses and of large-scale retailing through chain stores is salutary and (given not too much foolish legislation) abundantly promising—offering great economies through increase in the size of units and without raising any real problem of monopoly.

Enterprises like Consumers Research, Inc., may represent the beginnings of an almost revolutionary development. We may hope that such undertakings may flourish and that their growth may be promoted through private endowment. (It is hard to imagine a more worthy philanthropy.) Perhaps we shall see the establishment of endowed, nonprofit-making institutions, of unimpeachable disinterestedness, which will offer to manufacturers (freely or with moderate charges) the use of the institutions' certification or recommendation in the labeling of approved products. Ultimately, we may see the labeling and classification of the more staple goods on the basis of Bureau of Standards specifications, so that consumers may know (and insist on knowing) which brands of goods meet requirements for government purchase. Perhaps we may still hope for substantial development of consumer co-operatives, organized for collective research and consumer education.

Early correction of merchandising evils by restrictive legislation is perhaps impossible; and one resents the conviction that many proposed remedies would prove worse than the disease. The strongest case can be made for heavy taxation of advertising, provided rates can be made much higher than revenue considerations would dictate. There are interesting possibilities in progressive taxes on manufacturers and jobbers according to the percentage of selling expenses to total expenses. The important objective, however, is that of breaking down, first, competitive advertising and, second, the artificial separation between wholesale and retail markets. Consumers should be free to purchase commodities either with or without the services offered by existing retail establishments— just as they should be free to purchase milk, at substantially different prices, with or without doorstep delivery.

Little has been said so far about the immediate problems of the depression. Our first and second proposals indicate appropriate methods for preventing the recurrence of extreme depressions. For the moment, however, attention must be focused on the task of escaping from the present affliction of extreme unemployment and underproduction. Unless the immediate crisis can be dealt with, there is no sense in talking about long-run policy.

The depression is essentially a problem (1) of relative inflexibility in those prices which largely determine costs and (2) of contraction in the volume and velocity of effective money. The crucial characteristic of the situation is maladjustment between product prices and operating costs; and, given this condition, there is no necessary limit to the possible deflation and decline of employment. Sound policy will look, first, toward pulling the more sticky prices down and, second, toward pulling the flexible prices up, in order to create favorable prospects with respect to business earnings. Little can be accomplished quickly in the first direction; consequently, main reliance must be placed on "reflationary" government spending.

Inflationary fiscal policy is dangerous, to be sure—but not so dangerous as the alternatives. It should be undertaken with definite preliminary announcement of an objective, stated, perhaps, in terms of *moderate* increase in a specified price index. The program should be planned with an eye to maximum flexibility, for prompt attainment of the price-level objective, and to assure checking of the inflation within the limits designated. Measures of this kind must be undertaken, merely to keep running a system which banking and monopoly have brought to its present plight.

Such a program contemplates bringing the more flexible prices back into line with the prices which prove most resistant to downward change (freight rates, prices of steel rails, electrical equipment, and aluminum, wages in strongly organized trades, etc.), and it looks toward general increase in the volume of production. If the prices which have been most inflexible downward prove highly flexible in an upward direction with inflation, the whole undertaking will fail calamitously. While there may not be much which governments can do to bring the relatively high prices down, it is the supreme folly of a recovery program to facilitate their increase. If the uncompetitive prices are pushed up continually with inflation,[12] the effects of the stimulant will be counteracted, and more and more inflation will become politically inevitable. No diabolical ingenuity could have devised a more effective agency for retarding or preventing recovery (or for leading us away from democracy) than the National Recovery Act and its codes.

It is easy to devise phrases for denouncing the Roosevelt program and the so-called New Deal. On the other hand, one hesitates to condemn, knowing that condemnation will invoke applause from persons whose political philosophy has nothing in common with one's own. Moreover, one hesitates to alienate that now large group of earnest persons with whose general purposes and aspirations one has the deepest sympathy—whatever one may feel about their conception of means to the ends on which it is so easy to agree.

One cannot criticize the policies of the present administration without seeming to approve those of its predecessors. In fact, one must condemn the Democrats mainly for their wholesale extension of the worst policies of the past. The N.R.A. is merely Mr. Hoover's trust policy and wage policy writ large. The agricultural measures and many other planning proposals are the logical counterpart and the natural extensions of Republican protectionism. The gold policy and the silver legislation, like the Federal Reserve System, lead from a bad monetary and banking system only into something worse.

There is little point, however, merely in condemning particular measures and proposals. Real negative criticism must be judged in terms of, and will be significant for, the critic's conception, express or implied, of sound policies. In these pages we have tried to express criticism of current trends in economic policy in terms of definite specifications for a sound liberal program. For those who accept understandingly the position here outlined, it would be gratuitous to point in detail to the dangers of the spuriously liberal proposals which receive the benediction of our political leaders and journalist-economists; and for others, it would be pointless indeed.

The program here outlined should afford adequate outlet for all the enthusiasm and genuine idealism which might now be canalized so effectively. It seems drastic enough to satisfy the most ardent reformers, and it offers abundant opportunity for real economic planning. There is the whole field of transportation and public utilities for the gradual expansion of government enterprise. Competition enforcement and the reform of merchandising call for a generous measure of government control over private business. The designing and building of a mighty engine of income and inheritance taxation is an undertaking big enough and hard enough to occupy the capable people who are really concerned about inequality. There are endless possibilities for increasing and improving the community's "free income" in the form of governmental services, especially through extension of social welfare activities. Finally, and perhaps most difficult of all, is the task of constructing a sound monetary and banking system.

There cannot, of course, be general agreement in detail on the measures here proposed. No reader is likely to find all of them acceptable. (I must confess to serious misgivings myself at many points.) However, it has seemed desirable, if only for conciseness, to define problems in terms of possible solutions and to define the general objectives of a liberal policy in terms of fairly specific measures. We hope that there may be agreement, within a significant group, on these general objectives and that, starting from such agreement, we may be able to formulate specific proposals which are less inadequate and less ambiguous.[13]

This tract is submitted in the hope of promoting a consensus of opinion within a group which might now perform an invaluable service in intellectual leadership. The precious measure of political and economic freedom which has been won through centuries may soon be lost irreparably; and it falls properly to economists, as custodians of the great liberal tradition out of which their discipline arose, to point the escape from the chaos of political and economic thought which warns of what impends.

III

The Requisites of Free Competition*

THE requisites of free competition are the measures and policies necessary to survival of our established economic and political institutions. In putting this construction on the topic assigned to me, I am following not only my own inclinations but also the suggestion of the program committee.

My task is that of restating and presenting for discussion a position which I outlined some time ago in a pamphlet, under the subtitle of *Some Proposals for a Liberal Economic Policy.* Time permits only a sketching of that position and only meager reference to specific proposals. I shall try to define basic objectives; to describe a comprehensive policy; to translate general proposals in terms of proximate objectives and specific measures; and to criticize the current drift of policy and opinion. Attempting all these things, I shall be successful in none of them. But my function is merely that of opening discussion.

The preservation of freedom is, I submit, the most important end of policy and the most promising means to other valid social objectives. Abhorring violence, revolutions, and dictatorship, I believe that we must choose between freer competition and increasing political control and that, for real policy, the choice lies simply between a competitive system and authoritarian collectivism. Compromise schemes, and the so-called American compromise especially, are mirages luring us away from everything we really prize.

There are many routes back to authority. We may abandon economic and political freedom, either deliberately, or merely

* Reprinted by permission from the *American Economic Review, Supplement,* XXVI, No. 1 (March, 1936), 68–76.

by continuing to drift, to temporize, to experiment, without any policy at all. To preserve liberty, however, and, indeed, to protect all those things whose recent accretion defines human progress to modern minds—to this end a positive economic program and a sharp alteration in the long-established course of governmental policies are indispensable. And the insights of old-fashioned economic liberalism point the only possible way.

The more proximate objectives of a traditionally liberal economic policy, under modern conditions, may be defined in terms of the problems: first, of money; second, of monopoly and regulation; and, third, of inequality. These objectives I shall try to describe concretely. The proposals involved are radical, of necessity; a conservative policy now demands radical implementation. What is requisite, however, is not drastic measures but only a radical redirection of policy and the pointing of legislation toward definite long-term objectives. Repudiating gradualism, one repudiates the whole liberal faith. The proposals which follow must therefore be regarded as defining a direction of policy rather than as prescriptions for drastic reform.

I. MONETARY PROPOSALS

A. The establishment of definite, stable, legislative rules of the game as to money or, in other words, the creation of a national monetary system which will minimize monetary uncertainties and provide a definite, secure basis for monetary anticipations.

B. The sharp focusing of responsibility for observance and execution of the monetary rules.

These two proposals may be interpreted to mean, among other things:

1. Repudiation of central banking and, in general, of all schemes involving monetary authorities (dictators) with discretionary, policy-determining powers;

2. Establishment of the monetary rules as a sort of extra-constitutional mandate governing budgetary practices of the central government. (The monetary rules must be implemented through, and in turn must determine, fiscal policy.)

C. Financial reform (banking reform primarily) aiming at sharp differentiation between money and private obligations.

Increasing concentration in the hands of the central government of the power to create money and effective money substitutes. (By "money substitutes" I mean all obligations which are widely acceptable not only for use as circulating media but also for use in cash reserves or hoards.)

This is not the place to defend what some of you regard as a crank scheme of banking reform. A few general remarks must suffice.

We must abandon and avoid a financial system under which funds actually invested in production and trade are, at the same time, legally available to creditors on demand or on short notice. Not only must we prevent the periodic multiplication of money substitutes; we must also face the fact that substantial liquidation of investment is inherently impossible and remodel our permissible financial practices accordingly. Practical solution may be found merely in narrow limitation upon the borrowing powers of private corporations and in withdrawal of the special status which the state, through special charter, regulation, examination, guaranty, and innumerable other measures and policies, has conferred upon the obligations of banks.

A main reason for radical banking reform lies in the prospect that banking, if it persists in its present form, will be nationalized or, at least, subjected to increasing governmental regulation, the result in either case being political control over the direction of investment. If we could separate sharply between the function of issuing money, the function of warehousing and transferring funds, and the function of mobilizing funds for investment, then government control over enterprises performing the latter function (or the last two functions) might easily be confined to the provision of ordinary safeguards against fraud, and the threat of political influence in the allocation of investment funds minimized.

Monetary reform invites emphasis in this discussion, for it is both urgent and especially promising. Given release from a preposterous financial structure, capitalism might endure indefinitely its other afflictions; but, assuming continuance of our financial follies (which, without definitive rules of policy, are inevitable), it becomes academic to consider how the system might be saved.

The immediate necessity is the reduction of monetary uncertainty—the adoption of a generally acceptable rule of policy, through which it may be possible to prevent the chaotic financial boom which credit expansion and dishoarding now imminently threaten. A rule calling for stabilization of some inclusive commodity-price index—and, I should urge, at its present level—offers the only possible escape from present chaos and the only promising basis for a real monetary system in the now significant future. Given such a rule, we might obtain salutary fiscal and central bank action which otherwise will be politically impossible. The long depression has only put us in the mood to draw and quarter anyone who, wisely, would deny us the stimulation of an exciting prosperity. But a rule might save us from ourselves where nothing else will.

Monetary reform can be immensely salutary without being drastic or disturbing, and the political situation is relatively favorable. We have now no monetary system at all and have never had anything that deserved the name. The reactionary position on monetary questions is weak—though weaker intellectually than politically—and our friends on the left, fortunately, have no position at all.

II. MONOPOLY PROPOSALS

A. The deliberate creation and preservation of competitive conditions in all industries where effective price competition is possible.

There must be vigorous and vigilant prosecution of conspiracy in restraint of trade and, above all, thoroughgoing reform in corporation law. The right to charter large corporations must be vested exclusively in the federal government; and the powers conferred on these legal creatures must be carefully and narrowly limited. (From the viewpoint of practical reform, both our monopoly problem and our financial problem have to do largely with abuses of the corporate form, i.e., with the careless, extravagant dispensing of corporate powers.)

Sharp separation must be made between operating companies and investment trusts, with restrictions and prohibitions designed to confine the activities of each class of corporations closely to its own special, separate sphere. Operating companies should be denied the right to own securities of other such companies; and elaborate precautions should be taken both against interlocking control and against practices among the investment trusts which would tempt or permit them to influence the price and output policies of other corporations. Operating companies must be limited in size, under special limitations prescribed for particular industries by the Federal Trade Commission, in accordance with the policy of preserving real competition.

Among persons whom the Administration and the press have recently elevated and transferred to the status of leading economists, such proposals are ridiculed as products of a horse-and-buggy mentality and condemned as calling for sacrifice of the economies of mass production. But no sane advocate is asking for perfect competition, and no critic who is at once fair and competent will picture the policy as requiring drastic change in the organization of production. The requisite changes have to do mainly with ownership units and control devices, not with operation. There would be a breaking-down of enormous integrations into more specialized firms, with ownership separation among phases of production which are now largely separate in place and in management. For horizontal combinations, the policy would require ownership separation among operating units which are now connected by little more than common advertising and selling organizations. The need for organized, jointly financed industrial research can be met by special arrangements. If there are cases where real production economies require units too large for effective competition among them, some sacrifices ought to be made in both directions; indeed, one finds here a reason for proposing the generally objectionable expedient of an administrative authority with some discretionary power.

The other monopoly proposal I will submit in two forms.

B. Increasingly sharp differentiation between industries requiring and enjoying governmental control of prices and all other industries, and the narrowest limitation of the former category.

Avoidance of the regulation expedient, as a permanent solution for the railroads and utilities, and, above all, the utter repudiation of this expedient as a feasible, tenable compromise between socialization and free competition for other industries.

Given current trends of legislation and opinion, this is the important and distinctive article of a liberal creed.

III. PROPOSAL REGARDING INEQUALITY

The reordering of government expenditure (including subsidies, explicit and implicit) and of taxation, deliberately for the purpose of diminishing greatly the prevailing inequalities of wealth, income, and power.

The promising measures to this end would include: adoption of a broader and less casuistic definition of taxable personal income; closing of enormous, obvious loopholes for avoidance of progressive taxes; establishment of a normal tax rate of, say, 20 per cent; sharing of federal revenues from the personal income tax with the states; and abolition of all excises, save the gasoline taxes, from federal and state tax systems.

I should like to discuss the first two suggestions in detail; but I can only append here a few general observations:

1. Along the above lines, current sentimental liberalism finds its only safe and appropriate outlet.
2. The reduction of inequality, as an object of reform, can and must stand on its own feet. As a means for increasing purchasing power, for preventing overproduction, overinvestment, or oversaving—whatever those nice words may mean—it is utterly ludicrous; and to consider it seriously in this light is to reflect innocently and unwittingly on purely monetary problems and to study fantastic implementations for monetary policy.
3. It is urgently necessary for us to quit confusing measures for regulating relative prices and wages with devices for diminishing inequality. One difference between competent economists and charlatans is that, at this

point, the former sometimes discipline their sentimentality with a little reflection on the mechanics of an exchange economy.

To these three main objectives of liberal policy, I will now add two others which, while subsumable under the other three, deserve special attention.

IV. PROPOSAL REGARDING FOREIGN TRADE AND AGRICULTURAL POLICY

Gradual but complete abolition of the gigantic federal subsidies implicit in our tariff structure and rapid termination of subsidies and production control for agriculture.

Tariff reform, as a main step toward liquidation of the growing political interference with relative prices, seems utterly imperative. So long as internal trade was substantially free, tariff legislation might be regarded as a somewhat harmless outlet or catharsis for all the antisocial, pork-barrel, logrolling propensities of our political leaders and representatives. Now, however, if the whole field of internal prices is not to be opened up to orgies of political manipulation and democratic corruption, the practice of special legislation on behalf of particular producer groups must be attacked on the whole front and in its traditional applications especially. The open season on consumers must be abolished; for, if the direction of tariff changes is not reversed, we cannot hope to prevent wholesale extension of tariff politics into interference with internal trade. The N.R.A. is now, I hope, only an unpleasant memory; but we cannot rely upon the Supreme Court as our only protection against the suicidal proclivities of representative government.

With freer foreign trade, the maintenance of effective competition in domestic markets would be much easier and would require much less severe limitation on the size of corporations. Sound monetary reform, moreover, would greatly weaken the familiar apologies for tariff handouts and facilitate tariff reduction—and this is perhaps the place for some further remarks on monetary policy.

The stabilization of a price index at its present level would permit us to maintain indefinitely both free export of gold and the present gold price. Such a combination of arrangements, indeed, would invite deliberate recourse to a continued lowering of our tariff wall as a means for preventing any further accretion of our enormous gold hoard, for trading off the greater part of our monetary gold for something useful or remunerative, for promoting recovery in countries which have some need for gold, and for improving both world trade and the temper of international relations. Such a program would also serve, incidentally, to confine the gains from our recent debasement mainly to producers of our export staples. If, under established monetary rules, further reduction of our tariff eventually becomes incompatible with free export of gold at the prevailing price, tariff reduction should be continued and the gold price and exchange rates allowed to seek their own level.

My fifth and last proposal might be classified as another monopoly proposal; and it obviously exposes me to the charge of defining a policy merely in terms of its ends.

V. PROPOSAL REGARDING MERCHANDISING

Recognition of the enormous waste of resources in advertising and distribution and of the awful bewilderment of consumers as a major problem of public policy.

For discussion of this problem I have neither time nor competence. The main opportunities lie in organized consumer education or, as a poet friend puts it, in the development of protective coloration for the buyer. But one may be hopeful of other changes: the development of consumer cooperation and (more important) of agencies, governmental and private, for informing and advising consumers; the development of standard specifications, standard testing, uniform grades, and accurate and informing labels for consumer goods. There is much that governmental agencies can do, especially by way of facilitation and encouragement, to promote these and other movements toward efficient distribution.

Returning now to the subject of regulation, I must comment very briefly, if only because of the strain involved in obeying the dictates of polite discourse.

In my pamphlet I suggested early transition to government ownership for the railroads and gradual movement in that direction with the other utilities. Candidly, I feel that our situation with respect to these industries will always be un-happy, at best; and I have no genuine enthusiasm for public ownership. My advocacy of the change is motivated primarily as an attack upon the notion, now common in high places, that our arrangements with respect to the railroads provide a simple and admirable model for the control of other indus-tries generally. This is the substance (if any) of recent oratory on the subject of industrial planning and the essential position of the prominent advocates of "bigness controlled." This plausible compromise between competition and collectivism is merely an alluring mirage along a downward course from which there is no returning; and it could be conceived and proposed, out of intelligence and insight, only by an ardent Fascist.

A London economist, criticizing my position, has suggested that complete and unregulated monopoly is preferable to government ownership for the railroads. Waiving quite trivial dispute, I should add "and clearly preferable to regulation for other industries." Unregulated, extra-legal monopolies are tolerable evils; but private monopolies with the blessing of regulation and the support of law are malignant cancers in the system. The conception of regulation as a device for protecting the public against monopoly exploitation is significant, in the real world, mainly as an apology for governmental enforce-ment of minimum prices and wages at levels higher than monopolies could maintain without the support of law. (It may be interesting here to recall that railroad regulation used to be regarded as a means for keeping rates down.)

I am, indeed, not much distressed about private monopoly power. Given sound monetary and banking reform, our institutions could survive, and the system thrive against an enormous amount of private racketeering. Serious exploitation could be prevented merely by suppression of lawless violence and of grossly unfair competition (in the pre-N.R.A. sense of that phrase). Labor organizations, of course, may depopulate and deindustrialize our metropolitan areas and force us to abandon transport over steel rails; and enterprise organizations may impede economic progress. But the ways of competition are devious, and its vengeance—government intervention apart— will generally be adequate and admirable.

The real monopoly problem thus derives from the prospect that the state rarely will permit private monopolies to bear the consequences of their own actions. Monopolists will run to the government for protection against any threat to their unstable equilibrium, just as they always have done in the face of competition from abroad. The government is thus likely to be drawn into the enforcement of fair minimum prices; and, incidentally, among all the vague conceptions of popular, political economics, there is none quite so misleading, treacherous, and subversive to sound policy as the conception of "fair price." Competition, once long suppressed, threatens awful disturbance when it reappears and calls for readjustments which, while clearly required for the general welfare, are too painful for legislatures, with their infinite solicitude for articulate minorities, to endure.

This is the compelling reason for stamping out private monopoly. For every suppression of competition gives rise to an apparent need for regulation; and every venture in regulation creates the necessity of more regulation; and every interference by government on behalf of one group necessitates, in the orderly routine of democratic corruption, additional interference on behalf of others. The outcome along these lines is: an accumulation of governmental regulation which yields, in many industries, all the afflictions of socialization and none of its possible benefits; an enterprise economy paralyzed by political control; the moral disintegration of representative government in the endless contest of innumerable pressure groups for special political favors; and dictatorship. (I omit inflation, calling it a symptom rather than a disease.)

If you can envisage these things only in a distant future, I would remark that the United States is part of a larger world, and I would remind you of the recent silver legislation and, more emphatically, of the Guffey-Snyder Bill, which, incidentally, is the perfect case in point for my whole argument on monopoly and regulation. If such legislation can be pardoned on grounds of apparent expediency, the responsible leaders can vindicate themselves only by testifying to awful moral decay in the system and to awful errors of policy, however remote in origin. And if anyone believes that these beginnings picture unfairly the potentialities of an economy of planning, of organized negotiation, and of regulation, he is not burdened with political insight.

Against all apologies for tariffs and for recent legislation, economists may submit, as generally decisive, the presumption that any price or wage which requires the support of force or law is relatively too high; and others may join us in observing that, in a democracy especially, force and legality must be economized. Thus, the fundamental issue, for liberals, is the same old issue of protection, of governmental intervention on behalf of particular groups and against the community. If we cannot now create and maintain a powerful moral pressure against use of the power of the state on behalf of organized producer minorities, the game of representative government is up. This, I hope, epitomizes and explains the whole position which I have tried to present.

Our monetary problems are conspicuous and intriguing; but here, as with the problems of inequality and merchandising, liberal reform faces no great obstacles. There is here no strongly adverse drift of policy or opinion—only intellectual confusion and hesitation. In opposing political control of relative prices and wages, however, liberalism defines itself and its own and perseveres in its discouraging struggle— against powerful, cumulative historical trends; against the vested interests of innumerable sheltered minorities; against the persuasive sophistries of mercantilism, new and old; and against the efforts of its own misguided friends.

The stakes in this contest are now tremendous. The future of the liberal faith and of the democratic ideal is now in American hands. And, ignoring factors far outside my competence, I submit that the choice we make between freer competition and increasing regulation of prices and wages will largely determine whether we lead Europe out of the valley or follow it down and down.

IV

*For a Free-Market Liberalism**

THURMAN ARNOLD'S *The Bottlenecks of Business*[1] may be the important political tract of its time. Broadly interpreted, it is an earnest plea for restoration of free markets in the United States—for preserving our democratic way of life and preserving free internal trade as the basis of our political liberty. Proximately, it is a plea for larger appropriations to finance enforcement of the Sherman Act and, tacitly, for sparing the act, the Antitrust Division of the Department of Justice, and Mr. Arnold from the assault of collectivists whom the New Deal and the Defense Commission have drawn to Washington from the Left and from the Right. Arnold and his program are threatened with political liquidation; but he seems quite indisposed to accept that fate or to facilitate concealment of issues which his resignation would involve. His recent prosecutions have been planned, publicized, and carried through with consummate political tact. The book is an appeal, vigorously and adroitly presented, for continuance of the program. His liquidation now may not proceed on schedule; and it can hardly be accomplished at all without a clear revelation of issues and policy implications which his superiors would like to avoid. In any case, it may appear later on that Arnold, almost single-handedly, forestalled administrative legitimatizing of arrangements which have been only less open since the *Schechter* decision.[2] Extra-legal approval of "industrial self-government" still has much to commend it to politicians, with its simultaneous appeasement of both busi-

* Reprinted by permission from the *University of Chicago Law Review*, VIII, No. 2 (February, 1941), 202–14.

ness and labor leaders; and the military emergency provides an excuse which is as plausible as it is bad.

The large responsibilities and opportunities of his present position have transformed Arnold into a serious and responsible person. Readers of his earlier books,[3] if they have not followed his recent activities, may well be amazed at the transformation. A rather cynical, sophistical commentator on our political folklore and symbolism now appears as the zealous, skilful advocate of a great cause. Arnold long displayed possibilities as a satirist. But his efforts in that direction were, to some of us, always disappointing and often a bit suspect intellectually. One could seldom discover the truth which guided his sallies at vulgar error and myth; or, if one pieced it together inferentially in separate contexts, it was often as ridiculous as the objects of his ridicule. His was anormative criticism of normative persuasions. Yet, if he never bothered to examine or to reveal his own normative premises, he somehow evaded classification as the mere cynic or smart-aleck whom serious folk might properly ignore—reflecting perhaps only the moral boredom and confusion which was (and is?) public opinion in this apathetic, disillusioned democratic world. Arnold is now neither bored nor confused. Moreover, he has the distinction of being the only highly and strategically placed advocate of the kind of economy within which we might be able to preserve domestically what we propose so zealously to defend against the Axis powers.

There are other recent examples of people adapting their economic and political philosophies to the special tasks which have come their way. Conspicuous among them is Henry Wallace, who, in Washington, has naturally been unable to live comfortably with the free-market liberalism which was once his. So, Mr. Wallace has contrived and exhibited publicly another politico-economic creed which generalizes and thus justifies his agricultural program as permanent national policy. Any literate person may now identify Mr. Wallace as our leading advocate of the totalitarian or pre-totalitarian economy of negotiation among tightly organized, monopolizing functional groups—as the mystical, sentimental, emotional partisan of democracy who zealously upholds it internationally while championing the kind of internal policies which have undermined and destroyed it abroad. If Mr. Wallace has made a virtue of trade restraint, others prominent in the government have provided plausible rationale for the financial policies which are the proper complementary preparation for civil war. These colleagues have sophistically extended the sound case for temporary, emergency reflation and conjured up an argument for increasing the federal debt indefinitely—although Mr. Wallace himself has given this argument perhaps its most elegant and ingenuous statement. Other leaders, feeling called upon to justify promiscuous dispensation of subsidies and monopoly privileges, have favored the reading and listening public with engaging purchasing-power doctrines which reproduce almost literally the pompous nonsense with which Republican orators used to sell industrial tariffs to agricultural voters.

It is proper that responsible officials should thus reveal to the public their persuasions and the intellectual stuff of which they are made. The practice facilitates judgment of how dangerous they are in places of power and, in rare instances, brings to light an individual who can safely be trusted with the power he has and more. Out of the great literary flood which is the public relations activity of our governmental agencies and leaders, comes now at long last a vigorous, skilful, persuasive statement of a policy position consistent with preservation of our political freedom and democratic institutions. Thurman Arnold has discovered, in the free-market idea, something worth believing, something worth fighting for. The idea, of course, is not novel; and it is surprising that, of all the academic people whom this administration has raised to prominence, this lawyer should be the only one to rediscover and invoke it as a guide for policy. If an old idea is the substance of the book, the book, however, is still a very novel

document. Economists will not find here a superlative definition of the idea or of its manifold implications; indeed, they
may hardly recognize the thing in the dress Arnold has given
it; but they will discover what the thing looks like when it is
properly and modestly dressed for presentation to essentially
hostile electorates and legislatures at a particular point in
time.

The inner substance of Arnold's earlier books (if I mistake
not) was discursive dissertation on how to be, if not a dictator,
a successful politician—on how to get things done politically.
Some of us failed to learn much from these books, but not
Arnold. His ideas about strategy and tactics, if less than inspiring in the general, theoretical form of his sociological writing, are impressive and fascinating as he exhibits them in a
practical, concrete application. Having acquired a fundamental persuasion of his own, Arnold has contrived one of the most
skilful and persuasive arguments for free-market liberalism, as
an immediate, practical program, that can be found anywhere. If one looks at the book as a whole, there is enough
truth and wisdom to satisfy rather exacting academic readers;
if one looks at details, there is enough good hokum and engaging half-truth to meet the best current professional standards of good public relations; and, if one seeks to find where
the argument is dangerously exposed to counterattack, the
place is not easy to locate.

Superficially, this book is the most weaseling statement of the
general position that could well be put together. If one adds up
all the concessions Arnold makes to different groups, without
regard for the innocently general statements and the pervasive
overtone of the discussion, one might conclude that there is
nothing left for Arnold to be against but the Sherman Act.
Carrying the ball for free trade, he runs toward and behind his
own goal line whenever he imagines an opponent in the offing;
but he never gets downed behind his goal and somehow keeps
on the offensive throughout. In the end he is headed squarely
in the right direction and, unlike his opponents, exhausted

merely from watching his frightened rushes, is fresh and fit at the end as at the start.

Arnold, in other words, is unlike us quixotic orthodox economists who delight in attacking impregnable positions. This is a political situation dominated by minorities, and especially by minorities with vast stakes in existing restraints upon internal trade. A few of us may rail against them in our quiet, academic isolation; but Arnold is fighting a real political battle and against great odds. He cannot take on all the powerful minorities at once or even annoy one of them without risking his political hide. He can attack only gangsters (defining that category most narrowly) and relatively harmless, weakling monopolists whose unpopularity is notorious and whose monopolizing practices have miraculously escaped the general sanctioning implicit in current policy and opinion. The important thing is to prosecute somebody in the name of the Sherman Act, if only the devil himself. The attack upon restraint of trade must be gotten under way somehow and kept going against something; and Arnold, naturally, is more interested in keeping himself and the idea alive than in charting the ultimate limits of conquest.

It is not disparaging to say that Arnold's interest in existing restraints of trade varies inversely with their importance. He has a fine nose for sacred cows and a healthy respect for them. Such animals abound in the areas he traverses; but he never runs headlong into one and never passes near one without pausing to stroke it affectionately and to feed it something nice. He may let drop some very nasty crack about it while he is soothing some other cow far away; but his deportment in the immediate neighborhood is unfailingly respectful and deferential. The amazing thing is that, with all his deferring, retreating, disclaiming, and apologizing, the author still manages to get somewhere, to advocate something substantial, and to keep his colors waving no matter how often he hauls them down.

What Arnold is doing may be indicated by contrast. If I were writing a tract on his general subject, I should start (and end) by saying that our serious and ominous monopoly problem lies in the labor market and in the power of unions to behave monopolistically. Next, I should maintain that enterprise monopoly is largely and basically a problem of excessive corporate size, of corporate imperialism run mad, of the fantastic, monstrous aggregations of businesses which, like our cancerous metropolises, we mistakenly regard as monuments to our economic efficiency. Next, that we would not need to worry much about collusive pricing by manufacturers if ownership units were large enough only to obtain the economies of large-scale but highly specialized production; but that it is a hopeless task to prevent effective collusion in industries dominated by giant enterprise aggregations with vast concentration of financial power. Next, that a major barrier to really competitive enterprise and efficient service to consumers is to be found in advertising—in national advertising especially, and in sales organizations which cover great national or regional areas. Saying these things (and they all boil down to a size problem, in both labor and industrial organization), I should be telling the truth—and also rendering both myself and the truth a considerable disservice thereby.

Arnold, on the other hand, is prepared to tell, and perhaps to see, only as much of the truth as may safely or helpfully be told right now. He bows deeply before the "right to bargain collectively" and denies any intention of prosecuting unions as monopolizers of their own labor services. He promises, in this area, to observe the limits set by minority as well as majority opinions of the Supreme Court. The Sherman Act, in his view, is not concerned with union activities directed at wages, hours, working conditions, or union recognition, but only with racketeering and with flagrant collusion between unions and employers to fix product prices—that is, with the abuse of unions to police restraint of product trade. While such a program ignores the heart of the problem, it is still full of dynamite and, if pursued, would gravely disturb many organizations and leaders whose public relations have placed them at the opposite end of the scale from gangsters and racketeers. With all his concessions and disclaimers, Arnold still has his teeth in something here. Indeed, he has probably bitten off more than he can chew; but he has taken a position in which even labor is rather estopped from direct attack.

Arnold likewise pays deep respect to the economies of mass production and deplores popular notions of the Sherman Act as an attack upon bigness. He never raises the innocent question of whether production economies ever or frequently require really monopolistic size or have any place in explaining the actual corporate aggregations which are so large a part of our actual monopoly problem. Nor does he suggest distinction between those productional economies of great size which, if real, are socially desirable and the advertising and selling "economies" which, while possibly very real to the enterprise, are disastrous diseconomies and wastes for the community. Mr. Arnold has no designs upon bigness, save as it gets into the wrong hands and becomes patently wicked. Given the political situation and the prevailing popular myths, this again is as it should be—as is Arnold's discreet silence on the relation between advertising and monopoly.

A similar explanation may be offered for Arnold's snide and disparaging remarks about system-builders, about elaborate coherent schemes of reform, and about broad, general doctrines as to governmental policy. As against communists, socialists, and collectivist planners generally, his disparagement is appropriate and consistent. But what about proponents of schemes consistent with Arnold's own proximate program and purposes? What about advocates of the kind of world or institutional structure which is the proper distant goal of his own schemes and which alone gives real meaning and significance to his immediate measures? If, in this connection, Arnold is merely kidding the public, being the deliberate and rather transparent hypocrite, again well and good. It would be folly for Arnold to identify himself with any broad "ism" or to expose more than the surface implications of his own proposals.

It may be profoundly wise for an assistant attorney-general to exhibit himself as a plain, simple, ingenuous soul, suspicious of theories and systems and intent merely on following his nose and enforcing the law as he finds it. Discerning readers will find, however, if Arnold does not, that his book is full of general ideas and theory and, indeed, that these ideas account for its being a good book instead of a bad or inconsequential one. The free-market conception, among ideas which have content and relevance to our problems, is highly general and abstract; and, as a norm for policy, it has innumerable implications which Arnold is not reluctant to expound vaguely or, if the enemy is not too strong, in terms of definite particulars. Moreover, Arnold had many pointed things to say about the relation of trade restraint to fiscal policy and the monetary outlook. If these wise observations are not informed by clearly conceived norms of monetary and budgetary policy, they are simply a fraud.

I trust these remarks will not make Arnold afraid of his shadow or induce schizoid tendencies; but I must say that the difference between system-builders and persons who argue for particular measures in terms of norms of policy as to trade and money is tenuous indeed. One formulates a broad institutional pattern according to his lights and tastes and then appraises particular schemes in terms of whether they lead toward or away from his ideal; the other seemingly gets interested in particular measures and, to support them, constructs the general scheme of things to which they are proximate means. No responsible advocate of traditional economic liberalism, of free markets and stable money, hopes to see the necessary institutional structure built overnight or achieved by revolution. Such a faith commits one absolutely to gradualism and, in the face of strongly adverse trends, to the proximate opportunism which Arnold stresses to a fault.

If I belabor here a simple point, it is because it disturbs me greatly as I try to pass judgment on Arnold and his book. The appeal for an immediate, preliminary program is much stronger by virtue of being not patently doctrinaire—by virtue of the vagueness and flexibility of the norms on which the argument rests. However, I cannot avoid suspicion that Arnold is as much afraid of truth,[4] and of his own moral premises, in the utter privacy of his own thoughts as in the political arena. If so, he may be unworthy of great trust. For the moment, he is a more effective advocate of free-market liberalism because he distrusts big words and grand schemes. We need able people who will do the hard, dull work that can be done in Washington now. However, one must consider the possibility that Arnold, if supported in his present nose-following, may next year be following his nose into other activities which require a different set of normative persuasions and a radically different kind of world as a goal to justify them. Actually, I would trust the fellow; but I wish he would trust himself enough to permit my offering more than intuition as a reason why others should trust him too.

It is significant that Arnold wants no new legislation—even wants not to think about it. Here as elsewhere I have no objection to what he says unless he believes it. It would be unwise to ask help from Congress at this juncture, save for appropriations. Proposing that teeth be put in the Sherman Act, he might awake some morning to find that Congress had repealed it without roll call. While Washington is packed with business and labor leaders, old-fashioned liberals should mention the act only in whispers or obscure euphemisms; and, when others mention it, we should insist, with Arnold, that the act has no teeth save for wicked people and, in an emergency or out, is as flexible as the Constitution itself.

Arnold's tactics are meticulously correct; but are they informed or guided by any strategy? What I make out of Arnold is that monopoly prosecutions should be a kind of perpetual witch-hunt, tormenting and dislodging people who make too much money selling things or spend too much producing them; our antitrust laws should be reinterpreted administratively as simple proscription of unreasonable behavior. In other words, there should be no law at all but merely endless debate between government lawyers and counsel for hapless defendants, each trying to persuade the jury-sitting public that particular conduct lies outside or inside the moral pale as defined by emotive slogans currently in vogue.

Lawyers, with their characteristic distaste for government by law, will doubtless like this phase of Arnold's argument. (Only a crochety economist could sense resemblance between what Arnold is proposing and the more outlandish make-work rules which he and others have observed in, say, the building trades.) If he has his way, trade regulation must become the same wondrous mystery as constitutional law. Indeed, his more dithyrambic remarks about the Sherman Act do not avoid that ponderous ambiguity and impenetrable profundity which distinguish (or raise doubts about) the legalistic mind. The act, it seems, is very definite legislation; it is infinitely flexible; it opposes nothing that is good; it does not necessarily apply to anything in particular; it is a bulwark against private usurpation of power; it is our economic common law. But what is it really? Well—it is what the courts say it is, in cases which attorneys-general bring before the courts to find out what it is. All this, one gathers, is as it should be. Courts are a fine thing, as are attorneys-general and lawyers generally. They can be trusted to work things out. Legislatures and laymen, in such delicate matters, should defer to lawyers. The professional arguers can handle such things better if given free rein and left to themselves.

But I do not like the rule of reason (either Mr. Arnold's or the Court's); I am skeptical about this talk of the Sherman Act as a broad constitutional principle of government; and I am diffident about turning our monopoly problems over to a profession which has demonstrated almost infinite capacity to misunderstand them. We have never had an antimonopoly policy in fact; few lawyers or courts have ever condoned such policy; and the unsubstantial concessions which have been made to advocates of freer markets, in legislation, in court decisions, and in sporadic bursts of innocuous prosecutions, have mainly enabled us to postpone effective action until monopoly conditions have become so consolidated, until interested minorities have become so numerous and powerful, and until the public has become so enamored of other, incompatible causes that effective action seems now nearly impossible.

Mr. Arnold, in his present post, has been on a kind of honeymoon. The National Industrial Recovery Act inaugurated an orgy of price-fixing and invited businessmen to do as patriots what they had been doing before, on a vast scale, to be sure, but furtively and with slightly bad conscience. With the *Schechter* decision, those groups which were not sufficiently organized, disciplined, respectable, and experienced for "industrial self-government" went their way; others were spared the inconvenience of public hearings but evidently saw no need for restraining trade with any great care as to methods or with any real secrecy. Businessmen were justly proud of their collusive schemes and, I am told, explained them carefully to all kinds of people, even to old-fashioned economists—not to mention their careless filing of incriminating documents.

One cannot deny that Arnold has done a magnificent job. The record is impressive, even when one makes every allowance for the favorable circumstances which he faced. On the other hand, one must be careful about extrapolations. Arnold has skimmed off a rich cream of prosecution opportunities; he has lowered some barriers to recovery; and, above all, he has saved the free-market idea from the utter demoralization which must have ensued if open and flagrant restraint of trade had proceeded without check or punishment. If his program of prosecutions serves only to drive collusion underground, into some decent secrecy, that alone will be a precious gain. I think he may be able to do more than that. But I do not think he can make large or permanent contribution to solution of our monopoly problems, either with the procedures he has been using or with any which are available to him under existing legislation. What he offers, unfortunately, is the best that can safely be tried now or in the near future. On the other hand, only a defeatist attitude would counsel our ignoring now the question of what should come next if this succeeds.

Any substantial achievements by way of monopoly reform must start, I submit, by repudiating that timorous squeamishness which is the rule of reason. When lawyers try to draw a line between lawful and unlawful restraint of trade, they invariably end up with something that looks like the silhouette of a roller-coaster. The idea is that of proscribing behavior involving substantial restraint without otherwise inconveniencing anyone or narrowing his freedom. The purpose may be laudable; but the result is that a few people get caught, rather fortuitously, and the growth of monopoly, with perhaps some formal modification, proceeds apace.

I do not maintain that rules of reason can be dispensed with or that broad, general rules of policy are without value (what the courts have left of antitrust legislation is now a precious refuge or anchor in a collectivist storm); rather, that main reliance must be placed on definite, legislative implementation, on unambiguous rules of law; and that such rules, if they prevent much restraint, must also and incidentally keep many people from doing things where substantial restraint is neither intended nor possible. The problem is that of selecting for proscription certain practices and arrangements, highly useful or essential for restraint of competition, which are not essential or highly useful for the conduct of competitive enterprise. More narrowly, it is a problem of depriving corporations of powers and privileges which were unwisely granted, have been patently abused, and are quite unnecessary for effective organization or efficient operation and management. Our whole corporation law, like our patent law, needs complete overhauling.[5]

Mr. Arnold comes disquietingly near to saying that all our industries should be treated as public utilities, and the Anti-trust Division transformed into a super–public utility commission with power not to fix prices (rates) but to harass those who charge unreasonably until they abandon the practice. He will dislike this imputation, of course; but what else is meant when one proposes efficiency of service to consumers as the test of exposure to prosecution? Mr. Arnold has no designs on monopolistic business so long as it charges competitive prices! With his staff following actual prices and computing what the corresponding competitive prices would be(!), Arnold will be crouched ready to pounce upon discrepancies as they appear and to charge the offenders with I do not know what. It is my impression that railroads and public utilities, having enjoyed this kind of attention from considerably more specialized agencies for quite a while, do not present a picture that would encourage general resort to the control arrangements which are unavoidable in these industries. Price-regulation has no real alternative there save the perhaps more dangerous device of governmental ownership. Neither is likely to work very well. If the public utility category were much larger—as good collectivists would like to see it—our politico-economic setup would have collapsed long ago. Outside this category, however, we have the happy choice of preserving effective competition and letting competition fix prices. Presumably this is what Arnold believes in. If so, he ought to concern himself about maintaining effective competition, not about hammering monopoly prices down to competitive levels with grand juries.

As regards labor monopoly, I share Arnold's distaste for new legislation and his penchant for preoccupation with the short view. Until telepathy is disproved, even thinking about it is dangerous; and, from here and now, it is almost impossible to think constructively in any case. We might face and solve the problem of corporate size; we could repair the damage of bad patent laws, implementing monopoly arrangements utterly unrelated to the proper purpose of patents; and we could handle rather easily the problem of trade associations and collective bargaining among manufacturers. But what, I ask could Congress or courts really do, if they tried, to limit the power of national organizations of workers (whether organized on trade or industrial lines)? How shall particular organizations, once strong, be compelled or persuaded to accept their share of new and displaced workers—that is, to accept wage-rate terms that are consistent with free movement into the industry, occupation, or trade? And how can we preserve a workable democratic system without some approach to a free labor market and free occupational migration? I do not know—and I do not blame Arnold for not raising such questions.

The acuteness of our labor problem is suggested by the imminent danger of Arnold's political liquidation. He has done nothing against unions, and will do nothing, that any reasonable person could question. But labor resents what he has done and distrusts him, as it distrusts all free-market ideas. It wants tariffs; it wants complete freedom from the Sherman Act; and, in fact, it wants employers who can fix their selling prices collusively too. American trade and industrial unionism makes sense only for "well-ordered" industries—makes sense only as part of a tight cartelization of industries where it is strong. It wants no competition from abroad and none at home, either in its own markets or in those of its employers. If employers will not or cannot police their product markets against chiselers, unions will undertake that task themselves. Wage-fixing is price-fixing; labor monopoly means product monopoly even if employers compete effectively; and better wage bargains can be obtained from employers who do not compete with one another than from those who do.

On all sides one hears that the way to abundance is for everyone to charge more and sell less—that is, to organize, to restrict production, and to raise prices. Monopoly in agriculture is a vaunted achievement of humanitarian reformers. Monopoly in labor markets is a thing which one can question only on pain of being ostracized as a Tory or Fascist and an enemy of workingmen—even though one posits a maximizing of labor income and a minimizing of inequality as proper goals or tests of policy. Monopoly in product markets, if still condemned because its practitioners are economic royalists, is increasingly commended or condoned as necessary to protection of labor monopoly and to that orderliness and rigidity in particular industries which is the prelude to infinite disorder in our national economy and in our political life.

Into such a world, Thurman Arnold has introduced a skilful and persuasive plea for freer markets. His brilliant effort may serve to keep alive a precious idea or bit of wisdom which, if it survives an inauspicious era, may enable us to build that world of freedom and abundance which was foreshadowed a century ago in England and America. If we do not bow to German military power, we may sometime shake off an allegiance to German economic ideology which we accepted substantially before the last war and, with our Allies, accepted almost wholly afterward. I recognize how easy it is in wartime to find all kinds of devils in the enemy and to blame him for our own mistakes. However, as Arnold intimates, the great ideological conflict of the modern period is (was?) between English free-market liberalism of the early nineteenth century and a German politico-economic creed which stressed state control of economic life and industrial development. Germany never accepted English liberalism; and even her best scholars rarely understood Adam Smith and Jeremy Bentham and the tradition of thought identified with them. On the other hand, the German creed was always congenial to our own powerful minorities, seeking special favors from the state, and to politicians who lived by such dispensations. Its emphasis upon social legislation appealed to the finest sentiments and led us, sensitive about our so-called "backwardness," into imitative measures subtly but deeply incompatible with our democratic tradition. Appeasing greedy minorities, on the one hand, and sentimental reformers, on the other, we have ignored and seemingly repudiated, as a desideratum, that basic dualism of competitive and political controls without which our nation cannot long remain productive or united or free.

Modern authoritarianism comprises strangely diverse sects whose leaders bitterly contest their claims to power; its unwitting apostles are legion; but, practically and in principle, it has but one opponent, namely, English free-market liberalism. Rejecting this element in our political and intellectual heritage (as England itself seems likely to do), we may fight for the privilege of finding our own way back to government by authority; but we cannot wisely regard ourselves as defenders of any great world cause.

Smith, and Bentham especially, stand out, I think, as the great political philosophers of modern democracy. Their special insight was that political and economic power must be widely dispersed and decentralized in a world that would be free; that economic control must, to that end, be largely divorced from the state and effected through a competitive process in which participants are relatively small and anonymous; and that the state must jealously guard its prerogatives of controlling relative prices (and wages), not for the purpose of exercising them directly itself but to prevent organized minorities from usurping and using them against the common interest. It is such wisdom which Arnold's book and its bold popularization may keep alive in American opinion.

If I belabor him for being unduly preoccupied with a short view and unmindful of long-range considerations, I do this mainly for the purpose of raising questions which, I think, should be discussed, at least in academic circles—questions which Arnold would be unwise to raise if he wanted to. He has already been courageous to the verge of folly. He has said more, and spoken more candidly, than would be appropriate if he were wholly concerned about his own political survival. If the political finesse of his words and actions make it hard for trade-union and trade-association leaders to liquidate him, his transparent zeal and purpose also make it easy. If he has not escaped defeat, he has assured that it will be rather glorious if it comes. He would greatly advance a cause by keeping at his present job; but he might advance the cause still more by losing the job because of what he boldly stands for. This, among other things, will doubtless give his opponents pause.

V

*Economic Stability and Antitrust Policy**

THE proponent of a largely competitive, free-market, free-enterprise system is plagued incessantly, and often discredited in debate, by the claim that such an institutional system is, and has been, inherently and intolerably unstable. The wide fluctuations of employment, income, and production of the past are commonly attributed to competition and to decentralization of control. The facts of instability in the past are commonplace. It is likewise undeniable that industries (or better, enterprises) not characterized by effective competition have fared better in the face of general instability than have the more competitive areas of the economy (e.g., agriculture) —or, at any rate, better than they would have fared with more competition or more decentralization of control. From such evidence the layman readily (too readily) concludes that competitive conditions mean instability and that the remedy lies in removing competition in favor of some other instrumentality of control. The plausibility of this conclusion, moreover, has been assiduously exploited by special pleaders and apologists for innumerable producer groups. Such vulgar economic analysis is the main stock-in-trade not only of our radicals and revolutionaries on the left but of monopolists and cartelizers on the extreme right as well—not to mention the more ingenuous advocates of "planned economy."

The answer of the radical-conservative or traditional economist liberal is that general and acute instability is, on any soundly reasoned analysis, primarily attributable to faulty monetary institutions and, in the broadest sense, to unfortu-

* Reprinted by permission from the *University of Chicago Law Review*, XI, No. 4 (June, 1944), 338–48.

nate fiscal policy. Indeed, he may go farther and insist that monopolistic control of prices and wage rates has, in fact, served to aggravate monetary instability and substantially to counteract or to frustrate such soundly remedial monetary and fiscal measures as have been employed.

This, in any case, is not the place (if, indeed, there is any proper place) for examining controversial questions of business-cycle theory. For present purposes, we may concede that rigidity of monopolistic prices and wages does set limits politically, if not economically, to fluctuations of general prices (if not of output and employment). Moreover, and more important, we may concede that, failing deliberate measures of fiscal stabilization, there are no politically significant limits to the instability of prices and, especially, to the degree of deflation which might occur under the institutional arrangements of the past. Whether extreme instability of the price level would involve intolerable fluctuations of employment and real income, given highly competitive markets for all goods and services, is an empty, academic question; for such price-level instability is undesirable and disturbing in other decisive respects; and the degree of price and wage flexibility necessary to assure reasonable stability of production and employment in the face of great monetary instability is utterly unattainable.

The characteristics of the best scheme of financial institutions and fiscal policies remain highly controversial. However, only a small, intransigent group of academic economists would now question the imperative need for deliberate governmental action (national and supranational) to counteract the perversity of changes both in the quantity and in the velocity of effective money (deposits). The old economic system (so far as it was competitive) could be trusted systematically and automatically to correct disturbances in *relative* prices and *relative* outputs of goods and services. Unexpected changes set in motion forces which served automatically to adapt both production and prices and to reallocate resources economically. General price (price-level) movements, however, served quite as systematically to set in motion forces which served, not to correct but to aggravate the initial disturbance. Thus, the familiar phenomenon of cumulative inflation and, especially, cumulative deflation. If a free-market system is to function effectively in allocating resources and in determining the composition of output, it must operate within a framework of monetary stability which it cannot create for itself and which only government can provide. This amounts only to asserting the axiom that it is a proper and minimal function of government to control (i.e., keep stable) the currency.

The kind of stability of aggregate incomes and employment which everyone desires can be attained under either of two extremes in political arrangements: (1) essentially free markets for goods and services, combined with deliberate fiscal or monetary stabilization by government, or (2) total governmental control of all production (granting that political power can be wholly concentrated, wisely exercised, and securely held by those who exercise it). The former arrangement implies political centralization of control over the value of money and close adherence to rules of fiscal policy which minimize uncertainties as to price-level changes. It also implies, *inter alia*, an extreme decentralization of control over prices and quantities of particular goods and services—a decentralization which it is also a primary function of government to foster and to preserve, in accordance with "constitutional" rules of policy. The latter arrangement (2), of course, is simply the totalitarian, collectivist state.

Particular problems of economic policy are fairly easy to formulate and to analyze for either of these two systems. Both, of course, are ideal types which have never existed, and will never exist, in a pure form. English-speaking nations, however, in the recent past, have lived under a system which was close enough to the first type to warrant analysis of their policy problems as problems of that system type. If they have been moving away from it, in terms of market organization, they have on balance perhaps been moving toward it in terms of changes in financial structure and fiscal practice. Indeed, we may well attain, for the first time, a proper financial framework for a free-market society after we have lost or abandoned the requisite deconcentration of control over relative prices and relative outputs. In any case, the question of which type of system we should now move toward presents perhaps our central question of public policy.

The decade of the thirties naturally has bequeathed to us a sense of desperate need for protection against insecurity and economic fluctuations. While irresponsible war financing should now raise the awful specter of extreme inflation as the great danger for an indefinite future, we are still mainly concerned about the next depression and deflation—about repetition of recent afflictions of unemployment and private insolvency.

If we can face the deflation danger as a national or international problem, its solution should be relatively easy and costless. Indeed, we have perhaps left behind an era in which the main danger lay in private debt and its threat of recurrent, precipitous deflation and entered a period where great and growing government debt exposes us continuously to radical decline in money value. Recurrent desperate struggles for liquidity may be displaced by recurrent flights from the currency as the major threat to economic and political security. Similarly ominous, however, is the prospect that security and stability will increasingly be sought not through the sound and promising devices of over-all fiscal policy but through action by and for particular producer groups.

This unhappy trend is strengthened both by extravagant optimism and by inordinate skepticism about the possibilities and prospects of monetary and fiscal control. Proponents of the new monetary doctrines tend grossly to exaggerate the potentialities of such control, confident that fiscal devices can alone solve our major problems in spite of any untoward accumulations of governmental and private restraints upon trade. While sometimes asserting the (mistaken) view that rigid, administered, monopolistic prices and wages may facilitate over-all monetary stabilization, they usually assert that monopolistic restraints are at most relatively unimportant as an obstacle to full production. A justifiable enthusiasm for monetary reform thus leads to gross disregard for other requisites of political order and economic efficiency in a democratic society.

On the other hand, representatives of particular industries and occupations display gross skepticism about the possibilities of over-all monetary stabilization. Against recurrence of afflictions of the thirties (admittedly of monetary origin), they demand particularist measures of protection, group by group, minority by minority. These demands are in general sympathetically received. It is seldom seriously proposed that attention be focused on over-all monetary stabilization and that, given the prospect of success at that level, each producer group should be willing and obligated to take its chances without special favors or privilege.

What strategically situated groups (farmers, suppliers of basic raw material, producers of capital goods, *et al.*) may reasonably demand is protection against the specially severe deprivations of general depression and deflation. This, a democratic government can and should provide—but by general monetary measures and without gross or deliberate differentiation among producer or enterpriser groups. Surely our federal government can stabilize the value of its currency if that purpose is accepted and intelligently pursued. Its power of taxing and spending are surely adequate; and their exercise to that end involves no sacrifice of other accepted values or objectives. By proper variations in its spendings and, especially, in its tax levies, it can inject and withdraw purchasing power as monetary stabilization may require. Nor does this imply or necessitate continued increase in the interest-bearing debt—or preclude the steady amortization of such existing debt.

Along these lines, it certainly is possible (and desirable) to give stability to a competitive, free-market, free-enterprise system without impairing its competitiveness and without substituting political (monopolistic) for competition controls in the markets for particular goods and services. To attain stability for particular industries or producer groups, by particularist measures, on the other hand, requires, if not outright special subsidies, the displacement of decentralized, competitive control by central authority, governmental or private. It thus involves radical departure from our traditional institutional system and movement toward the collectivist type. Proximately it implies further degradation of democratic government in the promiscuous dispensation of special privileges and immunities to organized, articulate producer minorities. Formalists will, of course, distinguish sharply between control exercised by responsible government agencies (e.g., under "commodity agreements") and control exercised by irresponsible private corporations and cartels. While dangerous in both cases, it is likely to be exercised with less disregard to the public interest by private groups than by government agencies actually responsible to particular producer groups. There is, on balance, some advantage in having such power exercised, if at all, in a nominally irresponsible manner, since it is more likely to be exercised with restraint if precariously held.

The common public interest in over-all monetary stabilization, national and international, is, like consumer interests generally, almost unrepresented in the political process. While opposed only by irresponsible reactionaries, it is vigorously sponsored and promoted by no one prominent in affairs. Stabilization schemes for particular producer groups, on the other hand, are powerfully represented and espoused. Thus, farm leaders push international schemes for fixing prices, limiting outputs, and dividing export markets by quota allocations. Producers of basic industrial materials (rubber, tin, copper, etc.) demand larger governmental participation in restrictive cartels. Cartelized manufacturers (chemicals, steel, electrical equipment, etc.) sponsor similar arrangements, demanding either governmental assistance or, at least, immunity from prosecution for monopolistic practices. In all cases, the argument runs in terms of security and stability—in terms of indispensable protection against the horrors of *depression* competition.

If many such special demands are granted, it is hard to see how others can be resisted or, for that matter, how we can continue to have an antitrust policy at home or any prosecution of restraint of trade. Equally hard is it to see how we can have effective economic co-operation internationally or any enduring peace. If this *is* the wave of the future, we might well ride it deliberately, organize a trading system like that of Germany, and regard peace merely as an opportunity to prosecute trade as economic warfare, with purely military objectives!

If half the time and effort now lavished on proposed international cartels could be diverted to plans for national and international monetary stabilization, even the special-interest groups, not to mention the rest of us, would be far better served. Particularist stabilization proposals have diverted current international planning almost wholly away from its proper task or objectives. A promising beginning, to be sure, has been made in the Keynes and White *Reports;* but even these documents are primarily concerned with exchange rates and not with stabilization of the purchasing power of either the dollar or the pound (or of Unitas or Bancor). While properly concerned about nationalistic exchange control and its consequences for trade, these *Reports* have little to say about tariffs or about the trade restraints of private monopolies. Indeed, they explicitly accept "commodity agreements." Thus, real, fundamental planning for economic stability and international economic co-operation under less restricted trade seems to have bogged down completely, while international monopoly schemes are burgeoning and thriving all over the place. The early talk about reducing tariff barriers has subsided completely. A possible international antimonopoly program is now moving along rapidly in reverse. And the reason is simply utter lack of responsible political leadership. Failing such leadership, the only things that have promise politically are measures on behalf of special minority interests—cartel schemes with the usual polite invitations for consumer representation. Instead of a sound international program sponsored and carefully guided in its formation by a vigorous and alert State Department, with full executive support, we have in prospect, besides a rather trivial scheme for exchange rates, only a multiplicity of proposals for extending and legitimatizing private international monopoly. The sound urge toward international co-operation is being "satisfied" and perverted in the form of broader co-operation of producer groups to raise prices and reduce outputs.

Such schemes not only divert attention from monetary stabilization and other proper forms of international economic co-operation. They also aggravate the difficulties of all-over stabilization. The attempt to sustain employment and investment by monetary devices must operate against the restriction of output and investment which is the basic function of agencies, governmental or private, for "stabilizing" particular prices. Such stabilization is almost inevitably a one-way process—raising prices which are often considered too low and seldom, if ever, considered too high.

During depressions the stabilization of particular prices against a general decline serves to shift the burdens of depression heavily upon other groups, and thus, to increase the difficulties of effective monetary or fiscal counteraction. Sustaining such prices means larger curtailment of employment and, thus, of spending. It means drawing off a larger share of spending to the particular enterprises and, thus, deepening the depression in other areas of the economy.

Conversely, rigidity of "administered" prices during a boom is likewise mainly unfortunate—if (as in rare cartel instances perhaps has been the case) "stabilization" ever works both ways. If steel prices are held down during a boom, by virtue of normal excess capacity, one important check upon excessive boom-time investment is removed. (If they are held down by private rationing, the effects and purposes of the rationing devices are at least open to question.) Variation in costs of capital goods is certainly not an adequate substitute for monetary-fiscal stabilization; but one may not deny that increases would somewhat reduce boom-time investment or that decreases would help fill in the valleys of investment during depressions. Conversely, the task of monetary stabilization will be less difficult, and perhaps better discharged, if relative prices of capital goods and their major cost elements are responsive to changes in general business conditions.

On a more realistic view of the future, however, one must focus attention upon the contributions of monopolistic wage price controls to the difficulties of preventing or checking continued inflation. Too much attention has been directed to the influence of price and wage rigidity ("stabilization") when, in fact, the controls or "administration" work mainly or largely to prevent change only in one direction (downward). No amount of monetary or fiscal stimulation will give us adequate employment or investment, if strategically situated unions and enterpriser monopolists insist upon utilizing improved demand conditions to increase their wages and prices rather than to increase employment, investment, and output—or to hold up prices where improved technology is markedly reducing costs. And there is no reason why organized producer groups, holding adequate organizational and political power, should, acting in their separate interests, forgo the opportunity to improve their relative position in such circumstances. They may, to be sure, injure themselves along with the community, all or most of them being worse off by virtue of their restrictive measures than if none had practiced them. But each group may be better off than if it alone had behaved less monopolistically; and, short of dictatorship at one extreme and real competition at the other, there would appear to be no means for getting co-ordinated or co-operative action from such groups as a whole.

Ultimately, as producers become more and more effectively organized, and the economy increasingly syndicalist, only internal competition or authoritarian dictation can protect organized groups from the folly of their own aggregate restraints. To argue that monetary stabilization, or even continued inflation, can overcome the restrictive efforts of widespread monopoly or bring the flexible, competitive prices reasonably into line with administered prices and wages is to predict what is least probable. The experience with wartime inflation, as to wage rates, farm prices, and silver politics, should facilitate better predictions, if common sense does not yield good ones. Prices and wages which are most rigid in the face of depression and deflation are likely to be most flexible in the face of inflation. In either and all circumstances, monopolistically organized and politically articulate groups may be expected to look after themselves, to serve their special interests, and mainly to act contrary to the common welfare— and even contrary to their own common interests. So, we might inflate endlessly and still find ourselves with worse maladjustments of relative prices and relative wages than we had at the start.

No amount of monetary stabilization or stimulation can make an economy function better or tolerably as it becomes increasingly monopolized and syndicalized. Restrictive measures, widely applied, must add up to serious aggregate restriction, to unemployment, and to a stagnant or contracting economy. Given widespread competition, free enterprise, and free access to markets for particular goods and services, the economy would be sensitive and responsive to monetary controls and able to thrive on the limited measure of fiscal stimulation which is consistent with a stable price level and a stable or declining public debt.

Only in a substantially competitive economy can injections of purchasing power be counted on persistently to increase output rather than prices, employment rather than merely wage rates. Only competition can assure that prices which have been held up during deflation will not be pushed up during deliberate reflation—that those which have resisted general downward movement will not lead the way upward. To anticipate another pattern without competition is to count on stupid lethargy among the most aggressive and powerful and to suppose that groups possessing great power will not exercise it promptly and wisely in their special interest.

The main objective in national (and supranational) policy, of course, must be adequate and stable employment. This objective, in turn, must be attained without marked or continued inflation and without recourse to beggar-my-neighbor measures of economic warfare, aggressive or defensive. To these ends, we must seek to break down all artificial barriers and inhibitions against new enterprise and private investment.

Failure in this undertaking, moreover, is likely to prove cumulative and self-aggravating. If expansion of private output and investment does not provide adequate employment, governmental enterprise and investment must fill the gap. This, in turn, necessarily involves governmental encroachment in areas of potential private investment and, thus, further inhibition of private capital to enter into competition with subsidized governmental enterprise. It also involves aggravation of inflation dangers and ominous threats to political and property institutions, whose security is requisite to private investment expansion.

On the other hand, failing general prosperity and expansion, particular industries and producer minorities are certain to be both more demanding and more successful in protecting and defending their relative position by exploitative, beggar-my-neighbor measures, governmental and private. Tolerating and promoting the restrictive schemes of powerful, organized minorities, we shall not only sacrifice expansion potentialities in their sphere but shall expose enterprise and investment elsewhere to their arbitrary, monopolistic exactions.

New enterprise and investment, facing competition and irreducible uncertainties in their product markets, must be assured of access to reasonably free, competitive markets for their purchases (labor and materials). Otherwise, they face not only the inevitable risks of misdirection of their activities ("normal," competitive loss contingencies) but the forbidding prospect of forfeiting any possible profits to organized, monopolistic suppliers of things they must purchase. There obviously can be no adequate private investment in a community where such investment is, or reasonably seems to be, a giving of hostages to powerful protagonists in economic civil war. A vigorous and expanding system of private enterprise needs little, if any, pure profit on balance, to function effectively. Loss contingencies, however, must be counterbalanced by possibilities of somewhat commensurate gains; and such possibilities, for new and competitive enterprise, simply do not exist where it is surrounded by organized sellers (or faced by organized buyers). Besides the danger of having its legitimate profits appropriated by arbitrary power, there is also the risk of destruction through collusive action of its suppliers and its competitors in the product market.

There can be adequate investment and employment in a predominantly free-market economy with effective monetary-fiscal stabilization or, alternatively, in a predominantly collectivist system based on securely centralized power. Full production can be achieved either by extreme concentration or by extreme deconcentration of control over particular prices and outputs. Like economical allocation and proper relative prices, investments, and outputs, however, it is unattainable in the face of an undisciplined struggle of organized producer groups which usurp or abuse governmental powers separately to improve their relative positions. In any system which is orderly or prosperous, the public interest in full production must be protected either by competition within producer groups or by authority which compels them to accept reasonable prices and to maintain adequate output. We recognize at least vaguely the threat to world order and prosperity arising from beggar-my-neighbor policies in international economic relations. We do not recognize, save perhaps during total war, the threat to domestic order and prosperity arising from such policies on the part of functional groups organized to restrain trade or to secure special governmental restraints on their behalf. Abhorring total centralization of power, and unwilling to enforce a workable decentralization, we drift rapidly into political organization along functional, occupational lines—into a miscellany of specialized collectivisms, organized to take income away from one another and incapable of acting in their own common interest or in a manner compatible with general prosperity. Seeking security and prosperity, group by group within the economy, we have as little chance of obtaining these goods as we have of attaining peace among nations by analogous military measures.

We are attempting to argue here a case which seems so obvious that effective argument is difficult. The amazing thing is that anyone should entertain the opposite view. Surely a competitive economy would be extremely sensitive to monetary controls and relatively easy to stabilize by fiscal devices. That the same should be true of a highly monopolized or syndicalist system is improbable on its face and, on reflection, appears quite impossible. Monetary remedies can cure monetary ills. In excessive doses they may serve to conceal other ills. That they should counteract or greatly ameliorate the consequences of wholesale organization of producer groups to exploit one another (and the unorganized), by raising their prices relatively and restricting their respective outputs, is certainly not to be anticipated on the basis of any reasoned analysis. Syndicalism cannot be transformed into an efficient and orderly scheme of politico-economic organization merely by adding a suitable monetary constitution.

Monetary and fiscal controls, aiming at stabilization of the value of money or price level, are a proper and now indispensable element in the framework of a free-market society. In such a society they can produce adequate, stable employment and contribute to effective allocation of resources. Seeking full employment and economic allocation without effective competition, we must move all the way to collectivism. The inherent conflict of interest between each producer group and the community (to repeat) must be reconciled or avoided, either by the discipline of effective intragroup competition or by the dictation of absolute authority from above.

Monetary and fiscal measures are not a substitute for competition and free-market arrangements but a means for attaining greater over-all security, stability, and efficiency under such institutions. Centralization of monetary and fiscal controls is a sound and necessary means for attaining order and prosperity without other and larger concentration of power. It may be part of a program of total centralization (collectivism) or of a program of systematic decentralization and liberty. It cannot be expected to bring either peace or prosperity out of the economic civil war of monopolized industries and pressure groups. Monetary and fiscal policies are crucially important in the traditional system; they present interesting problems under collectivism. To discuss such policies under syndicalism, however, is to speculate about the workings of a system which is patently and inherently unworkable.

VI

Some Reflections on Syndicalism[*][1]

Students of social science must fear popular approval; evil is with them when all men speak well of them. If there is any set of opinions by the advocacy of which a newspaper can increase its sales, then the student . . . . is bound to dwell on the limitations and defects and errors, if any, in that set of opinions; and never to advocate them unconditionally even in an *ad hoc* discussion. It is almost impossible for a student to be a true patriot and to have the reputation of being one at the same time.—ALFRED MARSHALL.[2]

QUESTIONING the virtues of the organized labor movement is like attacking religion, monogamy, motherhood, or the home. Among the modern intelligentsia any doubts about collective bargaining admit of explanation only in terms of insanity, knavery, or subservience to "the interests." Discussion of skeptical views runs almost entirely in terms of how one came by such persuasions, as though they were symptoms of disease. One simply cannot argue that organization is injurious to labor; one is either for labor or against it, and the test is one's attitude toward unionism. But let me indicate from the outset that my central interest, and the criterion in terms of which I wish to argue, is a maximizing of aggregate labor income and a minimizing of inequality. If unionism were good for labor as a whole, that would be the end of the issue for me, since the community whose welfare concerns us is composed overwhelmingly of laborers.

Our problem here, at bottom, is one of broad political philosophy. Advocates of trade-unionism are, I think, obligated morally and intellectually to present a clear picture of the total political-economic system toward which they would have us move. For my part, I simply cannot conceive of any

* Reprinted by permission from the *Journal of Political Economy*, LII, No. 1 (March, 1944), 1–25.

tolerable or enduring order in which there exists widespread organization of workers along occupational, industrial, functional lines. Sentimentalists view such developments merely as a contest between workers who earn too little and enterprises which earn too much; and, unfortunately, there has been enough monopsony in labor markets to make this view superficially plausible, though not enough to make it descriptively important. What we generally fail to see is the identity of interest between the whole community and enterprises seeking to keep down costs. Where enterprise is competitive—and substantial, enduring restraint of competition in product markets is rare—enterprisers represent the community interest effectively; indeed, they are merely intermediaries between consumers of goods and sellers of services. Thus we commonly overlook the conflict of interest between every large organized group of laborers and the community as a whole. What I want to ask is how this conflict can be reconciled, how the power of strongly organized sellers can be limited out of regard for the general welfare. No insuperable problem arises so long as organization is partial and precarious, so long as most unions face substantial nonunion competition, or so long as they must exercise monopoly powers sparingly because of organizational insecurity. Weak unions have no large monopoly powers. But how does a democratic community limit the demands and exactions of strong, secure organizations? Looking at the typographers, the railway brotherhoods, and metropolitan building trades, among others, one answers simply: "It doesn't!"

In an economy of intricate division of labor, every large organized group is in a position at any time to disrupt or to stop the whole flow of social income; and the system must soon break down if groups persist in exercising that power or if they must continuously be bribed to forgo its disastrous exercise. There is no means, save internal competition, to protect the whole community against organized labor minorities and, indeed, no other means to protect the common interests of organized groups themselves. The dilemma here is not peculiar to our present economic order; it must appear in any kind of system. This minority-monopoly problem would be quite as serious for a democratic socialism as it is for the mixed individualist-collectivist system of the present. It is the rock on which our present system is most likely to crack up; and it is the rock on which democratic socialism would be destroyed if it could ever come into being at all.

All the grosser mistakes in economic policy, if not most manifestations of democratic corruption, arise from focusing upon the interests of people as producers rather than upon their interests as consumers, that is, from acting on behalf of producer minorities rather than on behalf of the whole community as sellers of services and buyers of products. One gets the right answers usually by regarding simply the interests of consumers, since we are all consumers; and the answers reached by this approach are presumably the correct ones for laborers as a whole. But one does not get elected by approaching issues in this way! People seldom vote in terms of their common interests, whether as sellers or as buyers. There is no means for protecting the common interest save in terms of rules of policy; and it is only in terms of general rules or principles that democracy, which is government by free, intelligent discussion, can function tolerably or endure. Its nemesis is racketeering—tariffs, other subsidies, and patronage dispensations generally and, outside of government, monopoly, which in its basic aspect is impairment of the state's monopoly of coercive power.

Trade-unionism may be attacked as a threat to order under any kind of system. The case against it is crystal clear if one thinks in terms of purer types of systems like democratic collectivism. A socialist government, faced with numerous functional minorities each organized to disrupt the whole production process unless its demands are met, would be exactly in the position of recent Chinese governments faced with great bandit armies continuously collecting ransom from the nominal sovereign. It would either deprive such minorities of the power to act as units in withholding services or be displaced by a nondemocratic authority which could and would restore monopoly of violence. There is no place for collective bargaining, or for the right to strike, or for effective occupational organization in the socialist state, save in the sense that revolution against established authority is an undeniable privilege and violent chaos always an imminent possibility; and every intelligent socialist, whatever his public utterances, knows as much.

I am arguing, however, not as a socialist, but as an advocate of the elaborate mixed system of traditional economic liberalism. The essence of this practical political philosophy is a distrust of all concentrations of power. No individual may be trusted with much power, no organization, and no institution save the state itself. The state or sovereign must, of course, possess great reserves of power, if only to prevent other organizations from threatening or usurping its monopoly of violence. But the exercise of power inherent in government must be rigidly economized. Decentralization of government is essential. Indeed, the proper purpose of all large-scale organization or federation—as should be obvious to people facing the problem of world order—is that of dispersing power.

Let me remark in passing that highly centralized nationalisms are peculiarly inimical to sound political order. Federalism or informal union of states has everything to commend it if the central government confines itself largely to preserving order and free trade among constituent states and to providing a stable, common currency. But federal governments like our own and the great powers abroad have become a great obstacle to world order. Originating largely as customs unions or agencies for securing free trade within their boundaries, they were rapidly exploited by minorities to provide subsidies via restraints upon external trade; they have undertaken all kinds of internal policies which must be abandoned if freer world trade is to be achieved; and, finally, they have been largely utilized to restrict trade among their own constituent states or sections. These monsters of nationalism and mercantilism must be dismantled, both to preserve world order and to protect internal peace. Their powers to wage war and to restrict world trade must be sacrificed to some supranational state or league of nations. Their other powers and functions must be diminished in favor · of states, provinces, and, in Europe, small nations.

Along these lines we may reconstruct a total political system in which organization becomes progressively looser and functions increasingly narrow and negative as one moves from local government (counties?) to states, to nations, and to supranational agencies. The good political order is one in which small nations and governments on the scale of American states are protected in their autonomy against neighbors and protected against federalisms or unions which appropriate their powers, take positive government farther from the people, and systematically subordinate common to special interests.

The great sins against world order, by way of trade restraint and military activity, are those of great, not small, nations. In spite of popular impressions to the contrary, the worst breaches of political morality, the worst patronage corruption, and the most glaring weakness against organized minorities are characteristic of great national or federal governments far more than of smaller units—and of our federal government, with all its "respectability" and "efficiency," especially.[3]

Governments can be trusted to exercise large power, broad functions, and extensive control only at levels of small units like American states and under the limitations imposed by freedom of external trade. Especially in the higher levels or larger units of government, action must follow broad general rules or principles. Only by adherence to "constitutional" principles of policy can the common interest be protected against minorities, patronage, and logrolling; and only in terms of issues of broad principle can government by free, intelligent discussion (democracy) prevail. Most important here are the presumptions in favor of free trade and against dispensations to producer minorities. Constitutional principles or accepted norms are also peculiarly important, and lacking, in fiscal (monetary, budgetary) policy.

Other implications of this older liberalism may be mentioned briefly. The government must not tolerate erection of great private corporate empires or cartel organizations which suppress competition and rival in power great governmental units themselves. (In Germany the great cartels, and the great banks especially, attained to power which no private bodies can enjoy under a sound democracy.) It must guard its powers jealously both against the combination of numerous pressure groups and against powerful lobbies like the present federal lobby of landowners. (The case of German democracy and the Junker interests is again excellently in point.) It must hold in check organizations designed for raiding the Treasury (witness the history of pension legislation and the political power of veterans' organizations). Finally, and most important for the future, it must guard its powers against great trade-unions, both as pressure groups in government and as monopolists outside.

The danger here is now most ominous, in the very nature of such agencies and also because the danger is least well recognized and commonly denied entirely. In other areas we are, if diffident and careless, at least on our guard; nothing is likely to happen that cannot be undone if we will; but labor monopolies and labor "states" may readily become a problem which democracy simply cannot solve at all. There must be effective limitations upon their powers; but I do not see how they can be disciplined democratically save by internal competition or how that discipline can be effected without breaking down organization itself. Here, possibly, is an awful dilemma: democracy cannot live with tight occupational monopolies; and it cannot destroy them, once they attain great power, without destroying itself in the process. If democratic governments cannot suppress organized extortion and preserve their monopoly of violence, they will be superseded by other kinds of government. Organized economic warfare is like organized banditry and, if allowed to spread, must lead to total revolution, which will, on very hard terms, restore some order and enable us to maintain some real income instead of fighting interminably over its division among minorities.

A community which fails to preserve the discipline of competition exposes itself to the discipline of absolute authority. Preserving the former discipline, we may govern ourselves and look forward to a peaceful world order; without it, we must submit to arbitrary authority and to hopeless disorder internationally. And, let me suggest again, the problem is quite as critical for democratic socialism as for the decentralized system of orthodox liberalism. An obvious danger in collectivism is that the vast powers of government would be abused in favoritism to particular producer groups, organized to demand favors as the price of maintaining peace, and available to support established authorities against political opposition. Adherence to competitive, productivity norms is, now or under socialism, a means for avoiding arbitrariness and, to my mind, the only feasible means.

Observance of such norms *does not* preclude wholesale redistribution of income afterward, if such redistribution proceeds even-handedly on the basis of definite, broad rules. There is room for much socialized consumption, made available without price restraints or at prices well below costs. The policy requires, for good results, both deliberate supplementing of earnings at the bottom of the scale (relief, family allowances, old age assistance, etc.) and, especially under free enterprise, progressive taxation of the most fortunate and their heirs and assigns. But the supplementing of public spending and the scaling-down by taxation must proceed even-handedly among functional groups, in terms of objective economic (income) circumstances and without arbitrary occupational differentiation. Thus, poor farmers may properly be subsidized, like others of similar income and needs, because they are poor but *not* because they are farmers; and wealthy manufacturers may be taxed heavily, not because they are manufacturers of this or that, but because their incomes are large. Incidentally, it is one merit of our present (past) system that inequality is measured closely by income and can most easily be modified systematically through taxation and spending. Inequalities of political power, which alternative systems are likely to produce in extreme form, are likely to be more obscure and certainly are not amenable to quantitative measurement or to continuous, systematic correction or mitigation.

The importance of competitive norms and the anomalies of control through voluntary association should be especially evident from recent experience. After 1933 there existed a most unfortunate dispersion between rigid, administered prices and wage rates and the sensitive, competitive prices and wages which deflation had lowered drastically. If, while sensitive prices were held up and raised by deficit reflation, administered prices and wages could have been lowered to levels more consistent with them, almost everyone would have gained. But no single group, able to hold up its own price or wage, could advantage itself by reductions unless other such groups acted similarly and simultaneously. Even if general reductions were in prospect, each single group could advantage itself by holding back. Competition would have forced all such groups to do what it was to their common interest, and to the community's interest especially, to have done. Failing competitive control, they naturally all sat tight, cutting their own throats and all losing absolutely in order to preserve their relative positions.

Every organized group of sellers is typically in a position to gain by raising price and restricting sales; the popular notion that they commonly are more exploitative than their own interests would dictate (that we need only more enlightened price and wage policies by organized groups) is simply mistaken,[4] for inadequacy of monopoly power usually leaves them far short of ideal monopoly restriction. When organization becomes widespread, however, the common interest in increased production may greatly outweigh particular interests in restriction, even for those practicing restriction; but, I repeat, the common interest may be implemented only by competition or by authoritarian dictation. There is little hope that mass organizations with monopoly power will submit to competitive prices for their services while they retain their organization and power. No one and no group can be trusted with much power; and it is merely silly to complain because groups exercise power selfishly. The mistake lies simply in permitting them to have it.

Monopoly power must be abused. It has no use save abuse. Some people evidently have believed that labor organizations should have monopoly powers and be trusted not to use them. Collective bargaining, for the Webbs, was evidently a scheme whereby labor monopolies were to raise wages to competitive levels, merely counteracting monopsony among buyers, but eschewing further exercise of organizational powers. A tradeunionism, affecting wages and working rules only within such limits, and doing all the many other good things that unions can do, would be a blessing all around.[5] No one could seriously question its merits in the abstract. But monopsony in the labor market is, I think, very unsubstantial or transitory; and it is romantic and unreasonable to expect organizations to exercise powers only within limits consistent with the common interest. All bargaining power is monopoly power. Such power, once attained, will be used as fully as its conservation permits and also used continuously for its own accretion and consolidation. The skin disease of monopsony is certainly a poor excuse for stopping the peaceful and productive game of free enterprise and free exchange in favor of the violent contest of organized producer-minorities.

I do not assert that our only monopoly problems lie in the labor market. Save for the monopolies which government is promoting in agriculture, however, no others seem comparably important for the future. It is shameful to have permitted the growth of vast corporate empires, the collusive restraint of trade by trade associations, and the gross abuse of patent privilege for extortion, exclusion, and output restriction. But enterprise monopoly is also a skin disease, easy to correct when and if we will, and usually moderate in its abuses, since its powers are necessarily small, and since the danger of political reckoning is never very remote. Enterprise monopoly, enjoying very limited access to violence and facing heavy penalties for unfair methods against rivals, is always plagued by competition, actual and potential, and must always operate against a deeply hostile, if lethargic, attitude of courts, legislatures, and the public. In exceptional cases it has acquired vast power and sustained power over long periods. In many cases it has transformed salutary price competition into perverse and wasteful "competition" in merchandising and advertising. But, to repeat, the proper remedies here are not very difficult technically or politically.[6]

Labor monopolies are, now or potentially, a different kind of animal. If much violence has been used against them as they struggled into existence, this should not obscure the fact that, once established, they enjoy an access to violence which is unparalleled in other monopolies. If governments have tolerated flagrant violations of law by employers, they are nearly impotent to enforce laws against mass minorities even if majority opinion permitted it. Thus, unions may deal with scabs in ways which make even Rockefeller's early methods seem polite and legitimate. They have little to fear from chiselers in their own midst; and they have now little to fear from Congress or the courts.

Patently restrictive practices are now commonly deplored and, perhaps because unnecessary, seem somewhat on the wane. But there have been many cases of severe limitations upon entry—high initiation fees, excessive periods of apprenticeship and restrictions upon numbers of apprentices, barriers to movement between related trades, and, of course, make-work restrictions, cost-increasing working rules, and prohibition of cost-reducing innovations, notably in the building trades—not to mention racial and sex discriminations against which effective competition in labor markets is probably a necessary, if not a sufficient, protection.

It is not commonly recognized, however, that control of wage rates *is* control of entry, especially where seniority rules are in force and, even failing such rules, where qualitative selection is important and turnover itself very costly to firms. If able to enforce standard rates, experienced, established workers can insulate themselves from the competition of new workers merely by making their cost excessive, that is, by establishing labor costs and wage expectations which preclude expansion of production or employment in their field. New and displaced workers typically migrate, not to high-wage occupations but to places where employment opportunities exist; high wages are less attractive if jobs cannot be had. Wage control, determining a major element in operating cost, also determines the rate at which a whole industry will expand or, more likely, with strong organization, the rate of contraction.

Frankly, I can see no reason why strongly organized workers, in an industry where huge investment is already sunk in highly durable assets, should ever permit a return on investment sufficient to attract new capital or even to induce full maintenance of existing capital. If I were running a union and were managing it faithfully in the interest of the majority of its members, I should consistently demand wage rates which offered to existing firms no real net earnings but only the chance of getting back part of their sunk investment at the cost of the replacement outlays necessary to provide employment for most of my constituents during their own lifetimes as workers. In other words, I should plan gradually to exterminate the industry by excessive labor costs, taking care only to prevent employment from contracting more rapidly than my original constituents disappeared by death and voluntary retirement.

If I were operating, as labor leader, without the valuable hostages of large sunk investment, I should be obliged to behave more moderately. But I should still seek, controlling prices via labor costs, to restrict production as rapidly as consistent with decline of my membership by death and retirement and, while permitting some return to investors, should try always to induce only as much employment and production as my original constituents could take care of without new members. If investors disliked my high wages, they would like the high prices which I could assure them by excluding lower-wage competitors. In both cases I should, of course, not serve my constituents well toward the end unless I utilized the opportunity of permitting some newcomers, by payment of heavy tribute, to enter, to acquire skill and experience, and to become established with my older cronies; for the initiation fees would contribute handsomely to our retirement annuities.

The situation is more complicated, of course, where unions do permit and facilitate entry, that is, where work is shared equally between newcomers and others. Here the advantages of high wages are dissipated by the sharing of unemployment; and annual wages may even drop below a competitive level, if workers value leisure highly or are usually able to find other remunerative work during their periods of layoff. The outcome resembles that of the pure cartel among enterprises, where price is fixed by voluntary agreement, output divided by quotas, and newcomers admitted freely and granted quotas on the same basis as old firms. No one gains, and everybody as consumer loses. There is great social wastage of resources, of labor in one case, of investment in the other; and the two wastes are likely to occur together, as in coal-mining.

But free entry and division of work are not likely to characterize unionism of the future and have rarely prevailed in the past. Employees increasingly seek seniority rights; employers prefer to exercise qualitative selection; and the demands from both sides are roughly consistent, especially in large established firms where workers are carefully selected in the first place and experience is important. Some conflict arises, fortunately, between the rank and file, who want the highest possible wage rates, and labor leaders, whose power and influence, in government and in labor circles, depends on the number of their constituents; but this conflict will usually be reconciled in favor of the interests of the rank and file or avoided via organizational imperialism (jurisdictional conquests). Sentimentalists will urge that strong unions should moderate wage demands, recognizing an obligation to permit entry of young workers and workers displaced in decadent industries; but I should not expect them to behave so or blame them for using power, if they have it, in their own interest; and I see no way to avoid severely restrictive policies save by depriving them of control over wages, that is, of bargaining power.

Personnel experts tell us that qualitative dispersion in labor markets is enormous; that among workers regarded as belonging to the same class (i.e., apart from the upgrading that accompanies large increases of employment) the best workers are worth several times as much to a firm as are the poorer ones. In any case, it is instructive to consider an analogy in agricultural policy to the device of the standard rate in unionized industry.

It is a familiar axiom that the existence of poorer grades of land serves to keep down rents on the better grades. The poorer grades, adding to output, keep down product prices and thus diminish productivity and rents of other land. Suppose now that wheat producers, protected by prohibitive tariffs, should organize and prohibit, by night-riding or by securing appropriate legislation, the use for wheat-raising of any land whose net annual rental value is less than $10 per acre. (Thus renters could not use land for wheat unless they paid at least $10 per acre; and owners could so use their own land only if annual net returns averaged above $10 per acre.) The effects of such a measure would be fairly complex, since some land excluded at the start would become eligible for use after output fell and price rose; but its virtues for owners of the best land, and its grave diseconomies for the community, are obvious enough. No one (outside the Department of Agriculture) would purport to defend such a policy or suggest that it would be less objectionable if extended to cover all forms of agriculture. In principle, however, there is little to distinguish it from the standard wage in industry.

The argument need not be extended to support extensive differentiation among employees within establishments. It is the proper business of personnel officers to classify employees by tasks and to standardize rates within categories, with perhaps some regard for length of service. Differentiation among individuals is to be avoided, in the interest of both workers and management.[7] A less strong case can be made for considerable standardization of rates within cities or localities. The issue becomes critical when standardization is enforced over wide areas, between small and large cities, and among regions in a vast economy.

The case for differentiation according to differences in living costs is commonly conceded in principle and need not detain us here. Trade-unionists will deplore any such concession as a confession of weakness or as impractical and, since it is clearly contrary to the interests of established workers and established centers in most cases, may be expected to prevent it if they have the power to do so. Moreover, the principle is much less simple and definite than it seems to most people, for even rough estimate of the relative value of money as between distant places is nearly impossible.

Even with such differentiation, however, the argument for standardization of wage rates between communities comes near to denying all advantages of interregional trade and is fundamentally on a level with the preposterous Republican (and Democratic!) principles of tariff policy. If standard wage rates are desirable, then tariffs should everywhere be adjusted to offset all differences in labor cost between domestic and foreign producers. This differs slightly from the Republican principle of equalizing all costs, but not enough to merit separate attention. If fully applied in tariff policy, it would practically prohibit all trade and all territorial specialization. One difference here may, however, be noted. If a domestic industry and its workers are protected by duties which compensate for wage differences, say, in Argentina, Argentinean workers are excluded from an American product market. If American workers can enforce their wage rates on Argentinean and other producers, they get both the American and the Argentinean markets—if they are superior workers and/or if they have access here to better and more abundant capital and management. If northern enterprises and workers can enforce northern wages in particular southern industries, they can largely exclude southern enterprises and workers from both northern and southern markets.

Southern workers may be intrigued by the wage expectations held out by organizers from northern unions and by the Fair Labor Standards Act. They may in a few cases get such wages; but, if they get much employment at such wages, it will be only in spite of the intentions of the northern unions and the Massachusetts senators. Again, it is simply contrary to the interests of northern workers to permit competitive expansion of southern industry in their respective fields; and prevent it they will if the power is theirs.

The great American problem of poverty and underprivilege concerns southern labor. Climate, culture, poverty, and scarcity of complementary resources (especially capital) account for chronically low productivity. A bad situation has been profoundly worsened by world changes which have narrowed the market for our great export staple. This, in turn, gave rise to governmental intervention on behalf of landowners—to a modern counterpart of the inclosure movement, which further diminished agricultural output and accelerated displacement of labor where alternative employment opportunities were inadequate even for slower adjustment.

Two growing southern industries—textiles and coal—offered escape from the hills in many areas; but both developments were alarming to northern workers and employers, who, using the slogans of sentimentalist reformers, obtained legislation which protected them against the South as tariff subsidies had earlier protected them against foreigners. The Fair Labor Standards Act was designed, and will serve primarily, to retard migration of textile production and textile capital into southern states. The Guffey-Vinson Act was intended to sustain a cartelized and unionized northern industry, which the competition of southern coal would have disrupted considerably, if only to the extent of restoring an approximation of competitive norms in its prices and wages.

It is significant that the first measure obtained nearly all the votes which would have supported higher duties on textiles and that early drafts of the Guffey bills were prepared by northern operators and indorsed without modification by labor leaders. Both measures will become obsolete and unnecessary, however, if and as northern unions are able to eliminate or to minimize wage differentials in the areas which concern them. The results will seem good to southern workers who remain employed in the particular occupations; they will be excellent from the standpoint of particular groups of northern manufacturers and laborers; but they will be very bad for southern labor generally and for our economy as a whole.

Mitigation and gradual solution of our major poverty problem depend mainly on industrialization of the South. Migration northward will help; but migration at best is a slow and painful solution and, because of high wages and high quality standards in northern industry, is especially unpromising in this case. The better solution is that of moving capital and industry to the South. But this movement cannot proceed satisfactorily without the attraction of low labor cost. Southern labor, on the whole, simply is not worth much, to enterprisers

or to the community. Rapid industrialization means converting to industrial employment a population which is simply not
habituated to such employment and not readily amenable to
the discipline of factory work. New enterprise must largely
train its workers as it goes along, being satisfied with poor performance until it has educated and habituated the population
to a new mode of life. Public education can help. In the main,
however, we must face the necessity of giving to people,
schooled only in primitive, subsistence agriculture, long experience with highly specialized, mechanical production
which is alien to their culture. If complementary resources can
be provided (plant and equipment) in reasonable proportion
to labor, and if labor can acquire the appropriate skills and
the cultural adaptation for factory production, labor standards
may ultimately approach and rival those of the North. During the transition, however, while labor quality remains low
and while capital resources remain scarce relative to labor,
high wages in those few industries with large growth potentials
are a tragic mistake.

There are few industries available to afford this preliminary
training and industrial education in the South. They offer the
only promising escape from the back-country. Their development must impinge adversely on particular northern industries, while advantaging everyone as consumer; but the necessary displacement of workers *between* industries in the North is
a small price to pay for displacement *into* industry in the South.
Northern workers, having acquired basic adaptation to industrial employment, need pay no heavy price in relinquishing particular employments in favor of southern labor. A wide range
of alternative industries and occupations are available to the
higher-quality labor of the North. Those who possess greatest
occupational mobility, flexibility, and adaptability must to
some extent sacrifice the particular employments which are
most readily available to those for whom southern agriculture
has ceased to afford mean subsistence. We may have high
wages in industries which compete with strong northern

groups; or we may have a steadily rising level of income and living standards in the whole South. The choice is about that simple.

I am here arguing merely the classical case for free trade, free markets, and free occupational migration. The argument is equally sound whether invoked against external or internal barriers, against governmental restrictions on trade, or against those imposed by private monopolies. If its application is more obvious when one considers problems of our South, the same argument may be invoked as regards our whole economy or as regards the special interests of the North itself. The public interest demands free exchange and free movement of workers among occupations. Above all, it demands the easiest possible access by workers in low-wage occupations to highly productive and unusually remunerative employment. Unionism implies ability of established workers in high-wage areas and occupations to insulate themselves from competition, excluding inexperienced new workers and qualitatively inferior labor from their markets. It enables an aristocracy of labor to build fences around its occupations, restricting entry, raising arbitrarily the costs and prices of its products, and lowering the wages and incomes of those outside, and of the poor especially.

In passing, let me propose, as something better than half-truth, the generalization that, by and large, employers get the kind of labor they pay for.[8] Highest enterprise earnings usually go with highest wage rates; and so-called marginal firms commonly pay both their workers and their owners rather poorly. Some people deduce from these facts the conclusion that wage increases, whether enforced by legislation or by unions, will be relatively costless, forcing economies in management and improvement in methods. This argument, unfortunately, can also be employed to demonstrate that excises are the best device of taxation, since, as some classical writers argued incautiously, they tend to be absorbed by inducing more economical methods of production! But the phenomenon in the labor market is not hard to explain on other grounds.

As between firms and even between industries, large differences in wage rates may persist without corresponding differences in costs. A single firm, offering higher wages than its competitors, may get better morale and co-operation which are well worth the cost; and surely it will be able to enlist and maintain a qualitatively superior labor force. A whole industry may accomplish the same thing, competing for labor with other industries. Depending upon prevailing rates of pay, one industry may get high-quality labor in all firms; another, very mediocre workers. Thus, wage concessions to organized groups may at the outset cost nothing at all, to a firm as against other firms or to an industry as against other industries. All that happens is that quality standards are raised and inferior workers more rigidly excluded.[9] But downgrading cannot go on forever; the trick works only if it is confined to a few cases; we should guard here against fallacies of composition. The automobile industry may employ only the best human material, leaving other industries to absorb lower grades. But beyond narrow limits wage increases will not permit corresponding improvement in quality, even for a single firm. When all industry or many industries try the trick, poorer labor is simply frozen out and driven into unemployment or into much less remunerative and less socially productive employment where standards are less severe. In the old days the steel industry, the garment industry, and coal-mining, with all their abuses, did absorb and train a great mass of low-grade immigrant labor. What industries will do this job for us in the future? Where, to repeat, is our surplus agricultural labor going to be absorbed? Surely not in steel, which has now little place for anything but the best.

Consider also the untoward effects of standard rates on new and venturesome enterprise. The most vital competition commonly arises from firms content to experiment with new locations and relatively untrained labor. Such enterprises must offer workers better terms than they have received in alternative previous employment but cannot offer the wages paid to highly specialized, selected workers in established centers. If compelled to offer such terms, they will not arise. Yet it is obviously one of the finest services of new and venturesome enterprise to find better uses for existing labor and to employ more productively than theretofore labor resources which need not be confined to activities of low value. Indeed, every new firm must do this in large measure. Old established firms have skimmed off the cream of the labor supply and have trained their workers to a substantial superiority over the inexperienced. If potential competitors must pay the same wages as old firms, the established enterprises will be nearly immune to new competition, just as high-grade workers are immune to the competition of poorer grades. Here again one sees an alarming identity of interest between organized workers and employers and a rising barrier to entry of new firms, as well as to entry of new workers.[10]

Let me now propose some generalizations about wages and ideal wage policy, whether for a democratic capitalism or for a democratic socialism. To avoid the confusion and sophistry of "purchasing-power" arguments, we may simply abstract from monetary disturbances and deflations, supposing that the government successfully maintains a sound and highly stable currency, that is, a stable value of money or price index. This means that we shall be largely concerned here with principles of relative wages, since changes in average wages at relatively full employment imply changes in the general level of commodity prices, wages being the predominant element in costs.

The proper wage in any area or occupational category is the lowest wage which will bring forth an adequate supply of labor in competition with other employment opportunities. "Adequate supply" is ambiguous as it stands but will usually be interpreted correctly if not defined. It may, of course, be defined as the supply necessary to equate the productivity of transferable labor as between the industry or occupation in question and other alternative employments. In other words, it is the wage which will permit the maximum transfer of workers from less attractive, less remunerative, less productive employments. Broadly, for factory employment in general, it is the wage or wage level which will condemn the minimum number of workers to casual labor and to subsistence agriculture. We imply that any wage is excessive if more qualified workers are obtainable at that wage than are employed— provided only that the industry is reasonably competitive as among firms. Reduction of rates would permit workers to enter who otherwise would be compelled to accept employment less attractive to them and less productive for the community or to accept involuntary unemployment. This amounts to saying that any relative wage may be presumed to be too high if it requires the support of force (organization) or law.

The basic principle here is freedom of entry—freedom of migration, between localities, between industries, between occupational categories. If such freedom is to exist—and it is limited inevitably by costs and by defects of training and experience—wages must fall to accommodate new workers in any area to which many qualified persons wish to move. Freedom of migration implies freedom of qualified workers, not merely to seek jobs but to get them; free entry implies full employment for all qualified persons who wish to enter. Whether the wage permits an adequate family scale of living, according to social service workers, is simply irrelevant—as, indeed, are the net earnings of employers. What really matters is the judgment of workers who would be excluded by an excessive wage as to the *relative* merits of the employment in question and of employment in the less attractive alternatives actually open to them. Other things equal, the wage is too high if higher than the wage in actually alternative employments. Ethically, one cannot go beyond the opinion of qualified workers seeking to transfer. If in large numbers they prefer employment here to the alternatives and cannot get it, the wage is excessive. A case may be made for supplementing, by governmental expenditure, the family incomes of workers of low productivity, but not for keeping them idle or for confining them to less productive as against more productive employment.[11]

Now freedom of entry is peculiarly essential in the case of unusually remunerative employments, if one believes in greater equality of opportunity. Only by permitting the freest movement upward through wage categories can we minimize economic inequality and maximize incomes at the bottom of the scale. But it is exactly the high-wage industries which invite and facilitate organization; and it is the favorably situated who have most to gain by exclusion, restriction, and monopolistic practices. At best, no labor organization is likely to be more unselfish or to make less use of its powers than the American Medical Association; and, considering its loose organization and small power, the comparison is surely alarming.

Organization is a device by which privilege may be intrenched and consolidated. It is a device by which the strong may raise themselves higher by pressing down the weak. Unionism, barring entry into the most attractive employments, makes high wages higher and low wages lower. Universally applied, it gets nowhere save to create disorder. Surely we cannot all get rich by restricting production. Monopoly works when everyone does not try it or when few have effective power. Universally applied it is like universal, uniform subsidy paid out of universal, uniform taxation, save that the latter is merely ridiculous while the former is also incompatible with economy of resources and even with order. But the dictator will be installed long before monopoly or functional organization becomes universal. Must we leave it to the man on horseback, or to popes of the future, to restore freedom of opportunity and freedom of occupational movement?

Unionism is only incidentally a means for raising labor incomes at the expense of profits or property income. Profits are usually a small moiety, sometimes positive and often negative;

and all property income is a margin whose reduction by particular wage increases reacts promptly and markedly upon employment, production, and product price. Increased labor cost in particular areas has its impact upon earnings; but, as with excise taxes, the burden or incidence quickly transfers to the buyer of products, if not to sellers of services, via output changes.

Labor demands may be rationalized and popularized as demands for a larger share of earnings—as part of a contest over the shares of labor and capital in particular outputs. But enterprises remain essentially intermediaries between sellers of services and buyers of product. The semblance of struggle between labor and capital conceals the substantial conflict between a labor monopoly and the community; between organized workers and consumers; and especially between established workers in more remunerative occupations and workers elsewhere. The masses of the unorganized and unorganizable lose as consumers; they lose by being denied access to higher-wage areas; and they lose by an artificial abundance of labor in the markets where they must sell, that is, by being forced to compete with workers who should have been drawn off into the higher-wage occupations. And let no one infer that their problem would be solved if they too were organized. The monopoly racket, like that of tariffs and subsidies, works only so long as it is exceptional—works only to advantage minorities relatively, with over-all diseconomy and loss.[12]

Let me now explain an earlier dictum that proper wages are a matter of alternative employment opportunities and not of enterprise earnings or profits. In wage negotiations and arbitration the level of business earnings is usually given much stress—by management if they are low and by unions if they are high. The implication is that the proper correction for large earnings, if not for losses, is wage increase. This plausible notion, however, does not bear much examination.

In a world of continuous innovation, change in relative costs, and change in consumer tastes, new industries appear and old ones vanish; and among enduring industries some are always rising and others declining in the economy. When one industry enjoys an unexpected or inadequately anticipated improvement of demand conditions or production methods, earnings will rise markedly; and, with strong labor organization, this will mean larger wage demands. But should the industry meet such demands and share its earnings more largely with its existing employes?

Such adjustment, at least temporarily, is to be commended so far as it would occur in a free-market system. Employers would naturally seek to expand their outputs by drawing workers from competitors and by drawing them from other industries. However, if workers are not highly specialized—as they are not in the longer view—the relative increase here would be temporary, serving to attract young workers and to induce transfer where costs and sacrifices were moderate; and the long-term effect would be, not increase in relative wages but increase in the quantity and proportion of various kinds of labor in this as against other industries using similar kinds.

Where labor resources are not much specialized, the proper correction for inordinate rates of return on investment is not higher wages, but larger investment, larger employment, larger output, and lower relative product prices. If the large earnings reflect monopoly restraint upon output by enterprises, as they occasionally will, measures should be taken to extirpate such restraint; monopoly in the labor market will only aggravate and consolidate restriction. Temporary increases in relative wages are justified if necessary to attract additional supplies of labor from other industries. If attained by collusive, collective action of workers where supply is adequate or redundant, increases will serve, not to facilitate expansion of output, but to prevent it.

With strong organization, increased earnings will always be accompanied by demands for higher wages. If the earnings increase is general, and if there is little unemployment, the wage increases will be economically necessary and desirable. Gradual secular increase is to be expected in a progressive economy. But note the awful effects of adjusting *relative* wages continuously to relative earnings. Even in a vigorous and healthy system, some industries and employments will always be contracting, relatively and absolutely. Given free markets, the slack will readily be taken up by industries where demand conditions are improving. Expanding industries will absorb the labor released by those which contract—but only if the opportunities for expansion are not blocked by arbitrary increases of costs, that is, if the stimulus of relatively high business earnings reacts mainly upon employment rather than upon wage rates.

With strong organization, established workers in expansible employments are in a position to prevent expansion and must do so to capture for themselves the full advantage of favorable changes affecting their industry or product market. Ethically, they should share their gains with the community as consumers and with outside workers for whom expansion of output would permit transfer from less remunerative employment. But no group will practice such sharing if it has power to prevent it.

The situation here is especially alarming when one considers it from the viewpoint of enterprises or investors. In a free-market world, every commitment of capital is made in the face of enormous uncertainties. One may lose heavily or gain vastly, depending on unpredictable (uninsurable) contingencies. For reasonably intelligent investors, however, the gamble, with free markets, is a fairly even one, with chances of gain balancing roughly the risks of loss—relative to a conservative commitment, say, in government bonds. The willingness to take chances, to venture with one's property, especially in new and novel enterprises, of course, is the very basis of our whole economic and political system. It is now gravely jeopardized by developments which tend ominously to diminish the chances of gain relative to the chances of loss.

Much has been made of our taxes as factors inhibiting enterprise; but their effects on this score are, I think, grossly exaggerated and, in any case, concern mainly structural faults in our levies which are, in the main, quite as inimical to equitable progression as they are prejudicial against enterprise. We can, by proper reforms, mitigate the bias of taxes against venturesome investment, while strengthening the progressive principle and applying it more fully. But the bias against new investment inherent in labor organization is important and cannot be removed by changes in matters of detail. Investors now face nearly all the disagreeable uncertainties of investors in a free-market world plus the prospect that labor organizations will appropriate most or all of the earnings which would otherwise accrue if favorable contingencies materialized. Indeed, every new, long-term commitment of capital is now a matter of giving hostages to organized sellers of complementary services. Enterprisers must face all the old risks of investing in the wrong places—risks of demand changes, of technical obsolescence in plant facilities, and of guessing badly only because too many others guessed the same way. Besides, they must risk being unable to recover the productivity which their assets would have if there were free-market access to complementary factors. The prospect for losses is as good as ever; the prospect of profits is, in the main, profoundly impaired.

If we are to preserve modern industrial production without totalitarian control, we must solve the problem of private investment. There is now much profoundly foolish talk of economic maturity and of technically deficient outlets for new investment. Such talk is plausible for those who would evade hard problems and unpalatable facts; and it is more than welcome to those who pray for revolution here. It invites defeatism among those who cherish democracy; and it counsels policies which eat away the foundations of democracy in our economic way of life. But the phenomenal deficiency of pri-

vate investment in recent years requires for explanation no recourse to factually unsupported (and, I believe, grossly false)
conjectures about "real" investment opportunities. I believe
that investment opportunities were never so large as now;
that our highest thrift would not for generations permit
enough investment to lower interest rates substantially, if
owners of new capital assets could be assured of free-market
access to labor and other complementary factors (mainly indirect labor). But the prospect of such access has diminished
everywhere. Every new enterprise and every new investment
must now pay heavy tribute to labor (and other monopolies)
in acquiring its plant and equipment; and it faces the prospect
of increasing extortion in its efforts to utilize facilities after they
are constructed. (Labor monopolies are highly concentrated
in construction and in capital-goods industries generally;
they are also peculiarly characteristic of the more capital-
intensive industries.)

I am not concerned here with corruption and dishonesty
among labor leaders, or with their salaries, although much can
and should be said on that score. The whole scheme of
monopolizing labor markets obviously invites abuses of bribery
and extortion and use of power by leaders for both political
and pecuniary advantage to themselves. But, for purposes of
argument here, I am willing to ignore personal corruption and
private extortion, that is, I am willing to suppose that unions
are always managed scrupulously and faithfully in the interest
of the overwhelming majority of their established members.
When I say that investors and enterprisers face an alarming
prospect of extortion at the hands of organized sellers of labor,
I refer merely to the prospect that bargaining or monopoly
powers inherent in organization will be exercised fully, in a
manner now recognized and sanctioned as proper and legitimate. There is every prospect that opportunities for collective,
collusive, monopolistic action in particular labor markets will
increase indefinitely wherever organization is possible. This
prospect alone suffices to explain the ominous decline of pri-

vate investment and the virtual disappearance of venturesome new enterprise.

In the name of equalizing bargaining power we have sanctioned and promoted the proliferation of militant labor monopolies whose proper, natural function is exploitation of consumers. The ultimate burden of their exactions will not fall mainly upon industrial investors or enterprises; but enterprises, as intermediaries, will bear the impact of new exactions and may expect to see earnings continuously pressed down to such extent that average expectations are utterly discouraging. For industrial investors, the result is much the same as though the state had promoted organized banditry and denied them all protection against it—while offering unusual safeguards to holders of idle funds (deposits) and large new investment outlets in government bonds (not to mention "tax-exempts").

We face a real problem in economic inequality. This problem can be handled easily and without serious diseconomies, if one is not hysterically in a hurry, by progressive taxation of income and inheritance. Merely by repairing a few structural flaws in our income tax, we could assure steady reduction of inequality in property incomes and continuous correction of wide disparities in nonproperty incomes. But radicals and power-seekers have little interest in such dull, peaceful, orderly, efficient, gradualist methods. So they have simply ignored critical issues in tax reform and plumped for labor organization. They have promoted the organization of innumerable industrial armies, with implicit sanction to employ force, coercion, and violence to the full extent of their power, at least to prevent competing sales of services at rates below their own offers. We are told that violence is essential only in the organizing phase; that it will disappear afterward as organization is achieved and recognized—which, of course, is true. Organizations which have attained power need use little overt violence to maintain it. However, it is only the middle phase of unionism or syndicalism which is nonviolent. There is much violence at the start inevitably; but there is more and worse violence at the end, involving total reconstitution of the political system. Somehow, sometime, the conflict between the special interests of labor monopolies and the common interest must be reconciled. Beyond some point their exactions become insufferable and insupportable; and their power must be broken to protect the general welfare.

Romantic socialists, having the political sense to support unionism, ask us to believe that the whole problem of functional minorities would simply disappear if ownership and management of industry passed into government hands. Organizations, having fought and bled to attain monopoly powers, allegedly will simply give up their powers on the coming of the socialist state, begging the good socialists to reduce their wages so that prices may be lowered and new workers inducted wholesale into their occupational preserves. All this, to say the least, seems highly improbable!

The political alliance between socialists and unionists is fundamentally anomalous. Socialism, if it is to be democratic at all, must utilize a price system and must adhere closely to ideal competitive norms. Unionism, on the other hand, rests basically on rejection of free pricing in labor markets—and this is no less true of industrial unions than of trade-unions. Socialism must preserve the greatest freedom of occupational migration. Unionism must, except by deliberate forfeiting of its powers, create barriers against competition and immigration. Socialism must concern itself about consumers and workers generally; unions must represent and promote the special interests of their own particular minorities.

But, to pursue my point, progressive taxation is a workable, democratic method for dealing with inequality. The alternative of unionists is to send workers out in packs to exploit and expropriate by devices which resemble those of bandit armies. The one device is inherently orderly, peaceful, gradualist, and efficient. It is the device of law. The other is inherently violent, disruptive, and wasteful in the extreme. One calls for debate, discussion, and political action; the other, for fighting and promiscuous expropriation.

Unionists are much like our Communist friends. They are good fighters and like fighting for its own sake. They are extremely effective at undermining the political and economic system which we have but are surprisingly unconcerned and inarticulate about the nature of the world which they would create afterward. In neither case is there much constructive thought. Communists are out to destroy capitalism; unionists are out to destroy competition in labor markets. The former talk a lot about the evils of capitalism but never tell us much descriptively about the good life. Unionists, on the other hand, have never bothered to draw us a picture of their utopia. In other words, they have taken unions for granted as necessary elements in the good society but have not bothered about the nature of the good society within which unions would be good.

Scholars will protest that these overstatements ignore a great mass of anarchist, syndicalist, and guild-socialist literature. However, one may assert categorically that such literature offers no democratic solution for the problems in question. Anarchism has the merit of stressing values which have proper place in any sound value scheme, although they can have major or primary place only in the constitution of heaven. It may be regarded as the idealistic conception to which traditional liberalism represents the closest practical approach. While anarchists deplore all organized coercion, liberals would confine it narrowly within the limits of impersonal justice, of rules of law imposed only on the basis of consensus arising out of free discussion. They would limit the range of governmental functions, especially for the larger units of government between which persons are least free to move; and they would defend competitive private enterprise as the only system of control compatible with that measure of decentralization of power which affords real protection against tyranny and chaos. Government by discussion of impersonal principles of policy and by the objective discipline of free competition is the practical answer, in a world of elaborate productional organization and intricate differentiation of human activity, to the perfectionist plea for heavenly freedom.

In spite of seemingly intimate connection between syndicalism and anarchism, they can be related closely in principle only by adopting the vulgar parody of anarchism as dynamiting and disorder. Syndicalism, in my humble opinion, simply cannot be formulated, as a scheme of political order, in such manner as to invite intelligent discussion or serious intellectual inquiry on details. Efforts in this direction, by English proponents of guild-socialism, may be commended as an honest attempt to define the outlines of the good society which might be realized by utilizing the actual institutional trends of their time. But the efforts must, on any realistic political analysis, be judged an utter, if magnificent, intellectual failure. I doubt if the Webbs themselves would now find convincing the proposals so laboriously worked out in their *Constitution*.

Guild-socialism, with all its surface appeal, remains, to realistic inspection, simply a projected chaos of pluralism—a multiplicity of industrial or occupational states, nominally disciplined by a legislature, representing the common interest but actually powerless against the stronger syndicates. The conception is perhaps less implausible to Englishmen, who have never lived with the syndicalism of American tariff legislation or experienced fully the democratic corruption of pension legislation. Here, we should clearly sense the fact that minorities, industrial or functional minorities especially, are the great nemesis to democracy and that democracy, if it survives, must, above all, learn how to discipline and de-organize such minorities as special-interest pressure groups. Guild socialism is the perfect prescription for exposing democracy hopelessly and fatally to a corruption which has spread endlessly even under the geographic basis of representation and organization that should have reduced the danger to a minimum.

Few Americans will straightforwardly espouse syndicalism or look with approval on Il Duce's corporative state. Few likewise will face the patent fact that we are rushing pell-mell toward and into that political order in the United States. Our formal political structure, of course, retains its traditional character. Our legislators, state and federal, still represent geographic sections of the nation. But alongside this formal political structure arises now a structure of powerful organizations of labor, immune to prosecution as monopolies and largely immune to the proscriptions or penalties of other laws. An essentially syndicalist order (or disorder) may, of course, evolve or arise without formal participation of industrial or occupational organizations in the legislative process. Indeed, such organizations may exercise greater power as extra-constitutional political agencies than they could if they had direct representation in Congress, in state assemblies, and in county and local government.

The intricate pluralism of modern democracies is, of course, a commonplace among students of sociology and politics. Equally commonplace, however, is the fact that organized minorities are a continuing threat to democratic order and internal peace. The danger may arise dramatically in the case of churches, secret societies, vigilante movements, a Ku Klux Klan, or less dramatically in the case of political machines, tariff lobbies, silver senators, veterans' organizations, and farm blocs. In the main, however, we have rarely or briefly endured political usurpation by minorities practicing violence and intimidation; and (save at federal levels!) we manage somehow to stop corruption and vote-buying short of insolvency and short of disintegration in political morality.

But, to repeat, we have never faced the kind of minority problem which widespread, aggressive, national and regional unions and their federations present. They are essentially occupational armies, born and reared amidst violence, led by fighters, and capable of becoming peaceful only as their power becomes irresistible. Other groups practice violence, of course;

but few others practice it with general public approbation or employ it at all without grave risks of punishment or loss of power. Peaceful strikes, even in the absence of overt violence or intimidation, are a meaningless conception when they involve disruption of an elaborate production process with intricate division of labor. What is obvious in the case of railways and utilities is similarly true of coal-mining, steel production, and ultimately of every important industry and occupation.

Some conservatives will defend labor organization in terms of the right of voluntary association as a basic privilege in a democratic system, while deploring the use of violence and intimidation. Obviously, the practical problem would largely disappear if laws protecting persons and property were enforcible and enforced against strikers, pickets, and labor organizers. But there are no absolute rights; and the right of voluntary association must always be qualified, *inter alia*, by prohibitions against monopolizing—against collusive action among sellers. Failing ability to use violence or to threaten it effectively, particular organizations could not practice heavy extortion or sustain it indefinitely; but they could often tax the community substantially for a time and subject it to substantial, if minor, disturbances. The grave diseconomies of the theorist's pure cartel situation, in labor and other markets, are relevant to real situations, actual and possible; and protection of the public interest demands limitation of the right of association where the association is of people as suppliers of particular commodities or services.[13]

The point, in any case, is rather academic, for labor organization without large powers of coercion and intimidation is an unreal abstraction. Unions now have such powers; they always have had and always will have, so long as they persist in their present form. Where the power is small or insecurely possessed, it must be exercised overtly and extensively; large and unchallenged, it becomes like the power of strong government, confidently held, respectfully regarded, and rarely displayed conspicuously. But, to repeat, this apparent peacefulness of a maturing syndicalism is unsubstantial and deceptive. It marks a fundamental disintegration of the very bases of political order —a disappearance of free exchange and of the state's monopoly of coercion. Individual groups, securely organized and secure in their monopoly positions, may levy their exactions without overt violence and merely through peaceful political maneuvering (via the arbitration device especially). However, they necessarily restrict drastically the normal flows of trade, destroying general prosperity in their struggle for relative advantage, and reducing enterprisers and investors to a defensive, defeatist task of withdrawing their property, on the least unfavorable terms obtainable politically, into the dubious security of government bonds. Ultimately, this means disappearance of all opportunities for remunerative enterprise and investment, governmental or private, via excessive costs, actual and prospective. Moreover, it means a drying-up of government revenues, whether derived by taxes from return on private property or from socialized enterprise. It means also vastly increasing dispensations by way of unemployment relief and other meliorative measures.

A maturing syndicalism is the mature economy of our monetary and fiscal extremists. It is inherently unstable and unmanageable. It may be kept going, at income levels far short of our potentialities, by sufficiently large fiscal and monetary stimulation; and no one may wisely condemn policies which postpone revolutionary upheaval if postponement alone is possible. But we should face the fact that nothing else is ahead along this route. Especially, we should be skeptical of economic analysis and prescription which rests on the political premise that mass monopolies (and increasing enterprise monopoly) are ordained and assured for the future beyond any recourse of democratic discussion and orderly political process.

Our great minority and monopoly problem of the present and of the discernible future is the problem of labor organization. One may stress the right of voluntary association or, rather, the right of free entry into occupations. One may stress the right to bargain collectively on a national or regional scale or, rather, the right of free occupational migration. In neither case can one sensibly defend both categorically. If one is accorded and exercised, the other is curtailed or destroyed. The issue is simply whether wage rates should be determined competitively or monopolistically.

The obvious struggle within particular industries over division of earnings tends largely to obscure the more substantial identity of interest and functional complementarity of labor and employer organizations. Popularly regarded and defended as counterpoises to industrial concentration or enterprise monopoly, unions in fact serve mainly to buttress effective monopoly in product markets where it already obtains and to call it into existence when it does not. Labor leaders have, indeed, a quite normal appetite for monopoly prices and for monopoly profits which bargaining power permits them to appropriate and to distribute among their members.

While extremely ill-informed, I know of no instance where a powerful union has proposed reduction of a monopolistic product price or given real support, singly or in federations, to antitrust policy. On the other hand, N.I.R.A., like extreme tariff protection, was strongly supported by organized labor. The formal and enforced cartelization of the coal industry may be credited largely to the U.M.W. And, if some proposals of C.I.O. leaders for labor participation in management are not pure cartel schemes, I cannot identify the beast when I see it. If labor remains and becomes increasingly cartelized along industry lines, enterprises must be similarly organized for bargaining purposes—not only to present a united front and to recoup wage increases from consumers but because labor itself will prefer, demand, and, in any case, compel such employer organization.

We have often been told that difficulties in collective bargaining, and mutual intransigence of the participants, were only vestiges of the frontier and would disappear as America caught up with European civilization. We have been chided for our backwardness and urged to seek that matter-of-fact acceptance of collective bargaining and that maturity in union-employer relations which have obtained in Germany, France, and England. It may seem unsporting, in these days, to note that history has recently played nasty tricks on condescending apologists for American adolescence and upon zealous importers of European institutions—but, in fact, these folk seem only more capable of ignoring history when it screams against their position than of misinterpreting it when it can be used plausibly for their purposes.

I do not maintain that German trade-unions caused I.G. Farben and the Nazi revolution, or that French labor caused the disintegration of the French army, or that I.C.I. and the awful state of English industry are attributable to national collective bargaining. I do hold that large and powerful labor unions are integral elements in a total institutional complex whose development is everywhere antithetical to economic freedom, to political liberty, and to world peace; that we should here stop the development short of the German or French denouement and short of the awful mess which is now the English economy; and that we cannot import and retain the labor-organization component of this complex or trend without importing the rest of it too. If western Europe had maturity in collective bargaining and labor relations and if England has it still, these facts argue strongly against abandoning our democratic adolescence.

We must alter our labor policy or abandon our antitrust policy—as English businessmen so urgently recommend. If one big union is a *fait accompli* in, say, the automobile industry, that industry is all through as a competitive sector of our economy—and damned to full cartelization, if not to General Motors. Thanks largely to Thurman Arnold and, now, to an unprecedented sprinkling of intelligent business leaders, the prospects for sound antitrust policy are perhaps better than they have ever been, here or anywhere. Even if these prospects materialize abundantly after the war, however, the achievements

must be frustrated and then sharply reversed unless accompanied or followed closely by reversal of recent trends in labor
organization. If labor is tightly cartelized or syndicalized, enterprises must adjust themselves to the political realities. Even
Arnold could not much deflect their deference or allegiance
from the real *loci* of power.

Business leaders, even when qualified in terms of tolerance
and wisdom, are hopelessly disqualified, by their fiduciary responsibilities if not merely by what they symbolize, for leadership in the hard part of this task. They can and may put their
own house in better democratic order. That is no small job;
but it is all that they can do toward reversing the syndicalist
trend in America. And it is not enough—not more than a
beginning. Labor-baiters of dubious repute will volunteer in
hordes for the real task, and thereby aggravate enormously the
sufficient difficulties. Much the same must be said of the conservatives who now dominate our two great political parties—
men whose negligible capacity for frankness and whose stupid
smartness in devious maneuver are perhaps a greater obstacle
to solution than are the prospective harangues of professional
demagogues on either side.

It is easy to argue that the whole problem is so hard and
ominous politically that no effort should be made to solve or
even to see it—that the real choice lies between a certain,
gradual death of economic democracy and an operation or
treatment which would cure if successful but is almost certain
to kill. I am no forecaster and am not in direct communica-
tion with the Almighty. Consequently, I can only maintain
that it is immoral to take such absolute dilemmas seriously.
Democracy would have been dead a thousand times if it paid
much attention to historical extrapolations; and it is perhaps
unnecessary to discuss now the shortcomings of temporizing
expedients or appeasement.

If we can win this war, we can also win the peace; but, for
world order even more obviously than for internal order, free-

dom of trade and exchange is simply indispensable. With free trade the world can gradually be welded into a securely peaceful, democratic whole; with it, we may work miracles in monetary and political co-operation, in raising standards everywhere by economic integration and by relatively unrestricted movements both of goods and of investment funds. We may become free, nationally and on a world scale, if we set as our goal the greatest possible dispersion of military, political, and economic (monopoly) power. Freer trade is, I insist, the *sine qua non* of a durable peace. Attaining it, we can, if we will, raise our own living standards indefinitely while raising standards throughout the world. Thus our momentary military dominance might be used, not merely to enforce peace upon the world but to create a world society which would gradually come to enforce peace upon itself, with America gradually discarding its military domination in favor of moral leadership and partnership in a common task of keeping open the channels of trade and preserving peace.

But there can be no free world trade without free internal trade in the dominant postwar nation. Free access to markets implies, not merely absence of tariffs, exchange controls, and quota limitations, but opportunity to sell to competitive buyers and to buy from competitive sellers in every national market. Free trade among collectivisms is a meaningless conception. Much the same must be said of free trade between substantially syndicalist nations. There can be no really free access to raw materials produced by monopolists or cartels or to raw materials produced by workers organized to price their services monopolistically.

Given free internal trade, we might prosper substantially in isolation from the world (if it would permit us that isolation!). Given that free internal trade, however, we can prosper far more abundantly as part of a world economy and can lead the whole world into durable prosperity and peace. Thus, I submit that the peace will be won or lost in the field of American domestic economic policy. Other groups will bitterly oppose the necessary dismantling of our tariff barrier. However, if the battle for peace via free trade comes near to being won, it will, I think, be won or lost on issues in the field of labor policy.

The immediate issues will, of course, have to do mainly with our tariff. But labor groups, more effectively than others, may be expected to resist drastic reduction or elimination of protective duties. Even if we succeed in establishing free external trade, these groups will still be able to prevent necessary internal adjustments and to drive us back to protection as a shortsighted remedy for depression and unemployment caused by cost-price maladjustments. True, we might assure reasonably full employment at any level of money wages by sufficient injections of money and raising of the price level. But wartime experience indicates (what should be obvious on its face) that price inflation is a hopeless method of lowering real wages of strong and strategically situated labor groups—that such policy means only an endless spiral of inflation. The postwar adjustment of wartime wages in our heavy industries will be enormously difficult in any case. Without sharp reduction in many areas, private employment cannot revive adequately, save at a much higher price level; and forcing that higher level means not only expropriation of holders of defense bonds and other creditors but great risk of runaway inflation.

The peace will be won or lost on the simple issue of economic disarmament. The extreme nationalism of high protection, quota limitations, exchange controls, and bilateral trading must be swept away, at least among the leading protagonists in the present conflict. But movement in this direction cannot come unless there is wholesale economic disarmament also *within* these nations. As nations, we must abandon the contest for dominance and subjugation, finding our proper places in a close-knit, integrated world economy whose markets and commodities are freely and equally available to all. As individuals, we must find and make our places in a domestic system of free exchange, instead of organizing into occupational or industrial states to pursue domestically a power contest which is the analogue of war among nations and perhaps its most important cause.

VII

Rules versus Authorities in Monetary Policy*

THE monetary problem stands out today as the great intellectual challenge to the liberal faith. For generations we have been developing financial practices, financial institutions, and financial structures which are incompatible with the orderly functioning of a system based on economic freedom and political liberty. Even more disturbing, perhaps, than the institutional trend is the trend of thinking and discussion among special students of money—the fact that economists have become accustomed to deal with monetary problems in a manner which impliedly belies their professed liberalism.

The liberal creed demands the organization of our economic life largely through individual participation in a game *with definite rules*. It calls upon the state to provide a stable framework of rules within which enterprise and competition may effectively control and direct the production and distribution of goods. The essential conception is that of a genuine division of labor between competitive (market) and political controls— a division of labor within which competition has a major, or at least proximately primary, place.

A liberal system adapted to modern conditions would be, of course, exceedingly complex, by comparison with an authoritarian collectivism. It would involve a large measure of political control: outright collectivism in some areas; deliberate enforcement of competition in others; prevention of extreme inequality, largely via taxation, in the distribution of property, income, and power. Moreover, such a system is attainable, through economic reconstruction, only by years of careful

* Reprinted by permission from the *Journal of Political Economy*, XLIV, No. 1 (February, 1936), 1–30.

planning and wise legislation; and, once realized, however perfectly, it would require continuous modification, with at least minor changes in the rules, to meet new developments and new conditions.

There is thus little point in contrasting a liberal system and a planned economy—except for the coincidence that the latter phrase has been appropriated by reformers who have little sympathy with, and less understanding of, the liberal position.

There is imminent danger, however, that actual governmental policies will undermine irreparably the kind of economic and political life which most of us prefer to the possible alternatives. This danger manifests itself mainly in three ways: (1) in the displacement of price competition by political (governmental or monopoly) control in many areas where such competition, if established, preserved, and properly canalized, is peculiarly competent for promoting the general welfare; (2) in the neglect of the unquestioned positive responsibilities of governments under the free-enterprise system; and (3) in measures and policies which involve delegation of legislative powers and the setting-up of *authorities instead of rules*.[1]

It is this danger of substituting authorities for rules which especially deserves attention among students of money. There are, of course, many special responsibilities which may wisely be delegated to administrative authorities with substantial discretionary power; health authorities, for example, cannot well be limited narrowly in their activities by legislative prescriptions. The expedient must be invoked sparingly, however, if democratic institutions are to be preserved; and it is utterly inappropriate in the money field. An enterprise system cannot function effectively in the face of extreme uncertainty as to the action of monetary authorities or, for that matter, as to monetary legislation. We must avoid a situation where every business venture becomes largely a speculation on the future of monetary policy. In the past, governments have grossly neglected their positive responsibility of controlling the currency; private initiative has been allowed too much freedom in determining the character of our financial structure and in directing changes in the quantity of money and money substitutes. On this point there is now little disagreement. In our search for solutions of this problem, however, we seem largely to have lost sight of the essential point, namely, that definite, stable, legislative rules of the game as to money are of paramount importance to the survival of a system based on freedom of enterprise.

Indeed, it may be said that economists, as students of money and banking, have accepted and propagated the first serious heresy among liberals. Managed currency (along with protectionism) is the prototype of all current "planning" schemes —in the sense of all the illiberal connotations of planning. To be sure, many economists still protest vigorously against proposals for currency management; but they and their teachers before them joined zealously in the movement for central banking—and it is precisely here that the heresy is clearly manifested.

This unwitting defection among custodians of the liberal faith is explicable, and may be apologized for, in terms of an unfortunate habit of distinguishing too sharply between currency and banking problems, and in terms of a disposition to look upon banking arrangements as merely a detail or subsidiary system within the supposedly automatic mechanism of the gold standard. Only of late is it clearly realized that the money problem has been swallowed up in the credit problem or that gold has long been reduced largely to the status of a decorative symbol within a welter of national policies as to central banking, government finance, and foreign trade.

Economist-liberals are now on the defensive. On most fronts, however, their position is, or can be made, very strong intellectually. Conspicuous weakness is to be found only with respect to the problems of money and banking. There is little agreement, and not much relevant discussion, as to how the monetary rules of the game might effectively be altered to prevent or greatly to mitigate the affliction of extreme industrial fluctuations. We cannot effectively answer radical critics of the present system, or expose the stupid schemes of plausible reformers, by saying that the problems which they find in other areas are really just problems of money (although this observation is usually correct and pointed), when we have no good solutions to propose, with some unanimity, in the money field.

Our problem is that of defining an adequate monetary system based on simple rules and of finding the way toward such a system. We cannot seek merely to return to some arrangement of the past. The monetary problem was never solved in the past. There is no adequate system of rules to be found in earlier arrangements—except in the sense that the specific form of the rules was formerly, in a more flexible economy, a matter of less importance. Moreover, we have become so habituated to the fact and to the idea of "management," especially with respect to banking, that we shall find it hard either to reject the palliatives which management offers or even to face squarely our intellectual task.

It is significant that the most stimulating contribution to recent discussion, namely, the conception of a neutral money, comes from a group of economists who have held most firmly to the essential tenets of old-fashioned liberalism. In this conception we have, perhaps, a clue as to how the practical problem may ultimately be solved—although it must be conceded that the conception rather defies precise definition or easy translation into concrete proposals.

An effort at such translation was made recently by a group, including the present writer, in connection with some tentative proposals for banking reform.[2] These proposals contemplated (a) putting demand-deposit banking on a 100 per cent reserve basis and, more tentatively, (b) eventual fixing of the total quantity of circulating media (currency plus demand deposits).[3]

The fixing of the quantity of circulating media is attractive as a principle of monetary policy for several reasons: (1) it avoids reliance on discretionary (dictatorial, arbitrary) action by an independent monetary authority and defines a statutory rule which might be enacted by the competent legislature without substantial delegation of its powers; (2) it provides automatically for downward adjustment of commodity prices as output expands through improvement in technical efficiency; (3) it represents a rule which, from the viewpoint of a contractual, enterprise economy, is ideally definite and simple; and (4) it is clear enough and reasonable enough to provide the basis for a new "religion of money," around which might be regimented strong sentiments against tinkering with the currency. It requires little or no judgment in its administration; it defines a policy in terms of means not merely in terms of ends; it is compatible with the rule of balancing governmental revenues and expenditures; and it gives to "inflation" a simple meaning which would be conducive to long-term stability in, and observance of, this section of the rules of the economic game.

With all its merits, however, this rule cannot now be recommended as a basis for monetary reform. The obvious weakness of fixed quantity, as a sole rule of monetary policy, lies in the danger of sharp changes on the velocity side, for no monetary system can function effectively or survive politically in the face of extreme alternations of hoarding and dishoarding. It is easy to argue that something would be gained in any event if perverse changes were prevented merely as to quantity, but the argument is unconvincing. The fixing of the quantity of circulating media might merely serve to increase the perverse variability in the amounts of "near-moneys" and in the degree of their general acceptability, just as the restrictions on the issue of bank notes presumably served to hasten the development of deposit (checking-account) banking.

This possibility is clearest in the case of savings accounts (time deposits), where one faces a real difficulty of preventing, and even of defining, effective circulation.[4] The questions which may be raised in this case alone are, indeed, sufficiently involved to dictate one's passing immediately, in discussion, to a broader and less practical approach.

The problem of synchronous industrial (employment) fluctuations is a problem (a) of rigidities in crucial areas of the price structure—of adjustments made through output and employment instead of through prices and wage rates—and (b) of perverse flexibility in the total turnover (quantity and velocity) of effective money. Assuming now a limited flexibility in prices and wages, let us try to see what would be the nature of better or ideal conditions on the financial side. What arrangements as to the financial structure would be conducive to lesser or minimum amplitude of industrial fluctuations?[5]

An approximately ideal condition is fairly obvious—and unattainable. The danger of pervasive, synchronous, cumulative maladjustments would be minimized if there were no fixed money contracts at all—if all property were held in a residual-equity or common-stock form. With such a financial structure, no one would be in a position either to create effective money substitutes (whether for circulation or for hoarding) or to force enterprises into wholesale efforts at liquidation.[6] Hoarding and dishoarding (changes in velocity) would, to be sure, still occur; but the dangers of cumulative maladjustment would be minimized.[7]

Not far short of the ideal is a financial system in which all borrowing and lending takes the form of contracts in perpetuity—contracts on which repayment of principal can never be demanded. Given a large volume of financing on such contracts, the mere burden of the fixed annuity charges might occasionally lead to extensive effort among enterprisers to become more liquid. The protection against demands for payment of principal, however, leaves the total of fixed claims relatively small. Moreover, these perpetuities, being subject to substantial change of selling prices, would be relatively unattractive as money substitutes in hoards.

Only a little farther away from the best system is one where all borrowing and lending contracts are entered into for long periods—say, for at least fifty years. Here there would be the added danger that such maturities as did occur during a depression would be availed of to augment money hoards,[8] but the percentage of total obligations falling due in any critical period would probably be small.

Coming on down the scale, the economy becomes exposed to catastrophic disturbances as soon as short-term borrowing develops on a large scale. No real stability of production and employment is possible when short-term lenders are continuously in a position to demand conversion of their investments, amounting in the aggregate to a large multiple of the total available circulating media, into such media. Such an economy is workable only on the basis of a utopian flexibility of prices and wage rates. Short-term obligations provide abundant money substitutes during booms, thus releasing money from cash reserves; and they precipitate hopeless efforts at liquidation during depressions. The shorter the period of money contracts, the more unstable the economy will be; at worst, all money contracts would be in the form of call loans.

Thus we move rapidly out of sight of ideal or even tolerable conditions if there develop special institutional arrangements for financing a large volume of investment commitments (which are, or, to permit steady and efficient functioning of the economy, would have to be, essentially permanent and continuing) through intermediaries (banks) which obtain funds for lending by issuing demand and near-demand claims to the original lenders (depositors). If the state gives special status to banking corporations, if their obligations become the established medium of payment, and, what is perhaps more important, if these obligations come to be considered as good as (or, for convenience, better than) currency for use as reserves, then the banking system acquires in effect the prerogative of currency issue and places the government under the practical necessity of giving these private obligations virtually the status of public debts. Demand-deposit banking represents a gigantic development of call-loan financing; moreover, the practical difference between demand deposits and time deposits (savings accounts) is slight indeed.

The fact that such a system will be exposed repeatedly to complete insolvency is perhaps not a matter of primary concern, for government intervention to protect at least the great majority of banks may be taken for granted. What matters is the character of the financial structure which banking creates—and the fact that, in the very nature of the system, banks will flood the economy with money substitutes during booms and precipitate futile efforts at general liquidation afterward.

Two special circumstances serve to make such a financial system still more sensitive to disturbances: (1) the maintenance by banks of relatively small cushions of owner equities and (2) the practice of making short-term loans which represent secondary, unsecured claims. Thus, a relatively small decline of security values properly raises question as to the solvency of banks and induces widespread effort to improve the quality of bank assets. Moreover, bankers as holders of unsecured claims naturally respond to signs of unfavorable business conditions with sharp contraction of loans. Certainly, it is an unhappy arrangement whereby those who can demand prompt repayment (can discontinue lending) are, because of the preferred position of other creditors in bankruptcy, compelled to attempt immediate liquidation in the face of the slightest uncertainty.

The notion has somehow become prevalent that banks ought to invest only or largely in short-term commercial paper; indeed, one finds here the rationale of a great enterprise in banking reform. Anyone who is not something of an economist can see that banks, acquiring funds subject to call should lend only upon promise of early repayment; but the notion, while plausible, is entirely spurious. Indeed, the adherence to this cardinal rule of conservative lending serves (would serve), not to mitigate the affliction of banking, but to compound it; for banks thus increase the volume of short-term debts, not merely in acquiring funds, but in lending them as well. It must be accounted one of the most unfortunate effects of modern banking that it has facilitated and encouraged the growth of short-term financing in business generally.[9]

The penultimate step away from the ideal financial system carries us to one under which all matured (demand) and maturing obligations are legally convertible into some particular commodity like gold, whose total available supply is only a trivial fraction of the amounts which creditors are in a position to demand. And, finally, the worst financial structure is realized when many nations, with similar financial practices and institutions and similar credit pyramids (and narrowly nationalist commercial policies), adopt the same commodity as the monetary standard. When one thinks of the total potential creditor demands for gold for hoarding, in and after 1929, it seems almost beyond diabolical ingenuity to conceive a financial system better designed for our economic destruction. The anomaly of such a system is perhaps abundantly evident in the strong moral restraints and inhibitions which dissuade many people from exercising their legal rights under it.

Given the vagaries of commercial, fiscal, banking, and currency policies in the various countries, and given the character of national financial structures and price rigidities, it is to the writer a source of continued amazement that so many people of insight should hold unwaveringly to the gold standard as the best foundation of national policies.[10] The worship of gold, among obviously sophisticated people, seems explicable only in terms of our lack of success in formulating specifications for a satisfactory, independent national currency—and certainly not in terms of the need of stable exchange rates for orderly international commerce. Indeed, it indicates how little progress liberals have made in showing, by way of answer to revolutionists, what kind of money rules might be adopted to make capitalism a more workable system.

On the other hand, the desire to hold to something, in the face of perplexity, invites understanding sympathy—for certainly we have made little progress in defining attractive alternative systems. Some students propose pure dictatorship, under powerful monetary authorities; others, the stabilization of various price indexes; not to mention the many irresponsible proposals for indefinite inflation, based on the notion that our ills are traceable to deficiency of consumer purchasing power. Of all these schemes, those which contemplate stabilization of price indexes are least illiberal; but they, too, are unsatisfying. They define programs in terms of ends, with little discussion of appropriate means; they call for an authority with a considerable range for discretionary action and would require much intelligence and judgment in their administration; and they would leave us exposed to continuous legislative (if not administrative) tinkering, since no particular price index has much greater inherent reasonableness than many others, and since most of them would serve badly the end of profit stability.[11]

In a free-enterprise system we obviously need highly definite and stable rules of the game, especially as to money. The monetary rules must be compatible with the reasonably smooth working of the system.[12] Once established, however, they should work mechanically, with the chips falling where they may. To put our present problem as a paradox—we need to design and establish with the greatest intelligence a monetary system good enough so that, hereafter, we may hold to it unrationally—on faith—as a religion, if you please. The utter inadequacy of the old gold standard, either as a definite system of rules or as the basis of a monetary religion, seems beyond intelligent dispute. But if that system lacks peculiarly the virtues which now seem important, they are also patently lacking in most of the systems proposed as substitutes.

Thus, traditional liberalism, if not hopelessly or more fundamentally decadent for other reasons, is at least seriously embarrassed by the difficulty of answering urgent monetary questions in a manner consistent with its central tenets. It is the purpose of this paper, not to present any simple answer or solution, but merely to define the problem more closely and perhaps to provide some basis for ultimate consensus on definite proposals.

The problem of booms and depressions is one which must be attacked from both sides (a) by policies designed to give us a more flexible price structure and (b) by measures which will minimize the aggravations attributable to the character of the monetary system and financial structure. The former attack, however, must always be regarded as primary. With adequate price flexibility, we could get along under almost any financial system; with extreme rigidities (reflecting widespread partial monopoly), the most drastic monetary and financial reform, even an ideal financial structure, could not protect us from serious disturbances of production and employment.

For the present, we obviously must rely on a large measure of discretionary money management—on a policy of offsetting and counteracting, by fiscal and banking measures, the effects of monopoly and custom upon prices and wage rates. Such a policy, however, must be guided by a more fundamental strategy and by the need for early abandonment of temporizing expedients;[13] otherwise, political control must degenerate into endless concessions to organized minorities, with gradual undermining of the "constitutional structure" under which free-enterprise economy and representative government can function.[14]

The possibilities of genuine economic reconstruction, and the requirements of sound liberal strategy, may be defined in terms of three objectives: (1) restoration of a maximum of competitiveness in industry (including the labor markets); (2) transition to a less preposterous structure of private money contracts; and (3) ultimate establishment of a simple, mechanical rule of monetary policy. As regards this third objective, the writer feels that his earlier persuasion as to the merits of the rule of a fixed quantity of money was fundamentally correct, although the scheme is obviously too simple as a prescription under anything like present conditions. Its limitations, however, have to do mainly with the unfortunate character of our financial structure—with the abundance of what we may call "near-moneys"—with the difficulty of defining money in such manner as to give practical significance to the conception of quantity.

Under what financial conditions would the simple rule of fixed quantity become reasonably satisfactory? In principle, the answer is easy: under the ideal financial structure described above. If this seems to be a counsel of despair, one may add that perfection is not necessary practically. On the other hand, it requires some temerity to specify how far the ideal conditions might safely be sacrificed.

To propose abolition of all borrowing, or even of all borrowing at short term, is merely to dream. It would seem feasible, however, to undertake gradual and systematic reordering of financial practices, to the end of limiting quite narrowly the amount and the possible quantity fluctuations of the generally acceptable near-moneys. This would mean, above all, the abolition of banking, that is, of all special institutional arrangements for large-scale financing at short term. Demand-deposit banking would be confined (in effect, at least) to the warehousing and transferring of actual currency. Savings banks would be transformed into strictly mutual institutions or investment trusts. Narrow limitation of the formal borrowing powers of other corporations would obviously be necessary, to prevent their effectively taking over the prerogatives of which banking corporations as such had been deprived. Further limitations might also be necessary with respect to financing via the open account (book credit) and instalment sales, although other prohibitions might provide adequate protection indirectly against these evils. If such reforms seem fantastic, it may be pointed out that, in practice, they would require merely drastic limitation upon the powers of corporations (which is eminently desirable on other, and equally important, grounds as well).[15]

Banking is a pervasive phenomenon, not something to be dealt with merely by legislation directed at what we call banks. The experience with the control of note issue is likely to be repeated in the future; many expedients for controlling similar practices may prove ineffective and disappointing because of the reappearance of prohibited practices in new and unprohibited forms. It seems impossible to predict what forms the evasion might take or to see how particular prohibitions might be designed in order that they might be more than nominally effective. But we perhaps approach insight when we conceive the problem broadly as that of achieving a financial structure in which the volume of short-term borrowing would be minimized, and in which only the government would be able to create (and destroy) either effective circulating media or obligations generally acceptable as hoards media. More narrowly (with reference to depressions), the problem is one of moving toward a system in which creditors would be unable quickly to demand, and to require enterprises generally to undertake, rapid and impossible liquidation.

Whatever the best-detailed solutions as to financial practices and their control, it seems that some arrangements compatible with rigid fixing of the quantity of effective money may be feasible as a long-term objective of reform. Given such arrangements, the danger of alternate hoarding and dishoarding tendencies, to be sure, would still remain; but it would remain as a problem to be dealt with exclusively via efforts to obtain greater flexibility (competitiveness) in the economy· The problem of industrial fluctuations cannot be solved, and should not be attacked, exclusively by monetary devices. The best monetary system, so to speak, would tolerate occasional disturbances without alleviation, accepting them as a reasonable cost of maintaining the best structure of relative prices and as a means for preventing a continued accumulation of basic maladjustments which could only issue politically in disruption of the system itself.[16]

In the present critical situation we should not balk at bold schemes for restoring the free-enterprise system to a securely workable basis. The requisite measures, radical in the money field and more radical elsewhere, will become possible politically only with the revival or development of a real religion of freedom, as a strong middle-class movement, and of values (and revulsions) of a rather intense sort. These necessary conditions, however, might soon appear, through popular disillusionment with respect to recently popular economic nostrums and policies, as the perhaps natural alternation in a cycle of opinion and prejudice.

If this favorable climate of opinion does appear, it will behoove liberals to make the most of the opportunity (otherwise probably their last) and, avoiding plausible compromises, to focus their efforts on basic reforms. In particular, this may be interpreted to mean (*a*) that no concessions can be made as regards the restoration of highly competitive conditions and (*b*) that few concessions can be made in the effort to remodel our permissible financial practices to the end of making feasible and easily workable a definite, mechanical set of rules of the economic game as to money.[17]

For the moment, of course, we must be reconciled to pure management in the money field. We must rely on government action—on political efforts to bring down the prices which remain far out of line; on such injections of fiscal stimulants as may be necessary to prevent recurrence of wholesale liquidation; and, above all, on the prompt and drastic measures for debt retirement which may soon become imperatively necessary to prevent a disastrous inflationary boom. It should be feasible, however, increasingly to concentrate the monetary powers of governmental agencies in fewer hands and, later on, to bring the appropriate agencies more closely within the control of law, through the adoption of rules, expressed perhaps in terms of price indexes. Such measures, at all events, seem essential in a program for avoiding revolutionary changes in economic and political institutions.[18] For the most sanguine view, however, they define only a proximate objective in monetary reform—a way of escape from present chaos and a step toward a more satisfactory ultimate solution.

The short comings of price-index stabilization, as the fundamental basis of a monetary system, are numerous and serious from either an analytical or an empirical viewpoint. It is easy to maintain that such a rule falls far short of the ideal in monetary arrangements—far too easy, indeed, when those who criticize are not obliged or inclined to define the better rules by comparison with which the one in question is so defective. The advocates of a stable price level (with all the irritating excesses of their advocacy) are proposing a solution which is genuinely consistent with traditional liberal principles—and, precisely on that account, are faring rather badly in the debate which the proposal has provoked among professional economists and journalists. The most vigorous and pungent criticism comes from specialists who themselves have no intelligible solutions to offer and who generally have been spared the suspicion that a solution in terms of definite rules is of any importance.[19]

If price-level stabilization is a poor system, it is, still from a liberal viewpoint, infinitely better than no system at all. And it seems now highly questionable whether any better system is feasible or possible at all within the significant future. Given the present financial structure, and given the present multitude of unco-ordinated monetary measures and monetary authorities, is there any other rule of policy around which some order and system might be achieved? How else may the present chaos of private financial practices, central-bank action, fiscal measures, and tariff changes be pulled together into something which resembles a monetary system? How else can we possibly escape from a situation where monetary policy is merely the composite of the uncertain daily actions of an indefinite number of agencies, governmental and private? Some ordering of this chaos is imperative. It may be achieved, either by setting up a superior, independent authority or by bringing the totality of monetary measures under the discipline of some rule; and only the advocates of price-index stabilization have offered a feasible way out along the latter lines.

This solution, if unsatisfying, is likewise not simple administratively. Question is often raised as to whether stabilization of a price level is possible. The problem is better formulated, however, when we ask by what agency it might best be undertaken and what methods would be appropriate in its execution.

The task is certainly not one to be intrusted to banking authorities, with their limited powers and restricted techniques, as should be abundantly evident from recent experience. Ultimate control over the value of money lies in fiscal practices—in the spending, taxing, and borrowing operations of the central government. Thus, in an adequate scheme for price-level stabilization, the Treasury would be the primary administrative agency; and all the fiscal powers of Congress would be placed behind (and their exercise religiously limited by) the monetary rule. The powers of the government to inject purchasing power through expenditure and to withdraw it through taxation—the powers of expanding and contracting issues of actual currency and other obligations more or less serviceable as money—are surely adequate to price-level control. At present, monetary powers are dispersed indefinitely, among governmental agencies and private institutions, not to mention Congress itself. Since the powers of the legislature are ultimate and decisive, a program looking toward coordination and concentration of responsibility must focus on fiscal policy as its mode of implementation.

The scheme clearly requires the delegation of large administrative powers. The Treasury might be given freedom within wide limits to alter the form of the public debt—to shift from long-term to short-term borrowing or vice versa, to issue and retire demand obligations in a legal-tender form. It might be granted some control over the timing of expenditures. It might be given limited power to alter tax rates by decree and to make refunds of taxes previously collected. How wide and numerous these powers should be, need not concern us here. Any legislation granting such authority, however, must also impose the duty and responsibility of exercising that authority in accordance with a sharply defined policy.[20]

Given the suitable mandate, the grant of administrative powers should err, if at all, on the side of generosity. The more adequately implemented the rule of monetary policy, the easier will be its actual execution. The greater the powers available for its execution, the smaller will be the probable demands for their exercise. If it is clear that the administrative authority is adequately equipped to make the rule effective, then the rule will be, to some extent, self-enforcing, in so far as the actions of enterprisers and speculators come to be predicated upon its enforcement.

Not only must the price-level rule be implemented through fiscal measures; it must also serve as a control upon all governmental measures which have significant monetary effects. In other words, it must be accepted by the community, and obeyed by legislatures, as the guiding principle of government finance—as the basic criterion of sound fiscal policy.[21] While the rule cannot wisely be written into our fundamental law, it must provide the same sort of limitation and mandate as would a constitutional provision. As things stand now, there is almost nothing which a dominant party may not do or leave undone financially, without rebuke. (There is still some moral pressure, to be sure, against outright issue of paper money; but this only invites evasion through the use of short maturities and through resort to the inelegant expedient of paying the banks to create money for the Treasury.) A federal administration can now spend far beyond its revenues, and grossly debase the currency, without even placing itself on the defensive before public opinion. On the other hand, the "principles" to which reactionaries would have us return are perhaps worse than none at all. That the old moral prohibitions have lost their force is here not altogether an occasion for regret. But we cannot get along without some such rules—without some moral sanctions and mandates which politicians must obey in matters of finance. And there is probably nothing more promising than the idea of a stable price level as a symbol articulating deep-rooted sentiments and as a source of discipline in fiscal practice.[22]

A serious practical shortcoming of stable money programs lies in the fact that they are sponsored most vigorously by persons who want the price level raised sharply before it is stabilized. Thus the scheme is likely to be realized, if at all, on the basis of dangerously large concessions to the demands of debtors, in terms of stabilization at a level involving serious maladjustments and internal strains, and under conditions which would present great difficulties in administration and execution. If the undertaking is to get under way auspiciously, it is imperative that the level chosen should be low enough to require only the minimum of action and display of power by the monetary authority during the trying first years. (The possibility that the level would be fixed too low is of theoretical, rather than practical, interest.) Drastic administrative measures to overcome the inertia of an upward movement would jeopardize the political security of the rule and would also involve unfortunate disturbances in lines of business exposed to the direct impact of such measures. The advocates of stable money will do well not to offer the community one last big spree after the pledge is taken and not to promise a perpetuity of blissful inebriation.

The issues which such proposals raise with respect to gold are issues which may largely be neglected for some years to come. In the United States we might stabilize on the basis of a price index, while maintaining indefinitely the present gold price. Indeed, unless the orgy of devaluation which we invited in 1933 does finally occur, we shall, with world recovery, find it easy both to maintain the present price of gold and to reduce continuously the enormous barrier to trade which our tariff legislation has erected. The possibilities of such a program are indicated in the report of the Commission of Inquiry into National Policy in International Economic Relations:

"It may be argued that, while there is unlikely to be any occasion for justifiable increase in the dollar price of gold, it might soon be expedient to lower the price: (*a*) to prevent a wastefully large accumulation of gold by the United States; (*b*) to promote distribution of our surplus stock among countries which have real need for additional reserves; (*c*) to check an over-rapid recovery or a potentially dangerous boom at home; or even (*d*) as one means of putting pressure on the reserves of a too rapidly expanding banking system. To any of these ends, however, a more attractive means is at hand, namely, reduction of our tariff duties, even beyond those already recommended. This strategy would afford us a better protection against an unhealthy boom and against over-large investment in gold; it would affect other nations in the same manner economically as would a lowering of our gold price; and it would probably be even more effective toward improving the spirit of international commercial relations.

"Not least of the merits of this procedure is the prospect it offers for raising the internal prices of the export products (notably, cotton and wheat) relative to other prices. Indeed, it might in the end prove to be an adequate justification of our recent gold policy, that it created this opportunity for gradually and systematically repairing the injury of our past tariff policy to agriculture. Our drastic devaluation, whatever its short-term effects, is likely to lead, slowly and over a long period, to a rise of our price level which could serve no good purpose and might work serious injury. However, if we undertake by tariff reductions systematically to correct favorable balances of payments, and even to send abroad part of our present stock of gold, we could avoid the upward pressure on many industrial prices, while allowing our export staples to enjoy the full effect of the devaluation.

"The scheme here proposed is perhaps more elegant in principle than it could ever be in actual application. But it may be worth noting that, just as devaluation offered to post-war France a means for returning to gold without internal deflation, so devaluation offers to the United States a means for scaling down its barriers to trade *without internal deflation*. This opportunity, moreover, presents itself, fortunately from the viewpoint of domestic politics, at a time when there is widespread demand for just the assistance to agriculture that it so clearly offers. Furthermore, an expression by our government of the intention to prevent, by this procedure, any enduring injury to foreign countries from our devaluation, would do much to smooth the way for future international understandings as to both monetary and commercial policy.

"In this connection two observations are especially in point. (1) It is likely, in view of the condition of our balance of payments prior to devaluation, and in view of the prospect that many of the foreign measures for resisting gold drains will disappear with world recovery, that our present price of gold will prove distinctly excessive, unless measures are taken to offset the long-term effects of its sharp increase. (2) There are many strong considerations, not heretofore invoked in these pages, against resorting to reduction of our gold price in the future. Many of those who bitterly condemn our devaluation program will readily agree that little is now to be gained by trying merely to retrace our steps. If the rise in the price of gold may be held to have worked injury and injustice, it is still unlikely that reduction of that price at a much later date would accomplish much toward repairing the inequities. Those who lost (or gained) by the increase would be largely a different group from those who gained (or lost) from the reduction. Thus, all in all, a number of strong considerations appear to support the proposal for utilizing systematically the potentially large opportunities for tariff reduction which our recent devaluation promises to yield in the future. On this view, tariff reduction might be regarded as an agency of monetary stabilization for the near future and, quite consistently, as a means for helping agriculture at the same time.

"The whole argument here may be regarded as supporting the position that our bargaining efforts should be directed especially toward concessions with regard to exchange controls, quota limitations, and similar barriers to our exports. These barriers, largely the product of the acute emergency, may be regarded in part as compensatory to our emergency gold policy. The prospect of their removal will depend partly on our willingness to make the concessions necessary to preservation of reasonable balance. The only major or equivalent concessions which we could offer are (1) reduction of our gold price and/or (2) lowering of our tariff barrier. There are reasons for our preferring the second of these, and no apparent reasons why it should not be equally attractive to other nations."[23]

Price-level stabilization thus seems, on the whole, extremely attractive as the basis of a liberal-conservative policy in the field of money and government finance for the next decade. Whether the price-index rule would be as satisfactory under conditions which could be realized only over a longer period as the rule of a fixed quantity of money may merit discussion in academic circles and may provide a promising point of departure for analysis and exposition; but the question is not of practical significance now. Given the inevitable limitations of any particular index, however, the former rule might ultimately acquire or manifest serious shortcomings. It is thus appropriate to observe that all the changes in our financial structure which seem necessary to make feasible the adoption of the fixed-quantity rule are changes which would also facilitate the operation of the price-index rule. The existence of a large volume of privately created money substitutes, with alternate expansion and contraction, might tax seriously the powers of a monetary authority seeking to prevent price-level changes. Thus, if the stability of an index is to be maintained with the least resistance and the minimum of disturbing administrative measures, it is essential that the power to issue money and near-money should increasingly be concentrated in the hands of the central government.

As regards policies for the significant future, it therefore matters little whether price-level stabilization is conceived as a definitive reform or as a transition expedient in a long-term program pointed toward ultimate stabilization of the quantity of money. On either view, the same radical (if not drastic) changes in the field of private finance are clearly appropriate. Most of them, moreover, are necessary, on other grounds as well, for the preservation of economic freedom and political democracy.

The following observations may now be submitted, to define the author's general position and to guard against misinterpretation:

1. A democratic, free-enterprise system implies, and requires for its effective functioning and survival, a stable framework of definite rules, laid down in legislation and subject to change only gradually and with careful regard for the vested interests of participants in the economic game. It is peculiarly essential economically that there should be a minimum of uncertainty for enterprisers and investors as to monetary conditions in the future—and, politically, that the plausible expedient of setting up "authorities" instead of rules, with respect to matters of such fundamental importance, be avoided, or accepted only as a very temporary arrangement. The most important objective of a sound liberal policy, apart from the establishment of highly competitive conditions in industry and the narrow limitation of political control over relative prices, should be that of securing a monetary system governed by definite rule.

2. To assure adequate moral pressure of public opinion against legislative (and administrative) tinkering, the monetary rules must be definite, simple (at least in principle), and expressive of strong, abiding, pervasive, and reasonable popular sentiments. They should be designed to permit the fullest and most stable employment, to facilitate adjustment to such basic changes (especially in technology) as are likely to occur,

and, secondarily, to minimize inequities as between debtors and creditors; but the problems here, while of first importance, should be conceived and dealt with mainly as problems of a transition period. Once well established and generally accepted as the basis of anticipations, any one of many different rules (or sets of rules) would probably serve about as well as another.

3. The responsibility for carrying out the monetary rules should be lodged in a federal authority, endowed with large administrative powers but closely controlled in their exercise by a sharply defined policy. The powers of the monetary authority should have to do primarily or exclusively with fiscal arrangements—with the issue and retirement of paper money (open-market operations in government securities) and perhaps with the relation between government revenues and expenditures; in other words, the monetary rules should be implemented entirely by, and in turn should largely determine, fiscal policy.

4. Political control in this sphere should be confined exclusively to regulation of the quantity of money and near-money, the *direction* of investment (the allocation of investment funds) being left to the control of competition and kept as far as possible outside the influence of political agencies (or central banks).

5. A liberal program of monetary reform should seek to effect an increasingly sharp differentiation between money and private obligations and, especially, to minimize the opportunities for the creation of effective money substitutes (whether for use as circulating media or in hoards) by private corporations. The abolition of private deposit banking is clearly the appropriate first step in this direction and would bring us in sight of the goal; but such a measure, to be really effective, must be accompanied, or followed closely, by drastic limitation on the formal borrowing powers of all private corporations and especially upon borrowing at short term.

6. A monetary rule of maintaining the constancy of some price index, preferably an index of prices of competitively produced commodities, appears to afford the only promising escape from present monetary chaos and uncertainties. A rule calling for outright fixing of the total quantity of money, however, definitely merits consideration as a perhaps preferable solution in the more distant future. At least, it may provide a point of departure for fruitful academic discussion.

VIII

Hansen on Fiscal Policy[*1]

THE decade of the thirties marks an abrupt break with traditions of monetary and fiscal practice. Most economists
who advocated bold fiscal measures for stopping deflation and
initiating recovery, while intolerant toward extremist brethren
who foresaw imminent financial doom, were nowise blind to
less immediate political dangers in the repudiation of accepted
fiscal norms. Their misgivings, first aroused by the senseless
gold policy, were increased by the avalanche of reforms which
discouraged investment and inhibited enterprise; by the unrestrained political momentum of spending which eventuated in
bonus legislation at the worst possible time; by the surge of
aggressive unionism and wage increases in 1937; and especially
by the subsequent recession which revealed how utterly deficit
stimulation had been frustrated by other policies and trends.
At this point early proponents of reflation became divided, as
their conservative brethren had predicted, over policy for the
future. One faction, led by younger economists close to the administration, found explanation of the recession merely in
fiscal policy and went on solemnly to argue for perpetual
deficits and uninterrupted increase in the federal debt. Their
arguments, of course, are heavenly music to political leaders
as opportunists and to collectivists as strategists. Now, from
the ranks of older, distinguished economists, comes Professor
Hansen to argue their case and to espouse their cause.

Fiscal Policy and Business Cycles has been or will be read by
every serious student of economics. It would be gratuitous to
indicate attributes of excellence which are as unmistakable as

* Reprinted by permission from the *Journal of Political Economy*, L, No. 2
(April, 1942), 161–96.

they are substantial. Few books in our literature can offer so much in terms of useful information and ideas or do more to bring readers abreast of important recent inquiry; and few will be found so engaging in clarity of statement and excellence of style.

But I come to bury Hansen—albeit respectfully and despairingly. Praise he will receive elsewhere, for learning and assiduous inquiry which merit all praise and because he accepts and applauds the powerful political trends of the day. His book is the academic apology par excellence for the inner New Deal and all its works. It may well become the economic bible for that substantial company of intellectuals, following Keynes and recklessly collectivist, whose influence grows no less rapidly in academic circles than in Washington. So, as an unreconstructed, old-fashioned liberal, I must counterattack as best I can, hoping thereby to diminish slightly the impetus which the book must give to trends of thought and action which to me seem wholly dangerous.

Being mainly concerned with issues of practical policy, I cannot here do justice to Hansen's underlying theories or to the (in my opinion) devastating case against them. What one finds is a strange amalgam of Keynes, Schumpeter, and Spiethoff. The Keynesian ingredients are nowise novel or surprising. The Schumpeter elements involve propositions which, I would suppose, Schumpeter is likely to disown in Hansen's extreme formulation and which, in less extreme form, have long been the object of controversy and disagreement which Hansen does nothing to clarify or to resolve.

Hansen boldly resurrects classical errors of capital theory, elevating the useful abstraction of the static state to the status of actual norm (destination of tendency) of the economic process. Free-market capitalism is always tending toward an equilibrium position of zero net investment and zero interest rates. Only fortuitous accidents of invention and discovery prevent attainment of such enduring equilibrium, shocking an unwilling structure of prices and production into fitful progress and spurts of capital accretion. Thus the Keynesian specter (or Elysium) of zero marginal efficiency is offered, not as imminent historical prospect, but as an indubitable technical characteristic of our economy in the past, after every period of boom. Prosperity, induced by innovation (or by population growth or territorial expansion?) exhausts itself naturally by utterly exhausting available investment opportunities, leaving only replacement demand (and why that, if marginal efficiency is zero?) and no outlet for net savings. But the consumption function is intractable. Failing compensatory action, income must drop to a level where saving becomes, not merely equal to investment at a low level of investment, income, and employment *à la* Keynes, but simply zero, since net investment is technically impossible! All that can usefully be done is (1) to draw off redundant savings by governmental borrowing for financing public works or public consumption outlays, (2) to induce the high degree of liquidity which will facilitate exploitation of new investment opportunities when and if they appear, and (3) to beseech the gods for another wave of innovations.

This paraphrase will suggest, if not describe, the cycle theory which Hansen vigorously proclaims and leans upon heavily at many points. Believing such things, he naturally urges that such a theory of dynamic development be incorporated into fundamental economic analysis, as co-ordinate with, or superior to, conventional monetary analysis and relative-price theory. Finding Hansen's revelations preposterous, I am strengthened in the conviction that the sooner we quit talking about cycle theory as a major field of inquiry, the better. Economic historians may well try to discover, not why we had ups and downs in the past, but why, given our monetary arrangements, financial structures, and fiscal practices, we had as much stability as we did have. What we need now to understand and explain is why our economy of the thirties, though flooded with money, failed to revive adequately or to function effectively. Bold and novel theories of history are likely only to confuse and to distract us at this task. That such tools are not necessary to discerning practical insights is nowhere better evidenced than in the last pages of Schumpeter's own book,[2] which, if not altogether to my taste in their distribution of emphasis, have everything to commend them over applications of "cycle theories." Let us leave such theorizing to historians, statisticians, and business forecasters, hoping that hard-bitten empiricists will turn up still more interesting correlations, while we get about the job of diagnosing the important maladjustments and diseconomies of our times.

Hansen's chapter xv deserves special attention, both for its summary statements of central ideas and because, more than other parts of the book, it purports to justify the virtual disregard of the price structure and of relative prices, actual or expected, in his analysis of the depression phenomenon. This chapter distinguishes bluntly between cyclical and structural maladjustments, maintaining that mitigation of the latter is essential to effective long-term allocation of resources but that downward revision of sticky prices has little to commend it during depressions. The supporting argument is that, as regards cyclical maladjustments, price dispersion or disparities are effects, not causes (which seems pompously question-begging), and that the appropriate remedy is not reduction of laggard prices and wages but increase of investment (a whimsica Keynesism for government spending), which, raising income, will raise the flexible prices and repair the disparities.

If nothing were wrong about relative prices at the boom's end (an implausible assumption, implicit throughout and nowhere examined), much could be said for this view, that is, for prompt fiscal action which would prevent deflation and keep the "cyclical maladjustments" from arising. But this approach falsifies the position which Hansen purports to attack. The controversial issue relates to policy—say, in 1933—after long and substantial deflation has already occurred and after fiscal reflation is at last under way. Should fiscal policy aim at raising sensitive prices to levels consistent with administered prices and wages of the boom? Or should adjustment be sought on both sides, with an intermediate general level as a goal? Against the case for reduction of rigid prices in this context of policy (as stated, e.g., in Pigou, *Economics in Practice* [London, 1935], pp. 95 ff.) Hansen's arguments are irrelevant and misleading.

The same may be said for the argument as far as it follows Hicks. The bottom of an uncontrolled deflation, for all practical purposes, is nonexistent—with adverse expectations causing price declines and with the actual declines aggravating expectations, etc. It is arguable that, failing positive measures, rigid prices and wages may retard deflations and stop them short of where they might otherwise go.[3] The point, however, is merely academic and likely to mislead in discussion where the need for fiscal or monetary counteraction is beyond dispute. "Combined, however, with monetary and fiscal policies designed to maintain the total volume of consumption and investment expenditures, an orderly program of cost-price readjustment does facilitate recovery" (p. 322). But why, conceding this, did Hansen write the rest of this chapter?[4]

The extremes of Hansen's position have to do with the influence of cyclical maladjustments in the prices and costs of capital goods. Keynesians generally will concede the case for reduction during depression of sticky prices and wages in this area—but not Hansen. He falls back on his revelation that there are no investment opportunities in such periods anyway. If outlets for net investment simply do not exist (in some mystical sense not concerned with prices at all!), price and wage changes will do no good. He concedes that reductions will strengthen and accelerate recovery, once it is under way; but only the exogenous factors can initiate recovery of private investment.

Being preoccupied with saturation in some mysterious, technical sense, Hansen seems never to recognize that prices and wages in the capital-goods industries probably become relatively excessive, under the impact of boom demand, before the crisis arrives—that is, that booms presumably leave the economy with prices and wages in these industries too high to permit adequate investment, even if other prices were maintained at the boom level. Hansen maintains that our problem is primarily one of eliminating depressions and that boom conditions are an approximation of health in the body economic. Earlier economic writing has stressed unduly the need for drastic measures in boom periods; but truth and wisdom probably lie well short of Hansen's position at the other extreme. Even if one accepts his strange diagnosis, one may still argue (as he does at times himself—see pp. 296–97) for spreading investment thinner during booms if opportunities are going to be exhausted shortly in any case.

Hansen has long criticized monetary theories of fluctuations as narrow and inadequate.[5] The semblance of his old position is carefully preserved, but the substance is gone entirely. Hansen, judged by his policy proposals, is the extreme advocate of monetary explanation. If one defines causes as factors which can be gotten hold of, as factors peculiarly eligible for corrective or remedial manipulation, then Hansen's causes are purely monetary. To be sure, he distinguishes bluntly between monetary theories and savings-investment explanations; but this is distinction without difference. Keynesian conceptions and formulations are perhaps especially congenial to persons of Hansen's earlier persuasions; but the implication that they are nonmonetary is indeed surprising. As monetary theorist, he is, like most of his contemporaries, mainly engaged in formulating propositions which attain to generality by not being about anything—propositions which describe the monetary functioning of a system which is simply undefined (undefinable?) in its monetary and other aspects.[6] But he has cut through the dilemma of his earlier position, which seemed at once to assert that the cycle was our major policy problem and that its causes were to be found in exogenous happenings, immutable and beyond reach of policy. If vestiges of the dilemma remain and marks of his struggle with it, Hansen now confidently proclaims the efficacy of monetary weapons.

But another distinction conceals the conversion, namely, distinction between monetary and fiscal measures. Hansen, advocating the latter, thus dissociates himself nominally from monetary theorists by representing such people as advocates of mere central-bank action.[7] This provides a lonely category for Mr. Hawtrey, while denying classification to those for whom central-bank action is a feeble, inadequate, and anomalous implementation of monetary policy. If the name at issue be granted to those advocating schemes of monetary compensation or stabilization which would employ all the borrowing, spending, taxing, and issue powers of the central government, then Hansen not only belongs among them but stands as an extremist in that company.

Amid all this confusion about names, however, some real issues may be discerned. Central among these is the choice between currency issue (or direct creation of government deposits) and ordinary borrowing.[8] Against straightforward money creation, Hansen argues along several lines. First, he fears excessive increase in money supply (which is dangerous ground for an advocate of indefinite increase of near-money federal debt, maturities unspecified). Second (perhaps not a separate point), he argues that continued multiplication of money, pushed to its logical conclusion, "means, in fact, the gradual 'euthanasia of the rentier' " (pp. 178–79), via decline of interest rates. Third, he maintains, largely on the eloquent testimony of recent experience, that making money abundant is simply not enough.

The second point raises many questions, especially as to banks, which Hansen does not discuss fully. The use of new currency to finance deficits would be a somewhat disturbing innovation in a community whose media for payment and for liquid reserves have been provided largely by private institutions. It patently requires that legal reserve requirements (for all banks) be raised sufficiently to absorb the reserves provided by new currency—which eventually would give us something like the 100 per cent reserve system. The problem of bank earnings would indeed become acute if interest income were not displaced by systematic charges for bank services; but no one doubts that banks could effect the displacement or that straightforward charges would be conducive to economical use of their services.

I am not disposed to plead the case for 100 per cent reserves as an isolated scheme of financial reconstruction. Such a scheme, in principle and for useful application, must be regarded as merely one phase or one step in a total reordering of our financial structure which aims at virtual elimination of private fixed-money contracts, especially those of short maturity. Hansen commends proposals for wide extension of equity financing in private enterprise. One hundred per cent reserves represents merely consistent, thoroughgoing application of this proposal, with emphasis on that class of enterprises which now maintains smallest-equity margins and shortest-term obligations. If currency issue will promote institutional modification of banking, so much the better.

As regards savings banks and life insurance companies, I cannot share Hansen's fears. The former should be transformed into investment trusts, that is, into strictly mutual form; and the same may be said of life insurance companies as far as concerns the investment aspect (the major aspect) of their current business. Pure insurance requires no large reserves; and, in any case, conversion of portfolios toward common stocks, as Hansen observes elsewhere (pp. 288–89), is highly desirable. Hansen comes near to saying that, to avoid institutional disturbance, the government should subsidize such savings institutions, using them to finance its own investments and paying them rates which their funds cannot earn in private investment. His dislike of issue thus leads him implicitly to commend savings subsidies and use of governmental powers to sustain interest rates. But perhaps I misconstrue his meaning here.

Deeper and more involved issues are raised by the argument that currency issue (or "monetary policy") is inadequate. Hansen points repeatedly to recent experience which is superficially persuasive. Few will question that we did have abundant money in the late thirties and high liquidity or that investment agged notwithstanding. Hansen would explain the phenomenon in terms of an ebbing tide of innovations, decline of population growth, and territorial saturation, that is, in terms of technical deficiency or absence of private investment opportunities. Simple and convincing explanation is available, however, along other lines and without recourse to incredible assumptions, for example, along the lines of the Schumpeter passage mentioned above.

Here, as with important elements of Keynes, we are faced with questions of fact; but the facts required for even tentative answers are inaccessible and perhaps inscrutable. To refute, as to assert, one must rely on vague intuitions and common-sense conjectures. Let me now indulge in some assertions of my own, if only as antidotes to those currently in vogue.

It is my conviction that, in the sense of potential "social yield" or of marginal efficiency under free-market conditions, investment opportunities are and have been nearly limitless. Holding fast to Cassel notions,[9] I believe that the productivity curve for new capital is extremely flat; that investment, proceeding at the maximum rate consistent with high thrift, would have little effect for the significant future, even failing large accretions of innovations, on yields in this sense. What we need to know is, not actual yields or prospective yields at prospective prices and wage rates, but what yields would be in a monetarily stable economy if costs of capital assets were purged of monopoly and racketeering elements and if assets, once constructed, were reasonably assured of the productivity (annual rent yield) which they would have in a free market for complementary factors. We need to know, in other words, what the marginal efficiency of investment would be, at different rates of investment, under an omniscient, benevolent dictator who allocated and accounted for resources (whether so remunerating their owners or not) on the basis of free-market values (or productivities at full employment). This is a large order for statistical inquiry; but, unless substantial confirmation is forthcoming from such inquiry, we should be utterly skeptical about novel doctrines which explain our difficulties without reference to politically unpalatable or unmentionable facts.

If there was no real shortage of investment outlets, why did low interest rates and abundant money fail recently to induce large investment and to eliminate large unemployment? The answer is suggested, I believe, by the Schumpeter phrases, "social [political] atmosphere" and "social drift." The period which exhibits this fabulous increase in money stocks also witnessed almost revolutionary change, profoundly adverse to investors and enterprise, in the political situation and outlook. In part, this was merely an aspect of world disorder and long-time political trend. Largely, however, it was a by-product of particular legislative measures, whereby the government and its supporting minorities practically defied people to invest privately or to behave enterprisingly. Earnings data may suggest that the fears of investors were extravagant; but everyone as vicarious investor or enterpriser knows that they were real. Conservatives differ widely as to which measures were most harmful and are often undiscriminating in attack. My inclination is to place emphasis overwhelmingly on labor policy, which, of course, only accelerated a powerful, pre-existing trend. Other legislation invites criticism on many counts; but there is good in much of it; and there are no great obstacles to modification and revision in the future. In labor policy, however, we have sown the wind. Government, long hostile to other monopolies, suddenly sponsored and promoted widespread organization of labor monopolies, which democracy cannot endure, cannot control without destroying, and perhaps cannot destroy without destroying itself. There is evidently no means of disciplining such minorities, once strongly organized, in conformity with the public interest or even of disciplining particular organized groups in conformity with their own common interests. We face a kind of unending economic warfare in which, save for workers with high seniority and high qualitative rank, no one's chances are very good, and the residual claimant's, deplorable. Every new investment must seem now like a giving of hostages to organized sellers of complementary services, whose costs usually represent, over the life of investment assets, a huge multiple of investment. Why anyone should now give hostages to the future, undertaking the long-term commitments essential to real prosperity, is not easy to understand—save in the case of corporate control groups, interested in salaries, perquisites of insiders, and power and relatively unconcerned about dividends.

The plight of investment is largely an incident of wholesale restraint of internal trade—of racketeering or exploitation. One may be pardoned for stressing an aspect of that situation which seems most important at the moment, most likely to become increasingly serious, and least amenable to legislative correction or control. Other monopoly conditions deserve serious attention; and other mass minorities (farmers, retailers) become ominously powerful. But, however one weighs different aspects, we may perhaps agree on two points: (1) that monopolistic restraints, labor and other, are highly concentrated in our capital-goods industries (and especially in those which have recovered least since 1928) and (2) that labor monopoly and the threat of excessive labor costs especially characterize our important investment outlets, the capital-intensive industries. Any theory of stagnation which distracts attention from such factors renders grave disservice to the future of government by discussion.

Hansen looks at the thirties and infers that "monetary policy" is not enough—which might be applauded if he meant that it is no cure for restraint of trade. The inference, however, merely leads him to advocate more and bolder monetary expedients. Here, perhaps, issue may be joined. Hansen urges us to go on, borrowing and spending governmentally the redundant savings which private business fails to absorb. A more conservative view would hold that, with easy and abundant money, fiscal measures have done their bit and cannot wisely be relied upon further. They should assure us against subsequent decline of the price level, cutting away the inhibitions of adverse monetary expectations, but should not be utilized to complement and consolidate policies and trends inimical to private enterprise and investment. Given cheap money, we should work out our minority and monopoly problems within the framework of general price stability, avoiding that dangerously easy solution of displacing private by governmental investment and avoiding debt increase like the plague.

Investment, of course, is the way out; but at some level the choice between governmental and private investment is the choice between ways of life, individualist and authoritarian. Most of Hansen's proposals for public works and public consumption are conservative and commendable; but such proposals can be carried out within a budget balanced by taxes and issue, without debt increase, and as rapidly as their best execution would permit. His positive conception of partial socialization is hardly controversial at all. What matters is the negative attitude toward private investment—his disposition to write it off as technically hopeless or unpromising and thus to evade or to minimize what is, save for reckless opportunism, our central policy problem. Unless prepared to abandon hope of a tolerable future, we must somewhere allow some savings and resources to run to waste, facing that wastage as a problem of restoring free markets and free occupational migration, not glossing it over by more spending. Public investment, freed from the exacting social accounting of private business, is a dangerous evasion—and, incidentally, one in which socialism can indulge more irresponsibly when it occupies a minor sector of the economy than it could if extended substantially.

Gradual socialization, displacing private by governmental agencies in areas where competition is notoriously inadequate as a device of control (public utilities, oil extraction, life insurance, etc.), has much to commend it. Such developments in policy, however, have little to offer by way of outlets for investment, involving in the main merely ownership and control displacement. On the other hand, Hansen's over-all scheme for governmental absorption of savings promises a flood of governmental investment which is unlikely to be directed with much (if any) regard for need of governmental, as against competitive, control. It promises a promiscuous spreading of governmental activities which, missing areas where large or complete political control is clearly indicated, gets the government involved in a mass of miscellaneous undertakings for which it has little competence and impairs or inhibits enterprise in many areas where competitive control is most appropriate. Moreover, a progressive society, in which only governmental enterprise can expand, will surely lose its complement of private business from sheer atrophy or stagnation.

"Were it not for the fact that a rapidly mounting public debt tends toward wealth concentration, borrowing is always to be preferred to taxation, since borrowing is always a more expansionist method of financing expenditures" (p. 179). Against this view, I should argue that there is never any excuse for borrowing save to *prevent* expansion. Borrowing is a means for displacing money (deposits) with less effective money substitutes (consols). If we want expansion, the way to get it is by noninterest-bearing issues—exchanging million-dollar bills for central-bank deposits, if one must think in terms of an anomalous separation between central banks and treasuries. Borrowing has little place in sound policy, save as temporary, temporizing means for checking incipient inflationary movements until taxation-expenditure adjustments can be made and for avoiding sharp taxation adjustments to quite temporary surges of spending.

Vulgar prejudice will support Hansen's implication that borrowing is less dangerous than issue. I am firmly convinced of the opposite. Injection of money, within limits, is like putting fuel in the furnace; borrowing, like accumulating dynamite in the basement, with the explosion risk growing as the pile accumulates. Or consider another analogy. A community which endlessly resorts to governmental borrowing is like one which, with abundance of fuel and great conflagration hazard, keeps itself warm by burning up its fire engines and water-works.

Currency issue, merely because its effects are more immediate and its dangers well recognized, is likely to be used cautiously and in moderation. Its excesses set off danger signals for everyone to see; and popular distaste for inflation sets proximate limits on legislative extravagance and reluctance to tax. What matters most, perhaps, is that the obvious short-term norms are also nearly adequate as guides for long-term policy. If we get along tolerably well year by year, we may be fairly confident about more remote prospects. Borrowing, on the other hand, permits legislatures to indulge freely their spending proclivities, piling up difficulties for legislatures of the future. Inflationary extravagance is countered by deflationary borrowing; and the trick can be made to work for quite a time.

The debt, of course, we shall owe to ourselves. We might have lower morbidity, valuable public assets, a larger tax base, and other good things to show for it. But the magnitude and rate of increase of internal debt is a measure of political instability and exposure to revolution. We cannot indefinitely and continuously add to the transfer obligations of our political system without jeopardizing political order. Somewhere, sometime ahead, taxpayers or claimants of governmental dispensations will revolt against deprivations in the name of bondholders, especially as free spending and repudiation of all fiscal norms relax pressure against minority demands. As soon as such possibilities become discernible ahead—which may be soon or decades away—the fright of bondholders will create a revolutionary situation.

I offer this, not as historical forecast, but as indicating the probable outcome of Hansen's program. For many years, the government, leaving private investment exposed to extortion, may be able to borrow cheaply and to spend with abandon.

Savers are left between the devil and the sea—with little hope of conserving or retrieving funds invested privately and with grave fears for the distant future of government credit. That they should prefer and gladly absorb government bonds for a time is natural enough; but the situation is highly unstable and will become increasingly unstable, especially if responsible people talk and write in the vein of Hansen's book.

The dangers of large debts, to be sure, have been exaggerated, with respect to communities which indulged increases only in great emergencies and deplored them with a profound financial puritanism. If our present federal debt were to rise in proportion to real income, one might, while disliking the trend, readily concede that it was not alarming. Hansen reminds us (p. 173) that, with increase of $2-2\frac{1}{2}$ per cent per annum, we should have an income exceeding \$200 billion in fifty years. But suppose we invoke the marvels of compound interest for fifty years of debt increase at the 1933–40 rate, which Hansen condemns as niggardly! To talk of increase at 2 per cent per annum is to dissociate one's self from the whole view and school of policy which he represents.

During the past century or more, a thriving economy, denied adequate proper media for liquid reserves, created and encouraged private agencies to provide what government itself blindly failed to provide. Thus, we evolved a fantastic financial structure and collections of enterprises for money-bootlegging, whose sanctimonious respectability and marble solidity only concealed a mass of current obligations and a shoestring of equity that would have been scandalous in any other type of business. In this unfortunate manner the economy was supplied, almost adequately in a secular view, with the flow of money requisite for rapid expansion—although the flow reached flood proportions at times and dried up most unseasonably. However, the financial structure and institutional monstrosities whose development provided us with money media, while sparing us rapid secular appreciation of money, also exposed us continuously to precipitous, catastrophic deflation, whose possibilities were sometimes painfully revealed but, by some miracle, never deeply explored. At any rate, proceeding without policy, we did avoid intolerable money shortage by recourse to a mass of *ersatz* moneys which could function only while the illusion persisted that they were really convertible into the real thing. In other words, we evaded long-term deflation by continuously courting deflation catastrophe.

For the future, following Hansen and his school, we evidently will correct a bad pattern of past fiscal practice by moving to an opposite extreme which is only more dangerous (and without correcting past mistakes in the control of private finance). Having long pursued our business beneath a mountainous structure of private money substitutes which threatened indefinite deflation whenever creditors insisted on their rights to currency and gold, we now propose to take up residence beneath another mountain of governmental money substitutes (debt) which threaten indefinite inflation if the confidence of creditors is ever impaired. As I see it, Hansen proposes with borrowing to avoid long-term, secular inflation by continuously courting inflation catastrophe.

The mistake in both directions lies in fearing money and in trusting debt. Money itself is highly amenable to democratic, legislative control, for no community wants a markedly appreciating or depreciating currency or is tolerant politically of departures from the norm of stable money value. But money is not easily manageable alongside a mass of private debt and private near-moneys whose aberrations fiscal policy must always work against, or alongside a mountain of public debt, short-term and long, which rises prodigiously in emergencies and is not reducible at other times. If the old system needed genuine instead of spurious liquidity, the new will need 100 per cent reserves of borrowing power and the greatest potentials of revenue increase and expenditure reduction.

Obviously, the future dangers of money depreciation are of a different order of magnitude from the old dangers of appreciation. Deflation possibilities in the old system were almost limitless. That we had only tolerable depressions is to be explained psychologically—by a persisting confidence that prosperity would sometime follow upon depression and that great bargains were to be had by those who took the long view when everything looked worst, that is, by persisting faith in prede-pression prices as norms which would be approached or attained again in time. To be sure, there was nothing in the financial structure to support such faith, and little in fiscal practice; but recovery of prices was at bottom always an excellent political speculation, for deflations always stirred up cheap-money movements and, if more prolonged and more severe, would earlier have produced fiscal and monetary counteraction on the grand scale we have just seen. Government was always there with adequate power to stop deflation if it would.

There is, of course, no corresponding ceiling to inflation, once governments have squandered their borrowing powers and undermined confidence of their creditors in the future of fiscal policy. Psychology is then all to the bad and expectations endlessly aggravating. If governments carefully conserve their borrowing powers for inflationary emergencies (wars) and promptly amortize debts incurred on such occasions, if they retain large reserves of unused taxing power and avoid politically irreducible expenditures (e.g., agricultural subsidies), then severe depreciation of the currency would be technically and politically easy to prevent, exhausting wars apart. What Hansen offers is a future of free spending with a minimum of political flexibility, of taxes near the limit of taxable capacity (largely a matter of political solidarity or morale), and of huge debt, growing at an uneven rate but always growing. And the gods are surely on his side. What he proposes is exactly what many of us, in our most realistic and despairing moods, foresee ahead as the outcome of recent trends. So, just as fear of money led to private usurpation of issue powers and grave deflations in the past, that fear now promises reckless recourse to borrowing with destruction of the political and financial system at the end. Having erred heretofore in not using issue powers and in not keeping them in governmental hands, we shall henceforth err more seriously in not confining the central government to taxes and issue as peacetime sources of funds.

An important criticism of debt expansion, as against currency issue, is that it facilitates a dangerous muddling of monetary questions and questions of socialization. Confined to taxation and issue, Congress would be reasonably restrained in its expansion of governmental dispensations and activities. Given real consensus of fiscal norms (a monetary constitution) and given a private economy free enough to benefit by monetary stabilization, the government could easily implement such stabilization by proper use of taxing, spending, and issue powers and without extending, for that purpose, the range or magnitude of its total activities. We might then face squarely and separately questions of policy which should be so faced, notably questions as to the relative merits of private versus governmental ownership and entrepreneurship in particular areas. If we must spend and borrow to absorb savings, finding outlets where we may, we are likely not only to neglect measures for revitalizing private enterprise and investment but also to extend collectivism indiscriminately, wherever private enterprise languishes from extortion or intimidation (coal-mining, housing, railways). Thus we shall neglect socialization or pursue it deviously and diffidently in areas where the case for it is clear and strong; we shall have no clearly defined socialized sector but only promiscuous intrusion of governmental enterprise all over the place; and we shall progressively incumber the socialized sector with acute minority and monopoly problems which socialization promises only to aggravate. The outlook in this respect should be even more distressing to good socialists than to old-fashioned liberals.

So I come back to highly orthodox views. Legislatures can be trusted to spend if required to tax accordingly. They must be trusted to issue freely, under mandate to stabilize the value of money, if we are to have the stabilizing element in our institutional system which it has long needed and utterly lacked. But the power to borrow, if not denied, should be narrowly limited, that is, used only in war emergencies and for major projects of socialization where net return on governmental investment may confidently be anticipated. Debts, however incurred, should be amortized and liquidated systematically, if only on the principle of conserving legislative powers. If these views seem narrow and dogmatic, what is the alternative principle of policy with which a community may hope to discipline its legislature or to function responsibly itself?

The importance of rules, and of focusing democratic discussion on general principles of policy, calls for emphasis at many points in criticism of Hansen's proposals. Only with rules of policy can common national interests be protected against minorities (as lobbies or as monopolies); only with issues of general principle can government by intelligent discussion prevail; only in terms of such issues can responsible intellectuals provide guidance and leadership in the community; only by adherence to wise rules of action can we escape a political opportunism which jeopardizes and destroys what we wish most to protect and to preserve.

Some friendly critics feel that I have exaggerated the dangers of delegation of legislative powers,[10] arguing that the legislature remains free to judge actions taken and to withdraw powers. Such argument can perhaps be extended logically to prove that tyranny is the most democratic form of government. (It is not difficult to imagine nearly absolute dictatorship functioning within a framework of free elections and legislatures with formally undiminished powers.) However, one might concede something to the criticism if the choice lay between legislative and administrative rule-making; but advocates of delegation are usually not interested in rule-making at the administrative level either. If agencies endowed with large powers were to adopt, to announce, and to follow definite principles of action, they might then become genuinely responsible, the principles—rather than the discrete actions—being proper objects of legislative and popular discussion and of acceptance or rejection.

Hansen favors large abdication of fiscal powers by Congress in favor of special agencies and their experts (esp. pp. 446–48) —with freedom, I infer, to use the powers for consolidating their own position and that of their patron faction. And what, pray, are the principles which their actions should follow and be judged by? As far as I can make out, they are (1) that federal debt should rise indefinitely and (2) that the rate of increase should be adjusted to the degree of unemployment. Such principles are objectionable as far as they are unambiguous, and more objectionable because they are vague and indefinite. Reasons for rejecting the former proposition have already been suggested. The latter is merely opportunism raised to the status of principle. It has the specious appeal of all proposals which are defined merely in terms of ends or purposes which, as such, are universally approved. On its face it suggests that excessive wage increases, whether of average rates or of relative rates in critical areas, be counteracted by increases of the price level—which program, like indefinite debt increase, has little to commend it for the minimizing of monetary uncertainty![11]

This proposal of a continuing contest between the monetary authority seeking to raise employment and trade-unions seeking to raise wage rates, with each side trying to anticipate and outguess the other, is superficially incompatible with an implicit Hansen principle, namely, that inflation should be avoided. But a moment's reflection will reveal a reconciliation, if not a comforting one. Presumably the private economy is to struggle along as best it can, whatever happens to wage rates, the unemployed being absorbed continuously into public employment, that is, into an expanding socialized sector which, supported out of taxing and borrowing, need not be seriously concerned about relations between wage rates and productivity. Thus movements of administered wage rates would determine, not movements of the price level, but merely the rate of socialization, that is, the life-expectancy of free enterprise!

This seemingly inescapable interpretation of Hansen's position further discloses the practical import of his thesis that monetary policy is not enough and of his preference for debt over currency issue. What he proposes, if you will, is collectivism via fiscal policy or fiscal stabilization whose implementation is promiscuous socialization, letting functional minorities do their worst until the socialized sector, grown too large to live parasitically and irresponsibly, itself cries out for protection against them—and gets it from the man on horseback.[12]

Given the pressure for increasing money wages, one may concede the case for monetary arrangements which assure gently rising wage rates as labor productivities (at full employment) increase—especially since it seems impossible to formulate satisfactory norms of fiscal policy otherwise than in terms of price indexes. Recognizing inordinate demand for liquidity in a political environment uncongenial if not hostile to owners of sunk investment, one may commend the total ordering of fiscal policy toward stabilization of a broad commodity-price index and provision of all the liquidity consistent with that norm. Stabilization, perhaps, is not enough. We need not merely a stable value of money, which might be compatible with widely different levels of income and employment, but rather the most expansive fiscal practices consistent with index stability.[13]

So far, I discern no basis for substantial disagreement with Hansen (or with most Keynesians). He clearly is disposed to avoid and to deplore inflation (when he is not dismissing the possibility as exaggerated or imaginary) and presumably would be content to define the negative desideratum in terms of some price index. By implication he is asking for the most expansive fiscal policy compatible with price stability; and it should matter little whether one argues the case in Keynesian language or with old-fashioned monetary terminology.

Disagreement perhaps relates less to the rule than to implementation. One finds here the analogue, for fiscal policy, of the old issue of qualitative versus quantitative control in the banking field. Hansen evidently is pleading for an infinitely flexible scheme of discretionary action, whereby agencies and their experts would direct, from day to day, the flow of expenditures and revenues, as well as open-market operations, according to their best judgment of the moment. The issue here includes questions of currency versus debt and, broadly, concerns a matter of degree. Monetary authorities must have powers and must not be narrowly confined by arbitrary formulas in their use. The question of degree, however, presents the choice between government by free, intelligent discussion and government by bureaucracy which only revolution can dislodge, that is, between democracy and "the managerial state."

The more I consider the problem here, the firmer becomes my persuasion, first, that monetary authorities must be bound by simple, definite rules (a price index) and, second, *that their only real powers should be those of conducting operations in the public debt.* If they are to have any control over spendings and revenue receipts, it should be exercised under formulas which prevent substantial allocational control over taxes or appropriations. But should they have any such powers at all? Facing that question squarely, one shortly asks how the discussion could have started unless in connection with proposals to abolish legislatures entirely!

The plain fact is that the ultimate monetary powers and the ultimate legislative powers are those of taxing and spending.[14] No monetary authority can function, and no principle of policy can be carried out, against opposition of a real legislature; and no real legislature will delegate or impair its powers to tax and spend. Indeed, it should be obvious from the start that the great task of a monetary authority is simply that of advising Congress—of representing the general public as an expert body, indicating to Congress and to the public what may and may not be done consistently with accepted norms of fiscal action (monetary policy). If Congress needs rules to discipline the use of delegated powers, the monetary authority is more gravely in need of rules to assure congressional co-operation. The only real authority is the public; and the only possible rules are norms which the community, guided ideally by consensus of competent specialists, accepts and demands to be observed in government finance. Given expert and popular consensus, given an authority competent to advise, and given disposition of legislators to observe the norms and to act upon recommendations of the authority, there would be no need for much delegation of power or for much use of power delegated. If Congress were expected to abide by the rules (e.g., a price index), anticipations would make them nearly self-implementing between legislative actions. Appropriate open-market operations, replacing consols by demand obligations or conversely, would ease adjustments and forecast budgetary changes. It might be unnecessary for the authority to take any overt action beyond that of giving publicity to index movements and some advance notice of its recommendations. Indeed, changes in money supply might become quite as passive and "automatic" as are changes in note circulation at present.

These remarks will suggest, I hope, the overwhelming importance of consensus upon general rules or norms of democratic fiscal policy—of our developing a kind of monetary constitution, grounded in expert and popular approval and binding upon Congress as well as upon executive and administrative officers. With a real monetary religion, the economic objective of minimizing monetary uncertainty would be attained and the perversities of finance, public and private, eliminated or minimized. Given consensus on fiscal norms, moreover, problems of implementation become simple and trivial; without it, no amount of delegation of powers could yield good results, even if there were no political dangers in such delegation.

The moral here is that responsible economists should now strive to achieve such consensus among themselves as to the fiscal norms appropriate to the future of American democracy, partly collectivist but predominantly free enterprise. If we could reach agreement among ourselves—excluding those who would use all proximate means, fiscal and other, to prevent survival of this kind of system—we might easily exercise decisive influence and rapidly induce a popular, political consensus. Indeed, the essential ingredients of sound popular consensus already exist, in profound disapproval of both deflation and inflation, and need only be articulated in sound, concrete proposals, indorsed by people recognized as competent and disinterested. In any case, seeking such consensus, we should be discharging our primary responsibility to the community and doing our part to preserve government by discussion.

Hansen's book, I believe, renders great disservice on this score. It offers no clear principles of monetary and fiscal policy for the future or, at any rate, none which is promising as a basis for academic or popular consensus. Indeed, it is admirably contrived to intensify already bitter controversy, to confuse what should be a sharper division along individualist-collectivist lines, and to divide us as supporters or opponents of a particular administration. Whatever his intentions, Hansen concedes all that extreme collectivists could possibly ask by way of proximate measures. He gives his full blessing to those whose economics is epitomized in the fashionable remark: "Don't worry about the debt; that will take care of itself"—as indeed it will if revolution is the highest desideratum. A prominent expert adviser of the administration, he attributes its failures to exogenous factors beyond all control and imputes blame only for financial niggardliness (especially in 1937) which the opposition can hardly disavow. As a political tract, the book resembles party platforms, evading awkward issues and hard problems, conciliating all the powerful minorities, and presenting not a program of principles but merely a plea that the public trust "the experts" and their present political patrons to determine what is best as they go along. If Hansen were an extreme collectivist, I might respect his persuasion and grant that he has made a learned and powerful argument, albeit sophistical, for the inevitable disintegration of private business and for a program looking toward rapid movement into full collectivism, with only the usual blindness of socialists to present problems as they would present themselves after the old order was gone. As conservative defense of fiscal innovations, however, the book reveals a sudden conversion to monetary extremism which has swept the convert utterly away from the mooring of an anticollectivist position to which he still imagines himself, and purports to be, anchored fast.

Hansen's discussion of taxation is surprisingly fragmentary. Chapter viii (pp. 125–34) offers a good sketch of changes in the tax structure since the turn of the century, with emphasis on the last decade.[15] Chapter xix discusses "The Effect of the Tax Structure on Investment" quite sensibly, with an abundance of investment data but with little regard for major tax considerations. A deal of statistical information is presented, all useful for illuminating problems which Hansen does not stop to formulate. Thus he wisely concludes that the capital-gains tax is not so important, and tax-exempt securities not so unimportant, as conservatives have maintained, but without ever bringing the real issues into any focus. He suggests that reduction or elimination of capital-gains taxes, while not likely to help much, would have some favorable effect on investment —without recognizing that drastic change in the other direction is imperative for consistent and equitable application of the progressive principle. Indeed, he stresses exactly the point (p. 391) which is most misleading, namely, that the Treasury has little to gain by fair treatment of capital gains and losses— as if equitable distribution of levies among persons was a matter of no consequence. Discussing the corporation tax, he wisely argues the case for averaging and/or for more generous loss carry-over, but he nowhere suggests that such changes are still more important in the personal tax. Moreover, no mention is made of the anomaly and the unhappy influence of interest deductions in the corporation tax. Thus, while illuminating controversial questions for readers who previously understood them thoroughly, his chapter will leave many misconceptions with other readers and perhaps aggravate those which have long impeded sound tax reforms.

Only in chapter xiii is taxation discussed in the aspects crucially important for his general subject. Here the treatment is peculiarly casual and doctrinaire. Hansen bluntly distinguishes two cases: the highly dynamic economy capable occasionally of attaining full employment via spontaneous private investment (the past?) and the economy facing chronic unemployment and able to reach full employment only with public investment continuing through all phases of the cycle (the present and future?). For the first (past) he makes interesting proposals for pay-roll or excise taxes in prosperity to finance relief and employment subsidies in depressions. For the second (future) he argues against cyclical adjustment of either excises or income taxes on grounds which, even on his own strange premises, seem quite unsubstantial. The general idea is that, in the first case, excise taxes during prosperity, by checking consumption, would check excessive induced investment; while income-tax reductions (or avoidance of increases) would permit wholesome financing of investment from savings instead of from credit expansion. But, in the second case, the propensity to save is excessive and consumption inadequate in all phases; and the tax problem is merely one of altering the consumption function secularly! One passage perplexes me especially:

"Question may be raised as to whether the progressive income tax rates, designed to raise the propensity to consume, should fluctuate with the cycle, being increased in the boom and reduced in the depression; or whether the rate structure, while steeply progressive, should remain fixed in the various phases of the cycle. On balance, the latter is to be preferred. Excessively high rates in the boom cannot help the basic problem of increasing the aggregate community consumption over the entire cycle, since higher rates in the boom presuppose lower rates in the depression. The total volume of funds tapped from the savings stream and diverted into community consumption would not thereby be increased over the entire cycle period" (p. 300). Why, one asks, do not such considerations argue equally well against cyclical adjustment of spending?

The argument of this chapter is evidently designed to support the view, common among Keynesians, that attention should be focused on spending adjustments and not upon taxes. This again involves, if it does not candidly represent, a collectivist bias in stabilization proposals which, I think, is justified no more by Hansen's argument than by the usual ignoring of the question. Stabilization in principle admits of action on both sides of the budget and, on its face, calls for rather equal reliance on spending and on taxing adjustments. Indeed, political considerations argue, I believe, for allowing to tax adjustments more than an equal share, for its seems much less difficult to maintain real political flexibility in revenues than in expenditures. (Pressure groups are a greater obstacle to expenditure reductions than to tax increases.) Moreover, as already suggested, to make spending the only variable— whether for currency issue or for debt expansion—requires, with increasing income, a continuous, rapid expansion of governmental activities which, even if desirable, ought not to proceed merely as an incident of stabilization.

Hansen surely would not deny that in the thirties we could have obtained similar results, with the same deficits and far less spending, if excises and pay-roll taxes, state as well as federal, had not been vastly increased. Our tax system, of course, is not well designed for minimizing inequality or for cyclical adjustment. Federal excises, being highly differential, seem especially to require stable rates, their impact falling mainly on a few industries and their changes involving undesirable uncertainties and unfortunate windfalls of gain and loss. And the income taxes, besides involving great lags between legislation and revenue changes, are least effective in promoting expansion when reduced or in checking expansion when raised.

Such considerations, however, do not justify not doing what

we can with the present tax system or not altering it to facilitate cyclical adjustment. The windfall problem is not serious for our important excises, where demand for the commodities is extremely inelastic and where imperfect competition assures full and prompt adjustment of prices to tax changes. Reduction of tobacco and liquor taxes is a very effective means for increasing consumption, not of the commodities in question but of consumption goods generally; and the same may be said for many less important federal levies. The perversity of changes in state excises was a major aggravation in the thirties and presents a serious problem for the future and, under a bold program, could easily be dealt with by opportune federal grants to the states in lieu of equivalent direct federal spending.

If one would plan for deficits indefinitely, new borrowing might well be used to permit, not continued growth of spending, but gradual reduction and ultimate elimination of all our excise taxes (save the gasoline tax). If we were to contemplate moderate average deficits, covered entirely by issue, and cyclical tax adjustments, much could be said for displacing all our special excises with a pay-roll tax, a general manufacturers' excise, or even a value-added tax. I have no stomach for such levies as mere additions to our revenue system or for the arguments usually advanced to support them. However, if they were to displace existing particular excises which would not otherwise be removed, we should have afterward both a less regressive system[16] and one far more amenable to cyclical adjustment.

With the income tax, much can be said for levying against current-year income, with substantial collection at source, or for continuous readjustment during the year of rates applicable to previous-year income. In any case, while other taxes can be altered more effectively for either stimulation or retardation, current discussion seems greatly to underestimate the potentialities of sharp changes in the normal tax (if it amounted to something!) or in the exemption levels. If it is not a perfect instrument for the particular purpose, that is no excuse for not using it so far as possible or for not making it more useful so far as that may be done without impairing its fairness among individuals. Incidentally, full taxation of capital gains (with every transfer treated as a "realization") and full deduction of capital losses, along with generous provision for loss carry-over and for averaging rebates on fluctuating incomes, besides eliminating gross inequities among taxpayers and major evasion loopholes, would vastly improve the cycle sensitivity of income-tax revenues. A strong case can be made for stability in the higher surtaxes, on grounds other than Hansen's, especially if the tendency for revenues to swell during prosperity and to recede during depression is developed to the full along the above lines.

So, while Hansen looks with approval to rapid increase of spending, I should maintain that strong argument can be made for continuous and ultimately drastic reduction, whether to diminish inequality, to stabilize prices and employment, or even to modify the consumption function, not to mention the specter of increasing federal centralization and the authoritarian state. Few of our recent social welfare expenditures are sufficiently meritorious to justify expansion (save to provide some medical service for everyone) or even continuance at recent levels where the alternative is reduction of our worst taxes. Their marginal cost, measured in terms of federal and state excise taxation, is excessively high, since these levies pump their revenues predominantly from mass consumption from the bottom of the income scale. For the future we should fashion our optional spending in such manner as to avoid and escape large recourse to deeply regressive levies. Increasing socialization (and centralization) is ominous in any case. It has less than nothing to commend it when it proceeds at costs which, even in the short view, leave inequality unmitigated or aggravated on balance. Good taxes *plus* even the annual net borrowing Hansen would commend (or the desirable net increment of currency) cannot begin to cover our minimal expenditures, that is, the cost of governmental activities whose maintenance is beyond dispute. New undertakings, save for moderate old age assistance and health "insurance," generally cannot begin to cover their added costs if measured in terms of our worst taxes. Thus, until we are rid of regressive taxes, we should talk very softly about otherwise lovely schemes for socialized consumption.[17]

One may accept Hansen's view, if not the supporting argument, that government of the future should be financed by progressive taxes on personal income. There are still large unexploited potentials of income-tax capacity in the so-called lower and middle brackets. However, there are limits somewhere, if one has any concern about propensity to invest; and the severest income tax one can contemplate as politically and administratively possible would provide only a minor fraction of the revenues required by future spending, even on the most conservative extrapolation. Granting that politicians *qua* spenders should be released slightly from the narrow confines of full budget balancing, one may still demand that their noisy concern about the masses should be accompanied by some concern about mass taxation and even about property taxes which create wide disparity between marginal-private and marginal-social efficiency of investment. Vested-interest considerations perhaps argue decisively for stabilization of real-property taxes at present levels; but there remains a vast task, whether for those concerned about inequality or for those concerned about the consumption function, of eliminating excises and, especially, of undoing the vast extension of such levies in recent years. Such reform is tedious for men of action; it has nothing to commend it politically, since spending purchases the votes and the loud applause of organized, articulate minorities, while tax reductions concern only the unarticulated interests of everyone as buyer of goods and seller of services. But its possibilities for progressive reconstruction are more substantial than those of recent spending and deserve overwhelming emphasis in policy discussions of economists who are more interested in offering sound guidance than in getting elected or appointed.

Whether investment stagnation is a technical phenomenon

or a consequence of legislative, institutional, or "sociological" trends may seem unimportant for action, if the latter trends be accepted as immutable or inexorable. On this view, Hansen's policy position may be supported by argument which, granted its premises, is beyond attack; and there evidently are prominent people who will make this argument, candidly if not publicly. They start with assertion (assumption) that there is nothing ahead but deluge; that we must write off nearly everything we prize and accept as inevitable a future which has nothing to commend it in terms of our old values and aspirations. But, they say, this future is not upon us yet. We can postpone its arrival, first, by not fighting or struggling against the basically revolutionary and disintegrating tendencies (Schumpeter's "sociological drift") and, second, by filling the dying order with the stimulants of vast federal spending and borrowing while the game lasts. Thus, we may provide ourselves with a tolerable national existence for a decade or more and win reprieve from a hell which otherwise will only claim us sooner.

Such argument may give pause. Perhaps it is now a grave mistake to discuss fundamental problems of political and economic reconstruction or to concern ourselves deeply about the requisites of enduring peace or freedom or national unity. Perhaps we should now seek only, first, to defeat the devil abroad and, second, to ransom ourselves from him briefly by appeasement at home. My impulse is simply to evade the issue, distrusting human revelations of inevitability and keeping humbly to the task of discerning and explaining what needs doing and undoing if we are to preserve a world consonant with our highest values. Whether there is a chance to preserve it, in a realistic view, is a question for people of inhuman detachment or intimate communion with God.

Hansen, of course, would disavow and repudiate any such defeatist persuasions; but I think his program is utterly defeatist, if not utterly collectivist. He wisely argues the case for a dual system—part socialized, part free enterprise—rejecting the (collectivist) argument that a mixed system is inferior to purer types at either extreme. His conception of future socialization is not alarming or unconventional, either as to kinds of activity or as to dimensions of the socialized sector relative to private business—although his direct proposals seem strikingly in contrast with what his fiscal program would bring about in a fairly short space of time.

Questions of how territory should be divided in the dual system, however, seem relatively trivial. What matters is whether the private-enterprise sector is to be an area of free markets or not. If so, it may be expected to take care of itself, holding areas conceded to it at the start and possibly expanding, relative to the socialized sector. If not, it cannot long survive at all, much less maintain itself in absolute or relative size.

Hansen's positive proposals, significantly enough, relate almost exclusively to the socialized sector. It is to be provided with abundant funds, from progressive taxes on the private economy and from uninterrupted borrowing. Thus it will raise interest costs in the private sector, raise costs of capital assets by governmental competition (not to mention the Walsh-Healy Act), drain off all savings not promptly absorbed privately, and continuously add its interest burden to tax charges. Besides competing for resources and for savings with government enterprise, not much limited by pecuniary accounting and heavily subsidized, private enterprise must proceed under ominous uncertainty as to where government enterprise will next appear as subsidized seller and purchaser.

How is private enterprise to be strengthened and revitalized to carry greater tax burdens and to override the inhibitions of adverse political risks? On this score Hansen has nothing to propose save larger governmental control of prices and wages!

"In a free market economy no single unit was sufficiently powerful to exert any appreciable control over the price mechanism. In a controlled economy the government, the corporation, and organized groups all exercise direct influence over the market mechanism. Many contend that it is just this imperfect functioning of the price system which explains the failure to achieve reasonably full employment in the decade of the thirties. . . . .

"There can be no doubt that these profound changes in institutional arrangements are significant. It is not possible to go back to the atomistic order. Corporations, trade-unions, and government intervention we shall continue to have. Modern democracy does not mean individualism. It means a system in which private, voluntary organization functions under general, and mostly indirect, government control. Dictatorship means direct and specific control. We do not have a choice between "plan and no plan." We have a choice only between democratic planning and totalitarian regimentation" (p. 47).

At another point (chap. xv) he sketches a desirable pattern of movement for administered prices over the cycle. Wages are to remain stable during depressions and to advance during prosperity, but only at the same rate as productivity (at full employment?). Industrial prices should not rise (should fall?) during prosperity and should not fall during depression. Presupposing prompt fiscal compensation, and making the dubious assumption that booms will not aggravate "structural dispersion" adverse to investment, one may commend this pattern—it being, indeed, what would happen under free markets and price-level stabilization. But Hansen is diffident and evasive when he touches questions of how this ideal pattern might be implemented or how structural maladjustments (which he calls very important for long-term policy and unimportant for recovery) are to be mitigated and minimized. He evidently favors extensive price control during upswings, with an institutionalized Henderson passing on all petitions for increases. On principle, if not in politics, he might be expected to advocate similar control over wage increases; but the idea is dismissed as impractical.

"It is quite impossible for administrative agencies to determine accurately the appropriate price or the appropriate wage. The flexible functioning of the economy requires that this be left largely to the private determination of the parties concerned. It is, however, probable that better price and wage policies could be implemented by a governmental review of proposed price or wage increases. The burden of proof would then be put upon the industry or the trade-union to show that the facts of the economic situation really justified the price or wage increase. In the case of wage rates, this problem has been attacked in various countries through the instrumentality of labor courts and through boards of compulsory or voluntary arbitration. The problem is, indeed, a difficult one and requires a high degree of voluntary participation through collective bargaining units. Experience indicates the greatest measure of successful achievement where the responsibility for the determination of the rate has been placed upon the parties involved—the employers and the employees or their representatives. The problem confronting the price review board would seem to be relatively simpler than that confronting the wage review board" (p. 325). To the last observation one might add: "and much less important, since competition, though very imperfect, may usually be relied upon to prevent gross maladjustments."

It is misleading, I think, to call what Hansen is proposing "the dual economy." A dual system, to make sense, must involve a sound combination of competitive and political controls. The public interest may be protected, as against particular producer groups, by the maintenance of free competition within such groups or by the direct and specific control which Hansen associates with dictatorshp. There is no other way. Doctrinaire socialists would use the direct controls everywhere, believing that liberty and abundance could somehow be preserved and enhanced under such arrangements. Old-fashioned liberals, distrusting all concentrations of power and centralization in great federal states especially, argue for a mixed system, fully socialized in many areas but relying mainly on the indirect control of enforced competition within functional groups. Both these schemes make sense in principle; at bottom they have much in common. Intelligent socialists would seek to approximate via political control the structure of prices and production which would obtain in an ideally competitive system; traditional liberals would seek to approximate that structure largely by keeping competition of the real world as free and unrestrained as may be. Both recognize the dangers of great concentration of power, economic and political, of patronage corruption, and of monopoly; and there is no very substantial disagreement as concerns proper areas for socialized consumption and relaxing in price restraints. These groups, while differing bitterly on matters of practical politics, have large areas of mutual understanding and large opportunities for common discussion of problems of their respective systems.

For either of these schemes, the minorities problem is crucial. Government must preserve its monopoly of violence and behave impartially toward different producers. It must deal even-handedly with all functional minorities, on the basis of definite principles which are the only means for avoiding arbitrariness, corruption, and disorder. It must not concede to any functional group the power ("right") to withhold its contribution to an elaborate production process or to exact tribute by threat of such collective action. With intricate division of labor, every large group can, acting collectively, seriously check, if not entirely stop, the whole flow of social income; and no community, socialist or other, can function tolerably if many groups have such power and must continuously be bribed to forgo its disastrous exercise. Government, to repeat, must preserve its monopoly of violence, if there is to be internal peace and orderly production.

Hansen's world of "voluntary associations" is no dual economy but a pluralism or syndicalism whose norm is chaos. He asks us to accept for the future a mixed system in which both private and socialized business will constitute battlegrounds for voluntary associations, contesting as pressure groups in government and as monopolists outside. The surface spectacle is one of bitter contest between workers and employers (private and governmental). Underneath, one sees community organization along functional, industry lines, with each group seeking to guard itself against the competition of newcomers (new enterprise and new investment, and new workers) and to advantage itself at the community's expense by increases of prices and wages and curtailment of output and employment. Bargaining organizations will contest over division of the swag, of course; but we commonly overlook the fact that they have large common interests as against the community and that every increase of monopoly power on one side serves to strengthen and implement it on the other. The future of sunk investment is not rosy; numbers will win over dollars in intra-industry contests; but would-be investors and enterprisers are in much the same position as the unemployed.

To devise monetary systems or fiscal norms for such an economy is utter waste of time, unless to gloss over the patent fact that it contains no basis of order and no possibility of survival. Private enterprise cannot endure in such a world; and, while socialized activities may thrive on instability for a time, government itself has no future, save as absolutism restoring somehow the monopoly of coercion which democracy has thrown away in misguided deference to the "right" of voluntary association.

There is no sense in designing elegant financial appurtenances for an institutional structure whose foundations of free exchange, free enterprise, and free occupational migration are disintegrating rapidly—unless one is prepared to give some attention to these foundations too. Hansen's prescriptions seem excellently contrived to hasten the disintegration.

IX

On Debt Policy*

I HAVE never seen any sense in an elaborate structure of
federal debt. The national government must, of course,
provide and regulate the currency—a task it has never faced.
It may perhaps, on some occasions, properly borrow money;
that is, open-market operations are a convenient, traditional,
and perhaps desirable temporizing means of currency regulation.

On the other hand, it is essentially improper and undemocratic (Schachtian) to confuse issues by proposing and using a
miscellany of debt forms. In wartime and in peacetime we
should issue currency and (or) bonds. We should never disguise
currency as bonds or conversely. Moreover, every issue of
bonds should be primarily an announcement of prospective
tax increases. (The converse here is not valid, since debt retirement may and should proceed secularly, at least if bonds
are outstanding in excess of the amounts necessary to facilitate
open-market measures.) Bond issues are properly a means for
checking incipient inflation and are, like currency issue, a
means especially well suited for prompt action by administrative rather than by legislative action.

Bonds, as the antithesis of money, here denote consols or
perpetuities, that is, obligations without *either* maturities or
"call" features. In the good financial society bondholders
could liquidate only by open-market sales; the Treasury could
sell only one interest-bearing debt form and only by open-
market sale; and it could retire such debt only by paying the
current, free-market price. (There would, of course, be no

* Reprinted by permission from the *Journal of Political Economy*, LII,
No. 4 (December, 1944), 356–61.

bonds save those of the Treasury or, at least, no trading of private debts on organized exchanges; but sane government finance obviously need not wait for sane reform in private corporate finance.)

There is little hope for sound monetary-fiscal policy under representative government if our representatives persist in confusing everybody, including especially themselves, by issuing moneys, practically moneys, and near-moneys under other names. Trying to steer a path between phobias about paper money and terror of high interest costs, they create only fiscal bedlam and intolerable monetary uncertainty.

The community is now almost persuaded, on Treasury authority, that it can, with the same dollars, buy ammunition to make things hot now for Germans and refrigerators to keep things cool later on at home. Economists may be less credulous; but their relevant persuasions cannot be said to have escaped the confusion which bad fiscal practice invites. It is indeed difficult for anyone to think quite straight about equipment-trust certificates issued to pay either for war materials or for food distributed to the unemployed.

The issues here come to focus upon the problem of interest rates. Should the Treasury offer better interest terms to its lenders now? What interest rates should be offered after the war, when and if we clean up an awful mess of debt by consolidations and refundings. If wartime borrowing, like wartime (non)taxation, is beyond repair for the duration, postwar financial measures cannot yet be dismissed as unalterably determined wrongly by momentum or political habit. Neither may one concede the impotence of academic opinion or the certainty that its influence will again be predominantly wrong at the crucial time.

One merit of these strictures about debt form is that, if sound or if provisionally accepted, they largely answer our interest problem by indirection. Borrowing or refunding via consols must mean higher interest rates; we must pay people something to give up the liquidity features of their near-moneys. If we will not pay taxes to stop inflation, we must at least pay interest!

It should not be inferred, however, that the devices proposed will necessarily increase the interest burden, real or nominal. Confining bond issues to consols, we must pay higher rates, to be sure; but we need not pay higher rates on so large a debt. Retiring short-term and redeemable issues, we may then safely have more debt in a noninterest-bearing form; indeed, we should certainly need more money to prevent deflation if we dispensed with moneys disguised as bonds. Indeed, there is even less sense in the Treasury's paying interest on demand or time deposits than in permitting banks to do so (whether in cash or in kind).

Come at in this way, the postwar problem (if not war finance!) becomes readily intelligible and discussible. Our federal debt should be refunded promptly and totally into currency and consols. In other words, we should remedy as rapidly as possible our wartime mistakes as to debt forms. (Our sins of omission taxation-wise cannot, unfortunately, be corrected so easily, if at all. Inflation will prove largely irreversible—although much may be said for stabilizing the indexes rather than the realities, that is, for deflating back to where the indexes tell the truth instead of revising the indexes so that they promptly cease lying when peace comes.) Some people evidently think that, having done everything wrong during the war, we should or must go on doing it all wrong afterward. I find little use for the hypothesis that error becomes truth merely by long or consistent practice.

This leaves the question of how much near-money should be converted into real, honest money and how much into consols. The answer is simple in principle and amenable to determination by experiment. It is only a matter of implementing monetary stabilization, that is, of doing what is necessary to stabilize some sensitive and reliable price index. The major variable, namely, private investment, is largely an independent variable for fiscal or monetary policy—assuming that

thrift is not undermined by extreme inflation and internal disorder. Investment is largely a matter of the fundamental security of property, including security against monopolies, labor and other. Another major variable is postwar banking
policy, especially as to reserve requirements or permitted devices of corporation finance. (It would certainly clear the air,
however, if banks as owners of federal debt were offered simply
a two-way choice between "unsupported" consols and fully
supported currency.) Finally, there is the relation between
federal tax revenues and expenditures.

The rule for policy as to consols and currency, that is, for
composition of the debt including money, is simply stabilization
of the value of money. Converting money into consols is an
anti-inflation measure; converting consols into money is a reflationary or anti-deflation measure; and that is that. The
problem becomes difficult or complicated only on the assumption that measures taken in other areas of policy will simply
prevent stabilization, regardless of debt policy. Considering the
amount of debt available to be monetized, the real problem
here is uncontrolled inflation. Until this whole game is hopelessly lost, however, it is the business of debt policy to assume
that it will *not* be lost and to *stick* to *its* appropriate anti-inflation measures *whatever the interest cost*. Above all, it should both
assume and imply that the Treasury intends to *stay* in business,
not just for ninety days or ten years but indefinitely, and issue
its obligations accordingly.

Simple debt management would almost certainly improve
policy and action in other areas. If Congress and the executive
could finance expenditures only by taxation, by currency issue,
or by borrowing, each in its most straightforward form,[1] we
might expect really responsible behavior not only in these
matters but in expenditure as well. Currency issue, as I have
argued elsewhere, is both a more effective and politically a
safer means of reflation or inflation than is (that compounding
of opposites) inflationary borrowing, if only because the process and its possible abuses are generally understood. It would

be hard politically to pursue obviously inflationary finance in the midst of actually inflationary conditions. Moreover, it would be politically more difficult to hold taxes down or expenditures up if the obvious cost was borrowing at open-market consol rates—with "danger" of having to pay through the nose later on to retire the current consol issues. On the other hand, it would be conveniently difficult to advocate or to pursue a scheme of combating deflation by selling *consols* to private issuing agencies (banks). The case for currency issue instead of indirect deposit creation would be very clear.

Many readers will have recorded their categorical dissent from our proposals because these all imply a price-index rule or guide for policy. I persist in the notions that stabilization of the value of money, however unrealized, is the only rule or principle of monetary-fiscal policy we have ever had, that it is the only rule really available to a democratic society, and that only by recognizing and by accepting this rule explicitly can legislatures be made responsible financially or business be spared intolerable monetary uncertainty. Be that as it may. One may, I presume, reject price-level stabilization without embracing its opposite. Opponents, in the main, do not advocate maximum instability or total monetary uncertainty. Rather they recommend crossing bridges when we come to them, that is, trusting to the authorities of the moment, or crossing, bridge or no bridge, and finding the bridge afterward if we did not drown. Consequently, it may be of interest to see what kinds of measures are consistent with stabilization and what kinds are not, since no one is proposing to go squarely in the opposite direction. The important fact is that so many people are actually proposing measures or stressing considerations which lead where no one wants to go.

Let us first belabor those numerous folk who, while applauding, condoning, or just not discussing the size of our debt, insist on keeping down its interest burden. The company is numerous, distinguished, and highly placed, both in government circles and in academic esteem. There is, to be sure, a grain of wisdom in their solicitude. First, the Treasury should never offer its issues on such terms that radical rationing measures are required; bonds should not be distributed like postmasterships. Second, the government should never raise interest rates by promoting, by encouraging, or by tolerating expectations of price inflation. These propositions about exhaust the truth in a mountain of foolishness. The truth assay is really very low.

Subject to these obvious reservations, the Treasury should seek always to pay as much interest as possible. (There may be impurities here, but I have not found them.) This merely amounts to saying that it should pay enough interest to prevent inflation. On the other hand, as a corollary, it should also always issue as much money as can be issued without raising the price level. Thus, it should simultaneously maximize the rate of interest payment and maximize the amount of noninterest-bearing issue, subject to the same condition, namely, a stable price level or index.[2]

Since it is difficult to argue about axioms, I shall attempt only some elenctic remarks. First, if one *wants* to minimize the nominal interest cost, one may best resort to paper money. It is admittedly improper to issue additional currency when inflation is under way. By the same token, it is wrong to issue short maturities or, indeed, any debt form save that furthest removed from the pure-money category. In such circumstances issue-yields will normally vary directly with maturities. Consequently, when we want to stop inflation, we should maximize interest rates; we should mop up money not with other moneys slightly disabled but with money contracts as much unlike money as possible. Conversely, stopping deflation, we should issue not near-moneys but the real thing without disabilities; and, issuing it, we should displace not near-moneys but as-far-from-money-as-possible moneys.[3]

During actual or imminent deflation, on the other hand, it may be better to borrow at short term than at long term; but it is best not to borrow at all, that is, to issue merely currency, not only for the desired immediate effect but also for long-term safety and minimal national misunderstanding. Borrowing is an anti-inflation measure, not a proper means for financing reflationary spending. Borrowing is properly a means for curtailing purchasing power, private and governmental. To use it for injecting purchasing power is (to repeat a figure I have used elsewhere) like burning the fire engines for heating purposes when there is an abundance of good fuel to be had free.[4]

To repeat, the right way to lower interest costs is to issue paper money—which sometimes is and sometimes is not a proper thing to do.

Let us now argue obliquely from another direction, namely, from the standpoint of the Treasury as central bank (which it alone should be). Here is the one aspect of the traditional monetary-fiscal pattern which has been mainly correct—indeed, the only one where perverseness has not prevailed. It is naturally also the phase of action with respect to which orthodoxy is most nearly sound. It is generally agreed that the Treasury, at least in disguise, should sell bonds to banks in boom times and buy them during severe deflation. This obviously means, in general, seeking to maximize capital losses over time, concentrating purchases at bond-price peaks and concentrating sales at the lows.[5] (Why such inherently lossful responsibilities were ever delegated to private corporations, I have never understood.)

Surely it is logically or heuristically permissible to treat such capital losses as part of the cost of servicing the debt. Indeed, in an institutionally well-ordered democracy, based on systematic dispersion of power, it would probably seem silly to regard them otherwise. One of the costs of living with near-moneys, even though they be no nearer than consols, lies in the necessity of forever buying them dear and selling them cheap, as monetary stabilization necessitates. Even if we evade the responsibility of rapid secular amortization, we must always be prepared to give money freely for bonds when they are most valuable and to take money for bonds when they are least valuable.

Thus, we may charge that proponents of minimal "controlled" rates on our federal bonds are inconsistent unless they also propose to reverse traditional rules about open-market operations. Surely the formal interest burden could be diminished or offset budgetwise if "perverse" rules of Federal Reserve practice were "put straight," if Reserve Bank capital-gain profits were recaptured, and if the revenues thus smartly obtained were used instead of taxes to pay bond interest! There should be no trouble in selling the scheme, for it only involves asking the Reserve banks to make more money and to follow accepted Treasury practice instead of attempting to stabilize prices—which, behavior notwithstanding, they have always denied trying to do and certainly have not the power to do. Indeed, even for intelligent people, it may seem wise to do everything wrong consistently, since the shortest political route to thesis may involve going all the way to antithesis first.

It is now fitting to pass comment on some minor variants of the antithesis. Some people, while commending and condemning mildly a little bit of everything in practice, have steeled themselves to accept postwar refunding into longer if not indefinite maturities but still lack the fortitude to accept possible high costs of debt retirement. Thus, they veer toward a consol form for the bondholder but leap back toward money for the Treasury via wide or indefinite "call" options. Here the inconsistency noted above is just reversed. The advocate of call features, while accepting higher interest rates, seeks to avoid the illusory misfortune of contingently high bond prices. Escaping one horn of a spurious dilemma, he impales himself on the other; or, in a better figure, he avoids Charybdis by smashing upon Scylla.

The proper way to avoid high prices for retired debt is to avoid deflations, that is, to maintain private investment and reasonably attractive alternative investment outlets for private funds. Labor and patent monopolies, among others, may make this difficult to achieve by monetary measures; but debt policy should do its best willy-nilly and stick to its price-level guns. If we must have deflations and high consol prices, the more the government has to pay for its debt the better. Surely it does not aggravate the task of monetizing debt to have opportunely high bond prices! With effective monetary stabilization and the sustained prosperity which it would assure in a free-market economy, there would be no wide sweeps in bond prices. But it will do no good, and some harm, to control this monetary thermometer when the task is one of stabilizing the monetary temperature. Even penny-pinchers should not complain if the community asks high prices to exchange its bonds for non-interest-bearing obligations and makes this conversion harmless by its increased demand for socially costless liquidity.

We are asking people now to buy war bonds which it is here traditional to default on substantially, via inflation—and with only optimists expecting a small default this time. Against this near certainty and the enduring risk of further wild inflation, there is the relatively small chance of nominal gain through eventual decline of interest rates. This remote favorable contingency the call feature is designed to remove! Save for indefinite forced lending (and do not suppose there will ever be none of it), call features can only raise the interest rate[6] and, besides, create an implied obligation to support the market, that is, to convert bonds into money at the worst times, if not, indeed, to make them really money all the time.

We have proposed, to repeat, that our debt be wholly and promptly converted into currency and consols, in whatever proportion is requisite for price-level stabilization. Such action, as already intimated, would place banks in a quandary. They would be loath to take consols, because of the loss of liquidity. They would be loath to take currency because of the loss of interest revenue, unless permitted to compound the currency by their own expansion of investments and deposits. The proper answer here is as simple as it is remote from our thinking or from our likely actions. Those institutions which choose cash should find their reserve requirements radically increased thereby (to or toward 100 per cent)—and should find their revenues in service charges. Those which choose consols should find their equity requirements increased (also ultimately and ideally to 100 per cent)—and should thereafter become largely or exclusively investment trusts. Thus, we only repeat proposals for the 100 per cent reserve scheme—for which I still have no great enthusiasm save as part of a gradualist program whose objective is recognized (and consistently pursued) as gradual reduction and ultimate denial of borrowing and lending powers to all corporations, especially as regards obligations of short term.

Misguided fiscal practice and unguided institutional evolution have placed us in a foolish quandary. Seemingly, we cannot afford prosperity or full peacetime employment because they would render our banks insolvent and increase interest costs of our federal debt! Conversely, one way to keep our banks solvent and our interest costs at a low level is to render private investment so unattractive, and property so insecure, that people will be glad to hold money and deposits in preference to real assets and delighted to buy money in an interest-bearing form. The dilemma again is wholly spurious, save for those who deplore increase in reserve requirements of banks (or our reluctance to accept collectivism). The government, instead of worrying about interest costs, should covet the large revenues which high prosperity and high interest rates bring along—while always eschewing, of course, the too easy route of deliberate or permitted price inflation, which must sometime produce astonomical interest rates if not eschewed. Let us pray for the highest interest rates consistent with monetary stability—for the highest possible "real" marginal efficiency of capital. Prosperity need not prove insufferable or disastrous.

There is urgent need for reducing discussion of monetary and fiscal problems to simple, common-sense terms. Our financial system is becoming simply too elaborate and too complex for the political system within which it operates. Both private financial institutions and fiscal practice are too complicated for government by law; that is, they are not sufficiently amenable to effective control through the democratic process of action out of discussion and deliberation. Needless complexity in the private financial structure is the heritage of bad policies in the past and should gradually be corrected and removed. Needless complexity in government finance can and should be dealt with by prompt, thoroughgoing measures.

Taxation, expenditure, pure debt, and pure money are, along with price level, quite intelligible conceptions. If institutional borrowing and, especially, institutional issue were exclusive governmental prerogatives, and if these governmental prerogatives were exercised only in the most straightforward way, both economists and the public might quickly and wisely distinguish between proper uses and abuses and, thus, democratic government might adhere to sound fiscal-monetary policies. The proper first step is simplification of our federal debt.

X

Debt Policy and Banking Policy[*]

THE scheme of putting our federal debt wholly into two
forms, consols and currency,[1] is obviously too radical for
early political consideration. Its virtue is that of indicating a
direction for policy which, wisely pursued, would perhaps involve numerous steps and only gradual institutional change.
Much can be said for focusing attention upon the radical, ultimate objective, namely, an economy where all private property takes exclusively the forms of government demand obligations (currency or full currency equivalents), government consols (always in process of elimination, save during total war),
corporate common stock, and fee interests in real assets (along
with an inevitable minimum of business accounts receivable
and interpersonal debts). In its more important, converse aspect, 100 per cent reserve banking is simply 100 per cent equity
financing of all incorporated enterprise. No one responsibly
proposes early or sudden movement into this financial mil-
lennium. But a strong case can be made for moving ahead now
in the banking field. Indeed, an approach to 100 per cent reserves now seems indispensable for sound debt policy—if only
for the purpose of eliminating the enormous excess reserves
which bank holdings of "governments" now actually represent.

Instead of converting all federal issues into currency and
consols, we might, as a moderate, practical policy, utilize also
a third debt form, namely, a completely liquid federal "bond,"
continuously redeemable and callable and "on tap" but eligible only for bank ownership and required as reserve against

* Reprinted by permission from the *Review of Economic Statistics*, XXVIII,
No. 2 (May, 1946), 85–89.

bank deposits. (A fourth form is perhaps specified by implication, namely, a zero-rate issue for the Federal Reserve banks.) All other issues held by banks should be convertible into such "bonds" on reasonable terms, for example, at actual cost or at market values as of some specified date.

New reserve requirements (of, say, 60–80 per cent) as to these bonds might be superimposed upon existing reserve requirements; preferably they would take the form of requirements (of, say, 80–100 per cent) as to such bonds *and* deposits in the Reserve banks, with till-money also counted toward the requirement. Clearly such requirements should apply uniformly to all commercial banks, not merely to "member banks," and to all savings banks—although a case might be made for exempting small, genuinely mutual savings banks. A perhaps adequate expedient would be that of making the required reserves a condition of deposit guaranty by the Federal Deposit Insurance Corporation—whose charges for guaranty might then be radically reduced or eliminated.

All other federal issues should be declared ineligible for bank ownership. They should all be converted ultimately into consols or, at least, into very long maturities—if one must make concessions to political expediency. While outstanding issues should, at least temporarily, be convertible on generous terms into the consols or long maturities, all other "support" should be removed and eschewed. Indeed, sound debt management requires just the opposite of support. It should seek rather the maximum capital-gain and capital-loss leverage in open-market operations, offering capital gains to those who bet on reversal of prevailing inflationary or deflationary aberrations (declines or increases) in bond prices.

A suitable rate of interest for these special "bonds for banks" might now be three-fourths of 1 per cent, if new reserve requirements are superimposed upon existing requirements, or six-tenths of 1 per cent if a single global requirement, satisfiable entirely with such bonds, is invoked. The proper level, in any case, is merely a question of what subsidy should be paid for banking services, in the form of interest on completely riskless and perfectly liquid "bonds."

The new reserve requirements, in either form, should be set at a level designed to freeze present bank holdings of "governments," and with a view to subsequent adjustment of these holdings in accordance with the changes in aggregate bank money which prove requisite for price-level stabilization.[2]

The immediate problem is admittedly awkward. If the new reserve requirements are set at moderate levels, one minimizes difficulties with respect to particular banks whose holdings of "governments" are exceptionally small—but at the cost of leaving other banks with actual excess reserves that would enable them not only to expand their own loans but also to provide other banks with new reserves for multiple expansion. To impose severe initial requirements would doubtless be politically suicidal; and it is certainly more important to move in the right direction than to move as far as an extremist would wish. The most feasible scheme would perhaps set a global requirement not above 75 per cent, with provisions for gradual increase at intervals. And it should err on the side of generosity, in special interim provision for banks with unusually small reserves of "governments," for example, with interim arrangement for impounding of other assets as temporary substitutes for the "required" bonds.

Note now the urgent current difficulties which these measures would resolve:

1. They would be uniquely effective in preventing bank-financed inflation of securities and real estate.

2. They would eliminate the vast excess reserves which bank-held "governments" now represent—and, Federal Reserve policy apart, which bank-held short-term "governments" will otherwise continue to represent. As things stand, the banking system has an ominous inflation potential. Banks may obtain the reserves necessary for multiple expansion of commercial, security, and real-estate loans, not only from the Reserve banks directly but also from the Treasury via the Reserve banks, by not replacing federal obligations as they mature.

3. They would leave the Treasury free to follow, if and as necessary, a suitable inflation-checking policy of borrowing from the public at interest

rates (yields) as high as necessary to the mopping-up of excess liquidity. The notion that suitable increase of interest rates[3] on consols or long maturities involves a threat to bank solvency is probably illusory; but, if so, the illusion is widely entertained and affords a powerful inhibition and political argument against necessary measures for combating inflation through debt policy. If borrowing from banks were sharply dissociated from other borrowing, we might expect better practices at both levels and better understanding of both tax and debt problems.

4. They would also bring elegantly under control the awkward problem of inordinate bank earnings—and thus eliminate an argument against increase of interest rates that is more substantial than the supposed threat to bank solvency.

5. They would largely dispose of the vexed problem of inadequate bank capital or thin residual equities—and, incidentally, of a plausible, spurious apology for excessive bank earnings. If deposits were supported largely or wholly by completely liquid "governments," there would be little need for much cushion of stockholder equity—save as banks chose to operate also as investment trusts with respect to their own capital.

6. They would offer a long-term prospect of retiring our interest-bearing debt at a more rapid rate, and within a shorter period, than otherwise would be possible. Suppose that we shall need, for stability at a proper postwar price level, only 100 billion dollars of money and deposits, and that, with rising real income, this amount must be increased secularly at 3 per cent per annum to sustain the price level. It thus appears that (save for nominal "interest" paid as subsidy for banking services) we might retire our present interest-bearing debt in thirty to forty years merely by extra-budgetary measures, i.e., without having any net excess of tax revenues over expenditures during that period.[4] Our debt being what it is, the government clearly should reappropriate its prerogative of issuing the country's money.

The immediate problem, to repeat, is that of preventing banks from feeding inflation in the stock market, in real estate, and in inventories. More broadly, it is that of preventing general banking inflation on the basis of liquid "governments" as virtual excess reserves. Still more broadly, it is that of removing obstacles, real and illusory, to an anti-inflationary debt policy of borrowing from the public at the substantial interest cost that long maturities or consols would involve, that is, of funding our debt into illiquid, unsupported, and firmly held bonds or, if you please, of paying interest on real debt instead of paying merely hoarding premiums on money in the nominal form of bonds.

These immediate problems are urgent and critical, for we probably shall have, in the near future, no substantial protection against inflation save that which debt policy affords. Even if one accepts the Keynesian dictum that inflation should instead be stopped largely or wholly by taxation, there is now really little or no hope of securing increases in federal tax rates, save possibly after high interest rates are shown to be the alternative. We shall be lucky to hold present taxes against the insistent political pressure for reduction. Even the quixotic bureaucrats who proposed to stop wartime inflation with their bare hands, that is, with direct controls amid fiscal insanity, have now few illusions about their future potentialities, even for creating illusions.

To be sure, we may ride through without disaster in spite of policy. Inflation may simply not take hold in the dangerous near future. But it is folly to lay all bets on that possibility. We should be prepared for any eventuality and for accelerated and explosive inflation among others. Strong anti-inflation measures in debt policy (e.g., large reduction in bank deposits) may prove unnecessary; but we certainly should be prepared to take them and to take them promptly if the need becomes still more acute. This means getting on with a funding program and cleaning up the mess that wartime debt policies or practices have left behind.

This much done, by the measures here proposed, there would remain interesting long-term questions, notably, the question of whether federal subsidy for banking services should be continued indefinitely or gradually withdrawn.

I can make out no substantial reasons for permanent subsidy, that is, no reason why the services of warehousing and transferring private funds should not be paid for like any other economic services—by appropriate service charges. Interest should not be paid on money or on any money contracts that one may purchase without sacrifice of liquidity; and this proposition is certainly as valid for interest paid in banking services (to demand depositors) as for interest paid in cash (to savings depositors). It is anomalous that banking services should be free only to persons with large balances and that customers should be left without financial incentive to economize their use of such services.

Subsidy may be defended only as a transition expedient—as a device for facilitating transition to reserve requirements of 90–100 per cent and as a means for avoiding abrupt change in an established but anomalous institution. In the process of change, it would be a great advance merely to create arrangements under which interest payments on bank-held "governments" would be recognized for the subsidies they are, and thus distinguished clearly from interest payments to the public on real debt (consols). The subsidy issue might then be faced squarely and dealt with on its merits. The government need not pay private institutions to create money; it need not pay anyone to hold money equivalents instead of money; but it must and should pay people to sacrifice liquidity and really to forgo the available (expected) returns on real investment (assets and equities).[5]

Given subsidy as even a temporary or transitional expedient, a nice question arises of what kind of services shall command subsidy. Shall it be available regardless of the level of service charges, or regardless of the minimum balances required for free services? If banks were mere service agencies, one might rely on competition to assure reasonable charges, whatever the actual subsidy; while they remain "financial department stores," and while national charters remain subject to rationing, competitive determination of charges is, at least, not a wholly satisfactory prospect.

A second long-term issue concerns the future of banks as sources of capital funds for private business. A 100 per cent reserve requirement would leave banks free to provide such funds out of their own capital. It would not preclude combination of the business of providing safekeeping and checking facilities with the proper business of investment trusts. Such combination, of course, while requiring great increase in bank capital for large survival of conventional banking business, would facilitate best use of existing enterprises and their established staffs. But it seems uneconomical to sustain this combination of such widely different kinds of business. Services to depositors surely could be rendered more cheaply by specialized enterprises, housed in modest premises, investing mainly in accounting machines, and officered by skilful accountants rather than by credit analysts, bond specialists, business forecasters, and political-financial leaders.

Even greater advantages of enterprise specialization are apparent when one looks at the other part of the present combination. If banks as lender-investors were dissociated from banks as depositary-clearing agencies, the lender-investor enterprises might then focus upon a vital and essential function of providing long-term capital and, at best, of providing it in an equity form. There is now little need for the old type of bank lending or the short-term commercial loan. Established enterprises no longer need place their working capital precariously on call; they can finance out of withheld earnings by issuing stock rights or by outright sale of shares (or bonds); and seasonal variations in working-capital needs can be minimized directly or met by trenching temporarily upon ample liquid reserves. New or ill-established businesses need long-term funds, and equity capital above all. Trading on a shoe-string of equity, and under a mass of current liabilities, is largely a thing of the past and should be for banks as well as for their corporate customers.

If existing banks were suddenly excluded from lending or investing activities, their executives might simply be driven to effect a most salutary institutional reconstruction, namely, to establish thousands of localized investment trusts. Such institutions might attract a mass of equity capital for purposes of equity participation in worthy, smaller, local enterprises. Big metropolitan banks probably would reorganize, without much change of their staffs and facilities, into big investment trusts, specializing in equities (listed stocks) of great firms that need no such institutional assistance. But smaller banks, whose executives really know something about local or community enterprises, might be converted into highly useful institutions, mobilizing local funds for local investment, much as building-and-loan associations once did but on an equity basis. In other words, the change in question might release a lot of useful, competent people to perform functions which their present institutional connections preclude their performing adequately or in a proper way.[6]

It is easy to become dithyrambic if, as a libertarian, one contemplates the possibilities of radical decentralization of our capital markets via such localized investment trusts. It might eventually undo, and even reverse, the present artificial economies of inordinate enterprise size, in differential access to capital funds. While giant enterprise aggregations were plagued by a volatile New York Stock Exchange, and supported only by the most inconstant investors, small and moderate-size firms might enjoy the steady loyalty of their communities, acting through local investment trusts, and also a salutary close scrutiny of management by interested local shareholders, indeed, by the whole community as a functioning social group.

If such local investment trusts really served, as they should, to mobilize mass, small savings in their communities, even our labor problems might be brought toward good solution. In such circumstances community pressure might inhibit wage demands that would threaten the relative prosperity of local industry, that is, impair its competitive position vis-à-vis other communities. On the other hand, such pressure would also be exerted against needlessly low wage rates that impaired a firm's ability to attract or maintain good-quality labor, or impaired the community's ability to hold or recruit good worker-citizens. But this is rhapsody!

The urgent first step, to repeat, is to replace bank-held "governments" with a new low-rate issue, eligible only for bank

ownership, guaranteed against any depreciation, available, redeemable, and callable continuously at par, and required as
bank reserves to roughly the amount of "governments" now
held by banks. We should then fund our remaining federal
debt into consols or very long maturities. In this process it
might prove necessary, in avoiding imminent inflation, to use
such consols to reduce the amount of bank-held "governments." Over forty years, however, it might well be feasible,
and necessary in avoiding deflation, gradually to convert all
consols into money and (or) the low-rate issue for banks. Over
such a period, if not sooner, the rate on this latter issue might
well be reduced gradually to zero. Thus we might arrive at or
approach an economy where all private property consisted in
pure assets, pure money, and nothing else. This, along with
fiscal stabilization of the value of money, is the financial good
society.

XI

Postwar Economic Policy: Some Traditional Liberal Proposals*

THE role of government in our national economy of the future may be usefully discussed only as one aspect of a total postwar program. Domestic economic policies may no longer be regarded, in the United States, as essentially national or parochial problems. To win the peace, our nation must accept responsibilities of world leadership and must make itself an integral part of a larger political and economic system. Domestic policies must be informed and disciplined throughout by the necessities of world order.

For the world, as for great nations, the possible forms of stable political organization are of two extreme types. There is, on the one hand, extreme centralization or imposed collectivism, based on overwhelming, concentrated power and guided always by the severe requirements of preserving an artificial and precarious power concentration. That such a system has great potentialities for doing good is obvious. That it has vast potentialities for evil and for degradation of both planners and plannees, the most romantic reformers will now concede. This kind of system Hitler hoped to impose by sheer military force. If we want such a system, or accept it as inevitable, it is hard to see why we are at war. The Germans are eminently qualified to run this kind of world; once established, under whatever auspices, it would find Nazis to do the job or soon collapse. Neither we nor the English nor any combination of the democracies could seriously undertake the task or succeed

* Reprinted by permission from the *American Economic Review, Supplement*, XXXIII, No. 1 (March, 1943), 431–45.

at it if we tried. Condemning ruthlessness and rule by force, we must also reject schemes of organization, national and international, in which such evils are inevitable and indispensable.

At the other extreme is a scheme in which political organization becomes looser and more flexible continuously and governmental functions narrower or more negative, as one moves through the political hierarchy from local bodies to states or provinces, to nations, and to supranational agencies or world state. In this kind of world, great national and supranational governments, while possessing large reservoirs of power, are narrowly limited in their sphere (or permissible kinds) of action. To put it more paradoxically, centralization of power is utilized primarily, if not exclusively, as a means for maintaining systematic dispersion of power.

The conception and operating characteristics of this system are difficult for the layman to apprehend. Liking and espousing it in a general way, he may repudiate it in political practice, without awareness of his own defection. Moreover, the argument of its proponents, resting on a simple, practical, common-sense judgment, has little appeal to subtle or sophisticated minds accustomed to the rarer atmosphere of theological speculation. This judgment or premise is simply that no one may be trusted with much power—no person, no faction, no nation, no religious body, no corporation, no labor union, no organized functional group, indeed, no organization of any kind. Political insight reveals that concentration of power is inherently dangerous and degrading; economic insight reveals that it is quite unnecessary. And, in a community which purports to cherish government by discussion, it has become (if only by default) the main function of political economy to assert and patiently to explain these homely, practical truths.

Traditional liberals have long been dismissed as intellectual escapists and political romantics, unwilling to face the realities of political process and historical, institutional trend. However, as we finally face the problem of world order, it is rather collectivist schemes which must meet the charge of being impractical and politically fantastic. On realistic examination, socialism turns out to be, in the larger context of world organization, an all-or-none prescription for peace. The all is what we are now fighting against. The threat of world collectivism will disappear with the defeat of Hitler. The possibility of getting it under other auspices will not exist while our nation remains the leading power. We will not impose such a system on the world; and we will not accept the gross impairment of national sovereignty required for participation in a world state with the power and sphere of action contemplated by supranational socialism. Socialists, like "planners" and isolationists, can and perhaps will frustrate efforts at postwar reconstruction along traditional liberal lines; but they have nothing to offer as their peace program that is even superficially plausible.

The collectivist danger lies rather in the development (and preservation) of great national or regional systems, either collectivist or highly centralized governmentally; that is, in the organization of the civilized world into a kind of "National League" for bigger and more continuous wars, along lines admirably sketched out by newsworthy specialists in geopolitics. In a world of great nationalisms, whether controlling trade under full collectivism or manipulating it under protectionism, the very distinction between war and peace loses meaning, as during the last decade. Reasonable access to markets is attainable only by political penetration or military alliance. Peace is merely ruthless contest of monopoly states for economic power; and every marked change in relative power must involve either war or coercive adjustment in territory or spheres of influence. World order could emerge only as one nation (i.e., its authorities) attained to predominant power, subjecting other peoples and making their economies tributary to its own.

If multiple collectivism or large-scale nationalisms promise everything bad, no mongrel system is likely to give us much peace. Peace is the limiting case at both extremes. Rejecting more government and more power concentration as the cure for our ills, we must move far toward the other extreme to find security. However, an extreme application of traditional liberalism, if hard to attain, is not politically impossible. It involves the kind of order in which the democracies can most easily assume their places. It affords the only kind of world system congenial to democracies, and the only kind they can hope continuously to operate and to control. While its establishment does not permit gradualist measures or diffident procedure, it requires initially the close adherence of only a few democratic nations. A democratic, free-trade block comprising the United States, Great Britain and the Dominions, the Low Countries, Norway, and Sweden would represent a magnificent and adequate beginning. Adhering to the rule of equal or nondiscriminatory treatment and inviting the widest national participation, it need not and should not induce other nations to form rival and hostile blocks. Moreover, other nations need only be asked, in return for free access, to maintain equal access and to avoid gross discrimination. Along these lines may be established an economic and political integration of nations which, resting on dispersion of power and responsibility, is indefinitely extensible and capable of enlisting all nations, either as full partners or as increasingly responsible participants.

The essence of this postwar program, in its crucial economic aspect, is free trade among nations. On the political side, incidentally, a major purpose should be that of preserving and protecting small autonomous nations. The Low Countries and Norway and Sweden rather than great national states are the ideal elements or nucleus for world organization. It is our great good fortune that such nations will now demand and attain an important role in postwar reconstruction. In them democratic institutions have their deepest roots and free-trade tradition remains relatively uncorrupted.

The important specific features of a liberal world program

are fairly obvious and familiar. Four requirements may be noted as fundamental and minimal:

1. Dismantling of tariff barriers by all the democracies, and elimination of quota restrictions, import preferences or discrimination, export subsidies, and bilateral or barter trading.
2. Organization for co-operative or united action in matters of monetary and fiscal policy.
3. Preparation and execution, by parallel and united national measures, of effective antimonopoly policies, involving systematic industrial deconcentration, dissolution of giant corporations and cartels, and effective prohibition of private monopolistic restraint of enterprise and trade.
4. Establishment of inclusive, supranational government, limited in its sphere of action but strong within that sphere, and designed specially and primarily (a) to prevent military aggression or resort to force in connection with international disputes and (b) to promote parallel action and to implement united action in the three areas of policy listed above.

American tariff policy is obviously the crucial, immediate factor in postwar planning. Failing prompt leveling of our own tariff barrier, we shall certainly lose the peace. The great world power cannot remain even moderately protectionist without squandering its opportunities and repudiating its international responsibilities. Our tariff structure must be dismantled immediately and as a whole. Dealing one at a time with particular duties or schedules is politically hopeless. Proceeding slowly or gradually, we cannot undermine a deadly pessimism or skepticism abroad as to the possibility of substantial change in our traditional commercial policy.

Even in terms of mere national interest, the case of gradualism will be inordinately weak. The disturbances or dislocations involved in tariff reduction must be slight relative to those of conversion from all-out war production. Our economy must be reorganized drastically in any case. A major part of our industrial resources must be radically reallocated. It will be little more difficult to reorganize for participation in a larger world economy than to reorganize for isolation. There was never, and never again will be, such a chance to adapt ourselves quickly and painlessly to free foreign trade. Squandering this chance, we cannot reasonably expect our allies, in a weaker trading position, to discipline their policies in conformity with the requirements of durable peace. If we go on preaching equality of treatment while ourselves excluding competitive imports, however impartially, we must expect our friends to resume bilateralism and to form rival trading blocks, isolating us if we continue to isolate ourselves.

Given sound commercial policies, monetary problems appear relatively simple. Monetary stabilization, with relatively full employment, surely is attainable, by fiscal and budgetary devices, in (and only in) a free-exchange system. International monetary co-operation faces no great barriers in diverse nationalistic interests or in the special interests of international minorities.

The broad policy objective would be the greatest stability of exchange rates consistent with reasonable stability of national price levels (or vice versa). The minimal purpose should be that of extirpating arbitrary exchange controls and avoiding sharp relative depreciation (or appreciation) of particular currencies.

A strong case can be made for nominal return to the gold standard; that is, for attempting (a) rigid stabilization (with occasional readjustments) of other currencies against the dollar and (b) stabilization of the dollar in terms of a price index heavily weighted with international goods. One may look forward to an eventually more flexible and less administered system in which the separate currencies of nations or groups of nations are stabilized fiscally in terms of internal price levels and freely traded, without fixed parities, in organized, unmanipulated foreign-exchange markets. Such arrangements, however, perhaps cannot be recommended as a proximate objective, since with them it might be nearly impossible to prevent (or to define) arbitrary, governmental rate manipulation.

That monopoly is a world problem should be evident, even apart from recent exposures of pre-war cartel agreements. Abandoning governmental restraint of trade, nations must also break down great private trading organizations, extirpating private collectivism and needless enterprise concentration within their jurisdictions.

Socialists and others will immediately claim that effective competition is attainable, in major industries, only at immense sacrifice of technical, productional economies of size. This is admittedly true of industries already treated as public utilities. These industries afford a proper field for experiments in all-out planning or socialization (although preferably by states and provinces, singly or in groups, rather than by great national governments); but there is no convincing evidence that this area, where enforced competition is impossible or wasteful, is much larger than it has traditionally been recognized to be or that it tends to grow with advancing technology.

If the supposed economies of monopolistic size are real in some sense of technical potentialities, they are still illusory and misleading for practical policy. The afflictions of bureaucracy and ossification fall no less surely on vast private than on governmental enterprises. The efficiency of gigantic corporations is usually a vestigial reputation earned during early, rapid growth—a memory of youth rather than an attribute of maturity. Grown large, they become essentially political bodies, run by lawyers, bankers, and specialized politicians, and persisting mainly to preserve the power of control groups and to reward unnaturally an admittedly rare talent for holding together enterprise aggregations which ought to collapse from excessive size.

The only substantial assurance of long-term efficiency lies in persistent external competition. On economic grounds alone, and clearly on political grounds, we should eschew concentration of power wherever dispersion and competition are attainable without gross, enduring diseconomies. The technicians' grand schemes, however sound technically, are utterly misleading as guides for policy, since progressive technique depends on competition, and gigantic undertakings must be humanly and politically organized and controlled. The absolutist enterprise must be repudiated, even by socialists, along with the absolutist state. Both have great potentialities for good; but their realizable potentialities are almost wholly evil.

Deconcentration need involve little or no dismemberment of productional or operating units. But needless combination, horizontal and vertical, must be undone and estopped. There must be narrow enterprise specialization, as to both phases of business and stages in manufacturing process. Selling must largely be divorced from manufacture; and industrial research must largely be dissociated from particular operating firms.

There must be wholesale sacrifice of the merely private economies of size in selling and advertising. While limiting, via size limitation, the opportunities for private exploitation of these socially false economies, the government should also seek, through its own agencies and by fostering appropriate private agencies, to strengthen the competitive merchandising position of moderate-sized firms and thus to facilitate their entry and proliferation. Reasonable access to markets is a proper slogan for domestic as well as for international policy. Markets now barred by the prestige of big names, by national advertising, by vast selling and distributing organizations, and by the uninformed consumer's rational disposition to "play safe," must be opened up by the development of sound mass-consumer standards and by responsible, disinterested certification of the good products of smaller manufacturers. Educating and informing consumers is a worthy and abundantly promising public enterprise, even if it has no indirect benefits; but it is also perhaps the most promising form of antimonopoly policy.

Industrial research obviously presents a special problem in a deconcentration program. One may question the advantage of great size in research organizations or the desirability of relying heavily on commercial enterprise for fundamental research or basic scientific discoveries. There is, however, no good reason why even commercial research should be tied closely to individual manufacturing firms. Combination of competitive firms for this exclusive purpose and corporate-owned research corporations may well be permitted and encouraged, subject to appropriate regulation, especially as regards patent licensing. A large measure of governmental research service for private industries is also desirable.

These problems merge into the larger problem of patent legislation and its administration—a problem which urgently requires attention but probably cannot be resolved by simplistic devices. However, there can be no question of the need for radical change, especially as regards patent pooling; and it seems inconceivable that sound reform in patent law should leave untouched the organization and financing of industrial research. Just as free trade requires free and equal access to markets, it likewise requires equal and reasonable access, if not wholly free access, to technical knowledge and patentable devices. If we must prevent firms from insulating themselves against competition by use of monopolistic sales organizations and selling practices, we must also prevent their appropriating vast areas of the market by patent pooling and the intimidation of infringement litigation. Extensive investigation would doubtless reveal that there are now few if any important industries where new firms may enter or smaller firms behave competitively without risks of infringement litigation which only foolhardiness would incur. When the facts about patent pooling and about world cartels are more generally known, the argument for great corporations, in terms of contribution to research and technical progress, should turn against and overwhelm those who have employed it. It would be interesting, incidentally, to know what fraction of commercial research expenditures is made merely to implement discriminating monopoly; that is, to develop an artificial technical basis for discriminatory, differential pricing of intermediate products as among different final uses.

Supranational government, to establish free trade, may well begin by destroying a pre-existing structure of irresponsible extra-national government designed and employed to restrain trade. The role of international cartel syndicalism in the pre-war period is only beginning to be recognized clearly, as is the prospect that, failing wise measures of prevention, the old cartels will re-establish themselves promptly when hostilities cease. Free or reasonable access to materials means, *inter alia*, opportunity to deal with competitive sellers. Removal of tariff barriers and exchange controls will leave us far short of free world trade, especially in chemicals, metals, sulphur, diamonds, electrical equipment, airplane and optical instruments, etc.

The proximate goal should be an antimonopoly policy in this country which will afford a model and bold example for parallel action elsewhere and for a supranational program. The special need for vigorous American leadership arises from the fact that other nations, notably England, have moved even further than this country into industrial concentration and cartelization. Between Tory demands for continued tight monopoly and Labour demands for socialization, the task of reconverting England to free trade may seem herculean. Even English businessmen are now perhaps better prepared to turn over their enterprises to government than to contemplate the ordeal of competing again, after all these years, with one another.

Great strides could immediately be made by wise policies on the part of the Alien Property Custodian (and his English counterpart), especially in the handling of patents of enemy aliens and enemy-controlled firms. Much will doubtless be accomplished under recent Supreme Court decisions in opening up patents by antitrust litigation. Reform in patent law and administration should be undertaken here and on a wide international front. Consumer education and consumer standards, to repeat, are a fertile field for social planning and governmental activity. New antitrust legislation and activities should be directed especially against collusive agreements and practices in restraint of important export trade, and particularly against agreements dividing foreign (e.g., South American) markets. The Webb-Pomerene Act should be repealed outright and other nations assured of our intention to prosecute domestic corporations quite as relentlessly for practices restraining trade abroad as for restraint of domestic trade.

Monopoly must be dealt with as a protean phenomenon, by diverse measures within nations and by action on a wide, international front. The best results may possibly be reached by indirection. But the size problem must also be attacked directly. Deprived of all formal, legal devices, monopoly and essentially monopolistic pricing in world markets will persist as long as industries are tightly cartelized intranationally or dominated by gigantic firms. Private monopoly, like governmental foreign-trade policy, is a cancerous growth in our democratic society. Merely homeopathic or medicinal treatment will not suffice.

The secure foundations of world order will be laid, if at all, in these three areas of commercial, monetary, and monopoly policy. Some planners would give equal or greater emphasis to foreign investment programs and reduction of immigration barriers. To do so, however, is to promote dangerous schemes and to encourage false hopes.

When hostilities cease, there will be urgent need for large governmental dispensations, especially of food, to areas of famine and devastation. These will be forthcoming and should be regarded as essentially unilateral contributions to peace, like our lend-lease contributions to the war. They should be allocated evenhandedly according to need, without discrimination against enemy populations and without much repayment being demanded or expected. However, we should prepare to distinguish sharply between contributions for relief or immediate reconstruction and foreign capital investments.

For long-term policy we should face the obvious dangers of politically directed capital movements—of governmental lending or of private investment governmentally inspired. The freest possible movement of private capital should be sought; equal access should be maintained; but private funds should venture abroad without expectation or hope of extra-territoriality. Where private funds cannot safely go, or will go only with a high risk premium, governmental investment, whether by national or supranational bodies, involves grave political risks. Wholly backward areas, administered and controlled by supranational agencies, are perhaps an exception to this rule. The same may be true, for very different reasons, of China. On the other hand, the greatest caution must be observed with respect to investment in areas like India and South America, where stable, democratic government or tradition does not exist, or where foreign debts and foreign enterprises are symbols of subjugation and national frustration. Grand schemes for dispensing American capital to the world may best be shelved in favor of schemes for exporting useful knowledge and transplanting specialized skills.

As regards immigration policies, the less said the better. It may be hoped that world prosperity, increased political security, and ultimate leveling of birth rates may diminish migration pressures. Wholly free migration, however, is neither attainable politically nor desirable. To insist that a free-trade program is logically or practically incomplete without free migration is either disingenuous or stupid. Free trade may and should raise living standards everywhere (and more if transportation were costless). Free migration would level standards, perhaps without raising them anywhere (especially if transportation were costless)—not to mention the sociological and political problems of assimilation. Equal treatment in immigration policy, or abandonment of discrimination, should likewise not be held out as purpose or hope. As regards both export of capital and import of populations, our plans and promises must be disciplined by tough-minded realism and practical sense.

The general program sketched above obviously calls for a strong international organization which, besides preventing aggression and international violence, would mainly concern itself with commercial, monetary, and monopoly policy. It is not for economists to discuss the technical constitution or structure of good supranational government. Within such organization, however, special sections or agencies, of co-ordinate status, should be established to deal with problems in the three areas. (I would dispense with an international bank.) There would, of course, be many other agencies and activities, even in a world state narrowly limited in its sphere of action. Attention may properly be focused on three areas of policy, however, since they would provide the fundamental policy framework for other activities. Consider briefly some questions of sanctions.

At the outset, the democracies, opening their markets freely to one another, should also open them freely and equally to the rest of the world. Some other nations would doubtless reciprocate fully, and others would move toward closer affiliation with the free-trade block. But we could not and should not impose free trade on all the world. In some areas large tariff revenues will be indispensable for stable government; in others, tariff autonomy will be cherished and exercised as an attribute of freedom. Offering free access, the democracies should ask equal access to the markets of other nations. These others might also be requested to suspend new tariff measures, pending investigation and report of recommendations by the international agency and pending full reconsideration by the competent local authorities in the light of the recommendations. Sanctions should be available, perhaps in the form of penalty duties but should be invoked only against flagrant discrimination or gross departure from the equal-treatment rule and only by united action, under mandate from the international authority.

In monetary stabilization the acute problem case is that of the nation which refuses to order its fiscal practices in the manner necessary to prevent radical exchange depreciation. Here the obvious, and dangerous, countermove or sanction is penalty duties against exchange dumping, imposed uniformly and through the established international machinery. Such a dangerous weapon, however, should be most sparingly used.

Diffidence about recommending its use will become Americans especially, since our gold policy was a major contribution to international chaos in the thirties and since our fiscal policies— recent, present, and projected—come uncomfortably close to describing what a sound world program must prevent. The main requirement for stabilization will be not machinery for penalizing nonconformity but development in America of fiscal practices (and a financial structure) which other nations might sensibly accept as norms or bases of co-operation and conformity.

A larger field for sanctions or direct, supranational action may be found in monopoly policy, since action here may be taken against private firms rather than against national states. Even here, however, successful international policy should rely almost wholly on co-operative national action in the competent jurisdiction and upon recommendations from above regarding measures of local policy. World courts should perhaps be available in antitrust cases, if only to resolve, by declaratory judgments, moot questions of jurisdiction. Surely, any remaining limitations or uncertainties as to jurisdiction of our own courts, under local law, in cases involving monopolistic practices by American corporations in foreign markets, should be removed.

A politically awkward case arises where a national state has a substantial vested interest in private, world monopoly. Familiar instances are nickel and diamonds, and similar instances are numerous. The looser, cartel monopolies, where no nation represents overwhelmingly a producer (as against consumer) interest, should not prove intractable. But would Canada provide the world with nickel at competitive prices; or the United States, sulphur; and would England resolutely disestablish monopoly in diamonds or tin?

One may consider, in this connection, the case for supranational price-fixing; that is, for establishing a special class of international public utilities, with appropriate regulatory agencies. That special agencies and activities of supranational government would be concerned with ordinary public utilities may be taken for granted. Some control over shipping conferences and ocean-freight-rate agreements is desirable, as is international supervision of locally regulated transportation rates and port charges (if only to expose concealed subsidies or discrimination). Direct international regulation of either ordinary utilities or artificial monopolies, however, should be avoided like the plague. Every persuasive effort should be made to secure appropriate local measures, aiming at internal deconcentration and effective competition in export trade; and publicity should be focused on cases where nations have evaded or repudiated their responsibilities on this score. In extreme cases, sanctions might be invoked against either firm or nation, in the form of penalty duties or of supranational subsidies designed to develop substitutes or alternative sources of supply. Direct international regulation or price-fixing, on the other hand, seems utterly dangerous, both as interference with internal national affairs and as precedent or opening for extension in the sphere (or kinds) of action of the international authority.

The larger the area of government, the greater are the dangers of its powers being abused on behalf of articulate minorities. To realize the good potentialities of a supranational state, every precaution must be taken, by constitutional limitation and adherence to definite rules of policy, to protect a common, consumer interest in free trade against special, producer interests in restraining trade. Using supranational agencies to hold down particular monopoly prices, we might shortly find that, like corresponding domestic agencies, they were actually serving to hold those prices up. Moreover, if international authority were invoked to lower excessive prices, it almost certainly would also be invoked to raise other prices plausibly alleged to be too low.

One should stress here the dangers of proposed postwar schemes of agricultural control. Underneath an unfailing preoccupation with political expediency, our often inspiring Vice-

President is perhaps an ardent free-trader. But his conception of the peace, as an opportunity to create international agricultural syndicates, involves repudiation of an indispensable constitutional principle of supranational government and rejection, on behalf of his functional constituents, of a rule of policy which he and they in turn would apply to other groups. There will be no peace, in America or in the world, until we all give up the business of organizing—geographically, industrially, and occupationally—to take things away from other people. If American farmers, who have so much to gain from all-out economic disarmament, refuse to take the lead, or even to disarm at all, their power may be as inimical to peace as was that of Prussian landowners in the past.

The discussion so far has ignored a major obstacle to free trade; namely, monopolistic labor organizations. Strong unions may be expected to exert their full power against both tariff reduction and industrial deconcentration. Failing in such opposition, they may prevent the wholesale labor reallocation necessary for our prosperous, effective participation in a larger economy. Maintaining excessive relative labor costs and cost expectations in critical areas (i.e., in capital-goods production and the other industries with large expansion potentials), they may fasten upon us an acute unemployment problem which, politically, would drive us into beggar-my-neighbor policies, fiscal and commercial.

It is a weakness of the whole scheme of policy here sketched out that it must rely mainly on faith and hope for warding off labor syndicalism and for mitigating trade restraint in what is, on a realistic view of present and future, its most important form. Some of the legislative, administrative, and judicial implementation of large-scale labor organization might helpfully be cut away. In the main, however, direct political action must be confined to attack upon other concentrations of economic power, in the hope that the technical and political basis of labor monopoly will be eaten away as power is otherwise dispersed. On principle, one may concede nothing to the demands of the union partisan that other forms of monopoly be destroyed first, for the different forms are highly complementary, not counterbalancing. Surely no one believes that we can all live peacefully or prosperously on monopoly gains exacted from one another, or as a collection of mutually exploiting syndicates. All functional groups must submit to the peaceful, democratic discipline of intragroup competition or, following intergroup conflict, to the odious and precarious discipline of absolutist, centralized authority. However, for practical politics, enterprise deconcentration must come first. If only industrial leaders could see that deconcentration involves little or no loss to security-holders and that the alternative is control by government and/or by unions, they might wisely accept and support deconcentration.

The central purpose of postwar planning, to repeat, should be that of establishing, among the democracies, a free-trade front, so organized as to promote their prosperity and to facilitate steady recruitment of other nations as increasingly cooperative and responsible participants. In formal political organization the supranational government should, from the start, be extremely inclusive. Full opportunities should be offered to all nations for consideration of their special problems and for airing of grievances. But there should be no concealment or hypocrisy about the intention of the democracies to maintain a united front and dominant power. There can be no peace without power. It may be dispersed among democratic nations; its exercise will be conditioned, if they remain democratic, by the duty and necessity of exercising it beneficently; and inevitable distrust of great nations may be mitigated by giving to the small democracies a large voice in all major policy decisions. The United Nations, however, must remain the locus of dominant power for an indefinite future.

But will Russia permit establishment and extension of such a world system? Having suffered most from the war—and done most toward winning it—she may seek to secure herself by radical territorial expansion and by sustaining total political dominance of the Continent. There is reason to hope, however, that she will remain essentially nonexpansionist—that she will insist on ruling the whole of Europe only if we fail to develop a program which will guarantee her security. And recent experience should leave her receptive to the idea of having a noncollectivist Germany next door.

Russia would present real difficulties of detail in the operation of a great free-exchange system in the Western world. Free trade (not to mention exchange control and monopoly policy) has little or no meaning where a collectivism is involved. Russian foreign trade, however, will not be of major importance to herself or to others. She may willingly eschew discriminating monopoly or monopsony and adhere roughly to the rule of equal access and equal treatment. In any case, her interest in access to markets of the democracies would be commensurate with their interest in her trading practices. At worst, but only as a last resort, they could always set up a special corporation to bargain and barter for them collectively with Russia.

The critical area—for Russian policy immediately and for the long-term future of Western democracy—is Germany. She must be disarmed and kept disarmed indefinitely. (One hopes this may be accomplished without extensive use of quota limitations on ordinary industrial facilities or output.) German government must be radically decentralized. Prussia should perhaps be dismembered into two or more *Länder* or states and subjected to thoroughgoing land reform. The Reich should be compelled to abolish all protective tariffs (on foodstuffs especially) and to eschew quota restrictions, export and other subsidies, and arbitrary exchange control. Germany should be compelled to carry through drastic economic disarmament, dismantling her cartels and industrial combines and enforcing systematic industrial deconcentration and decentralization of enterprise control.

Such should be the central terms of the imposed peace. Reparations, save for transfers of existing industrial equipment to now occupied areas, should not loom large among impositions. There should be no dismemberment of the pre-Hitler Reich. Every reasonable effort should be made, in imposing governmental and industrial deconcentration, to facilitate reestablishment of democratic institutions and responsible government at all levels. Impositions should be explained to the German people as means to this end. They should be assured that, observing and executing faithfully the treaty terms, Germany would enjoy reasonable or free access to markets of the democracies and, so far as their good offices permit, equal access to other markets. Fulfilment of imposed treaty terms and secure re-establishment of responsible, democratic government should be recognized from the start as entitling Germany to reassume a prominent place in world government and international affairs.

Democracy is unlikely again to be the vital, advancing, world-integrating ideology unless it is securely re-established in the nation of skilled, educated, and cultured people where, while never securely established, it received its only sharp setback in modern times. To sit on Germany for generations and to prevent her reacquiring power commensurate with her human and material resources, would be a brutal and unrewarding task. As defenders of world order, the democracies will be shorthanded at best. The Czechs may again lead wisely and vigorously in Central Europe. Russia may become a bulwark of democracy and world order. France may establish a more secure and stable democracy than she previously attained. But Germany remains, on a sanguine short-term view, the crucial area for long-term policy.

If one posits sound postwar economic policies in England and America, the long-term outlook becomes very bright. The substantial reasons for pessimism are to be found within the great democracies, not outside. Development in other nations will largely depend on the prevailing world trend; and that trend we could largely determine. But England, tired of inordinate responsibility, lacks now both strength and will. And

America, save in gravest crisis, is irresponsible. Both nations, moreover, are divided internally by angry contests for power. If recent world disorder leaves other nations still amenable to wise leadership, its incidence upon thought and action in the democracies has been such that they perhaps cannot lead.

The ominous prospect is not that America will provide bad leadership but that it will provide none at all. Having assisted tardily in disarming aggressors and indulged in an exulting outburst of generosity, we may promptly retire from the world, leaving it to chaos while we busily create chaos at home. If our interventionists or participationists develop no sound or definite program and attain no fundamental consensus, the isolationists will take over, without a real contest, from the moment that shooting stops. Postponing their planning for peace until the war is won, American proponents of world participation will do their planning after they have politically been put to rout.

Traditional economic liberalism has as its characteristic feature a workable program for peace. As sketched in these pages, it is doubtless full of flaws. (Efforts to forestall attack have led the writer far outside the range of his pretended competence.) Some such program, however, affords the only promising basis for a united domestic front against isolationism, minimizing the concessions that different factions must make on behalf of unity and consensus. It also defines a plan for using our national power to establish a prosperous, durable peace, at home and in the world, and for reducing and dispersing gradually the military power on which peace must initially be rested.

XII

Money, Tariffs, and the Peace*

THE academic specialist in international finance is a creature of strange circumstance. Among practical bankers he is an academic specialist on commercial policy and trade. Among politician-practitioners of commercial policy, he is an academic specialist on banking. Among economic theorists, he is a clever practical fellow, full of strange lore about the world of affairs and yet skilled in an esoteric sort of economic analysis or controversy.

The intellectual level of his mystery is indeed high, relative to other fields of applied economics—if one may indulge calculated understatement. It has recruited many of the best economist minds and, by the way, the most intelligent and most confirmed apostles of traditional liberalism. But the mystery imposes grave ordeals of adjustment upon its high priests. As financial experts, they are thrown with bankers whose conception of sound finance is its antithesis. As experts on commercial policy, they are thrown with politicians and bureaucrats whose conception of sound trade regulation is its antithesis. Since free trade has outranked monetary stabilization among the imperatives of their economic-political creed, they have accepted ostracism or frustration in political discussion, while stultifying themselves by accommodation to the misconceptions of bankers.

Making no peace with bad commercial policy, and offering no apologies for stupid trade restraints, they have embraced bad finance and become its leading apologists. Unable to fight on both fronts, they have idealized a half-good society,

* Reprinted, by special permission of the editors, from the September, 1944, issue of *Fortune* magazine, in which this essay, with substantial revisions, especially of the first few pages, appeared under the title of "The U.S. Holds the Cards" (copyright, Time, Inc.).

good in its free trade and bad in its gold-standard construct
of a world banking system in which each national currency is a
fractional-reserve bank. Thus, they have integrated and per-
petuated both the greatest wisdom and the greatest error of
Adam Smith, apostrophizing an institutional complex of free
trade and maximal monetary instability.[1]

The specialists have now been called upon to lay plans for
monetary reconstruction. As might be expected, they have responded vigorously and with cultist *esprit*, to this relaxation
of their political ostracism. Their prescriptions, naturally
enough, center around a supranational bank—which may be
good tactics, since everyone defers to the experts and no one
much pretends to understand their elaborate institutional con-
trivances. Natural, too, is their scrupulous observance of a
tacit injunction against meddling in commercial policy—and
their offering to the statesmen as a bank what is really just
the nose of a good Anglo-American commercial policy!

While admiring their skilful dissimulation and their ingenious gadgets, one may still question their faith in such tricks and
their cautious avoidance of emphasis upon fundamentals of
policy. If only a little change were needed, such devious cleverness might bring it off. But such change will do little or no
good when radical alteration of Anglo-American commercial
policy is necessary to reverse a powerful world trend. The
chance of getting substantial change may seem very small, but
responsible students should play it for everything now. It may
be a small chance, but it is still a chance, and it will not last
long unless grasped. It is small, moreover, not merely because
of general misunderstanding but largely because there is no
evident consensus among economists on what, political feasibility apart, *ought* to be done. The clever action schemes of
specialists only serve to dissipate and to obscure this consensus.

Such persuasions, at any rate, may excuse the efforts of a
nonspecialist to discuss the monetary problem more straightforwardly and in the larger focus which is necessary to indicate its importance for the peace.

The major need for international monetary stabilization will be simply the internal stabilization of the dollar itself. This is the central prescription from which hopeful planning should proceed. Almost certainly, the dollar will be the predominant world currency[2]—backed by a vast hoard of gold and by a great foreign-investment potential. If the dollar again is violently unstable in purchasing power or commodity value, and especially if it is again debased irresponsibly by tragically inopportune tariff increases or devaluations, world economic order, large international trade, and decent national behavior in commercial policies or practices will be unattainable. If we can securely and closely stabilize our own price level and prevent recurrent aberrations of inflation and deflation, we can thereby eliminate the major obstacle to reasonable stability of foreign-exchange rates. Here is perhaps the best single contribution we can make to resumption of orderly international trade—to the ending of arbitrary exchange controls (rationing of foreign exchange), bilateralism, discrimination, and direct national control or governmental monopolizing of foreign trade.

If this view is sound, it deserves emphasis in domestic discussion and in international negotiation, for it raises no awkward questions of conflicting national interests or of "impairments of American sovereignty." The policy in question should be supported by both participationists and isolationists, since it is equally important for international and for merely domestic purposes. We shall need a stable dollar for our domestic economy as much as other nations need a stable international monetary unit. Serving well our national interest in this matter, we may also serve well the cause of world order and reconstruction, and conversely.

The place of gold in the monetary future is hard to discuss quite seriously. All talk about currencies based on gold is a bit silly. Gold producers, and would-be sellers of redundant, useless hoards, have a special interest in the continuance of prodigious subsidy. Nations as a group have a common need for stopping the squandering of world resources in gold production. This aspect of the matter, however, need not be stressed, for only South Africa has a major interest in the subsidy racket; and the world diseconomy is of relatively small dimensions.

There is no strong reason for not "re-establishing the gold standard" if that is the line of least resistance. It is pointless to attack bad religions if they have actually become innocuous. Under the old gold-standard system, the value of gold depended mainly on its convertibility into major currencies, not conversely. The real substance behind the fact that currencies were convertible into gold was the convertibility of currencies into one another—and the status of each national currency as a kind of fractional-reserve bank whose alternate expansions and contractions were dictated by the mainly perverse behavior of the world "banking system" of currencies. Like domestic fractional-reserve banking, it was the apotheosis of bad trading-on-the-equity and, as a system, admirably designed to induce intolerable, cumulative, self-aggravating deflations.

Now, monetary gold is almost monopolized by one nation which is also the creditor of almost everybody and the predominant international lender or investor as well. The value of gold is thus merely a fact of the official American gold price and of the commodity value of the dollar, that is, of our fiscal policy. We may hitch gold to the dollar if and as we choose. To think of hitching the dollar to gold is almost not to think at all; one does not hitch a train to a caboose!

However, there are perhaps good reasons of expediency, that is, mainly of innocent deception, for tying gold to the dollar indefinitely. The continued subsidy may keep South Africa on our side in the next war, too, besides humoring Russia and Canada. A gold-plated greenback—a dollar standard with a façade of gold—may prove more acceptable to other nations than the reality and thus facilitate international co-operation. Indeed, if we have sense, we shall assiduously promote such co-operation, seeking the largest fiscal assistance from other nations in our own fiscal stabilization and seeking to make the dollar a really international currency and to make its stabilization a multinational responsibility. Moreover, such tricks may permit us to palm Fort Knox off piecemeal on other nations in exchange for more useful commodities or higher-yield investments—that is, for things whose value rests less precariously on hocus-pocus or fiat.[3]

It seems likely, in spite of all our follies in war finance, that the dollar will still be too strong, at exchange rates which other nations will wish to establish, after the war. There is no need to humiliate other nations by forcing on the world a national currency of invidiously high nominal value. Much can be said for our lowering sharply the price of gold. Far more can be said, however, for our invoking first the alternative device of lowering our tariffs, that is, abolishing protection. This action would be equally satisfactory as a monetary adjustment; besides, it would get us out of the politically demoralizing business of subsidizing particular industries indiscriminately; that is, it would largely make an end of the worst manifestations of federal logrolling, vote-buying corruption. (If we must retain such subsidies, for either military or campaign purposes, they should all be transformed into wholly straightforward subsidies and handled openly as matters of appropriations and expenditures financed out of general revenues, that is, financed by lower income-tax exemptions instead of by concealed, regressive levies on consumers.) Republicans, having long practiced concealed subsidies, deplore open ones; and, having in effect repeatedly devalued the currency by tariff increases, they deplore the raising of our gold price. We have now the opportunity, with the predominant currency position, to make a clean sweep of past errors of both parties, reversing our devaluation by tariff reduction and terminating both newer open subsidies (e.g., to agriculture) and older concealed ones.[4]

Along these lines we may move simultaneously toward relatively fixed exchange rates and toward a stable international currency. Our own currency may be stabilized in terms of some broad price index. We should convert our federal debt wholly into consols (perpetuities) and currency (demand obligations), sterilizing increases of currency by increasing the reserve requirements of all private banks. While seeking secularly rapid retirement of the consols, we should stand ready to convert them rapidly into currency when deflation threatens and to absorb currency by net issue of consols when price inflation occurs or impends. This means pursuing boldly a traditional open-market policy, but pursuing it preferably by direct Treasury action, or by action of Reserve banks as branches of the Treasury—although such devices should be regarded as secondary or temporizing measures. The main implementation of monetary stabilization should be found in changes of the relative flows of federal revenues and expenditures; and, if large changes prove necessary, they should take mainly the form of large revenue changes around a relatively stable flow of federal spending. If the personal income tax were our major federal levy, the desirable changes, while partly automatic, might best be effected by raising and lowering the personal exemptions and without change of marginal or bracket rates of tax.

Given such internal fiscal policy and effective internal monetary stabilization, we would offer the world a dollar standard, disguised as a gold standard, to which other nations, given initially proper exchange rates, might willingly and prosperously adhere. Internal fiscal stabilization of currencies by separate nations or blocs, with uncontrolled futures-trading on highly organized private foreign-exchange markets, is perhaps closer to the ideal scheme of things than a stabilized dollar and fixed rates of exchange. But the latter is a more readily attainable arrangement and would perhaps largely eliminate the old difficulties of fixed parities. A dollar stabilized in terms of a good, broad index of domestic prices would, in the very nature of a good index, actually be quite stable in terms of internationally traded goods. Thus, the small and gradual adjustment of national economies, consequent upon shifts in international demand and in capital flows, might be accomplished easily and without inordinate delay by the "classical" methods of change in wage levels or income structures. Large disturbances (and initially mistaken determinations) probably would necessitate occasional alteration of exchange rates; but large disturbances are not to be expected with monetary stability in a substantially peaceful world. Monetary stability and the decent commercial policies it promotes are, moreover, necessary if not sufficient conditions of peace.

Within such a framework of policy, the Keynes and White plans begin to make sense[5] and can be readily explained to the mystified senator or businessman. These plans, and the American one especially, are not really monetary plans at all—or, as monetary plans, they are like *Hamlet* without the Prince of Denmark. They are, properly conceived, just commercial-policy schemes, designed to facilitate orderly resumption of decent trading practices. In spite of their anomalous solicitude about capital flights and their demand for "good" exchange controls, they are really intended mainly to facilitate abolition of exchange controls and of governmental exchange-rationing which, of course, were the great invention of the devil during the thirties. If we provide nations with available loans or overdraft facilities, if we make moderate devaluations respectable by international sanction, then we may hold off a resurgence of bilateralism and totalitarian trading until monetary order and commercial decency have a chance to prevail.

Whether such stop-gap devices are worth the trouble is mainly a question of whether America will handle the world currency responsibly and itself behave decently in commercial policy. The best augury of American responsibility would be radical reduction of our tariff barriers; at the least, we must undertake gradual reduction and avoidance of tragically inopportune increases.

There is also the ominous question of British policy, especially as regards bilateralism, cartels, and imperial preference.

One may sympathize with the English because of their weakness in bargaining with us, and because of their naturally skeptical estimate of our willingness to behave responsibly. Here again our tariff level assumes critical importance. We cannot hope to restore equality of treatment by other nations ("most-favored-nation" practices) or to prevent a deadly resurgence of bilateralism, if we persist in practically excluding imports, however impartially and multilaterally. On the other hand, we can, with promises of over-all reductions, easily trade England out of her bilateralism and arbitrary trade controls— and probably with applause from the Dominions. If we fail even to try, England will probably retrogress into totalitarian foreign trading, if not into unmitigated collectivism—which is perhaps the easiest and surest route to our losing the peace disastrously. Let us hope that the English will bargain skilfully— but that they will not in the process themselves become persuaded by their bargaining apologies for English isolationism![6]

There is probably no possible or prospective English policy which we cannot trade them out of with moderate concessions. Only when one posits our refusal to improve our own commercial practices does the outlook become alarming. And, to repeat, the improvements in question should be made if only on grounds of domestic policy alone. What we get for them by way of concessions from others will be merely bonuses on top of sufficient local gains. One should recognize always that the usual temporary disturbances of radical tariff reduction are now of little moment when we must, in any case, reorganize drastically from wartime to peacetime production. It will be little harder to reorganize for responsible participation in the world economy than to reorganize for economic isolation and irresponsibility.

Reduction of the American gold price, even total undoing of our awful devaluation of 1933, would find perhaps enthusiastic support among American conservatives. It should not prove impossible for wise leadership to make it clear that reduction of our tariffs would serve much the same purposes and have substantially the same effects internationally. If some minorities must be bought off, and some concessions made to military considerations, straightforward subsidies may be utilized for such purposes—and with sound hopes that, as straightforward disbursements of tax revenues, they would not have long or abundant lives. The remaining bitterness of conservatives about our 1933 action might thus be utilized effectively for a good cause. Conservatives might be made to see that tariff increases and devaluations are much the same things and that their case against subsidies is also a case against protection.

Even more promising is the prospect of showing conservatives that our real policy choice lies between substantially free trade and governmental monopoly of foreign trade—and that their case against federal centralization and interference with business is a case against governmental manipulation or control of private foreign trade. We cannot have the traditional federal interference with private importation without being driven into other governmental economic policies which are anathema to conservatives and simply incompatible with liberty, individualism, or free enterprise. The dominant national economy cannot remain protectionist without driving other nations, even its close allies, into more and more totalitarian control of their trade and thus itself being driven there too because it failed to go the other way. We may want undiscriminating protectionism and equality of national treatment (a tenuous conception if not a sheer contradiction of terms); but the world will not let us have it. We may want internal free trade and free enterprise and no collectivist control of our domestic economic life; but, again, the world simply will not accord us the possibility unless we create the larger scheme of free trade within which our own institutions might survive. America cannot persist as an island of economic individualism in a radically different world context. Institutional isolation is quite as impossible as is military isolation.

American protectionism is simply done for. It is *the* utterly unrealistic prescription for the future. If we try to maintain it, we shall find ourselves with an institutional anomaly wholly unsuited to its world environment. It will drive other nations, as did our needless deflation and then our gold policy as a final catalyst, into wholly different schemes of commercial policy which in turn will produce radical changes here. There can be no enduring issue, in the predominant nation, between free trade and protectionism. The real issue concerns a more extreme and epochal choice, namely, a choice between free external trade and national, collectivist monopolies of foreign trade. Surely conservatives would repudiate congressional manipulation of trade via tariffs if they knew it must lead to creation of a federal authority which would administer all our purchases and sales abroad and, in effect, prohibit all private negotiation of such contracts. Let them seriously contemplate the Export-Import Corporation which would fix all terms for import and export transactions, recognizing that such an agency would in fact be an executive agency, unamenable to action by rule of law and essentially beyond reach of legislative control.

Other nations simply will not follow our lead in the half-discriminatory, half-collectivist control which is tariff protectionism. The alternative to freer trade, achieved by bold American leadership, is a resurgence of bilateral trading, quota restrictions, and exchange controls—which in turn will tend to be consolidated in single national trading authorities. Thus nations will seek, if only from defensive necessity, to manipulate foreign trade as a national monopoly-monopsony. Private competitive trading, even with much protectionist restriction, is essentially a peaceful and productive process, serving to promote economic division of labor and generally higher real income. The collectivist trading of national monopolies, on the other hand, is essentially exploitative and essentially a power contest, imperialist in the worst sense, and conducive to lower real income (and militarism) everywhere. If such economic warfare again gets strongly under way, no nation may escape participation. If we, as the leading power, let the world go that way, we must go that way too, organizing for global economic war, if only to preserve the dubious security of our separate relative power. Our foreign trade must be nationally regimented to meet such regimentation elsewhere and to assure us our share of economic-political conquest and of vassal economies.

It goes without saying that, to play this game effectively, we must also regiment our economy internally. Total warfare is efficient warfare, whether in a military or an economic form. Free internal trade would be, or surely would seem, incompatible with the best use of our potential as a national trading monopoly vis-à-vis other strong rivals.

Viewing these possibilities in the light of the immediate prewar developments and of Nazi trading methods especially, one realizes how much real international organization we had formerly when it seemed that we had none. We see now that English hegemony of a century produced not merely cessation of major wars but a substantial institutional organization for peace, especially in the area of commercial policy. This organization was manifest in mutual self-denying ordinances among nations—inhibitions which, in spite of tariffs, preserved the spirit of free trade. Commercial policy, to be sure, was used to favor powerful domestic minorities; but it was not extensively and openly used as a weapon in the power contest. Peace as well as war had its rules; they were different rules; and some precious rules were well observed perhaps because not very precisely formulated: A first task of world reconstruction is the rebuilding of that international commercial organization, implicit in national inhibitions or self-denying ordinances, which was devastated by the Great Deflation.

The argument of these pages reflects no "philosophy" of economic determinism; neither does it intend an inordinate emphasis on economic policies by comparison with the considerations stressed by students of social psychology and the history of cultures. Economic legislation may, in the sweep of history, play a minor, derivative role. It may have as little influence in determining the underlying values of a society as it has, say, on the structure and evolution of a language. But a responsible economist, unlike Mortimer Adler, is not much interested in sketching the millennial course of war and truce which may precede the kingdom of heaven (or hell) on earth, just as he is not much concerned about mere forecasting or immediate political expediency which properly occupy national committees and improperly preoccupy most academic economists.

Economic policy, however, is the main area in which governments act. It is the main focus of discussion in that action-out-of-discussion which is the democratic process. It is really our major business as citizens, just as earning activities are our major private preoccupation. Moreover, it is the crucial or marginal area in the ideological conflict of individualism and totalitarianism. If our economy is largely absorbed into the state, if "political" comes again to include "economic," then State will in fact largely *be* Society, not its servant or instrument. Other areas or aspects of our liberties are not promising for defense against authority, save for defense in depth where the front line of economic liberty must be held as a whole and quickly consolidated if seriously breached. One does not necessarily undervalue the defenses behind in asserting that they need a front.

The breakdown of the last peace was mainly an economic breakdown—a consequence of errors in economic policy which at bottom or in the beginning were no less errors domestic than of international action—no less errors of isolationists and jingoists than of participationists and utopians. Their main causes were just ignorance and stupidity, unintelligent action and inaction, not bad motives or wrong values. To believe otherwise is to be a romantic planner or authoritarian and to distrust the democratic, societal process as a means for getting the big things done over time if the little things most amenable to deliberate planning and governmental action are half-well attended to.

Reflect casually on what the thirties might have been if only we had not permitted the stock-market crash to initiate a long and precipitous deflation in the United States—if we had maintained by proper fiscal measures the essentially stable dollar of the twenties. The not inconsiderable world progress and international reconstruction of the twenties *might* have proceeded without any grave setback. Hitler and National Socialism might have been merely a ludicrous episode in the early growth or consolidation of German democracy. The French Revolution, after a century and a half, might have redeemed itself in a sound domestication of the democratic process. Russia, likewise seeking a short cut to democracy, might by now have modified her authoritarianism and begun really to import the political institutions of freedom as well as machinery and industrial organization. Who can tell how long peace might have lasted or deny that it would have lasted much longer than it did? And, lasting longer, might it not have lasted very long?[7]

Such sanguine, "if-only" speculations become more implausible in total as they are multiplied. There is no need to imply that sound fiscal-monetary measures in this country would have carried the world straight into the good society. One may, however, insist that a little difference at the beginning of the thirties might have meant a big difference at the end; and that monetary stability, which was easily attainable save for misunderstanding, might have been such a crucial little difference.

In any case, the thirties should make it clear (1) that American deflations, devaluations, and high protection are inimical to world order and (2) that they are, by comparison with totalitarian trading, poor instruments for economic-military defense in a disordered world of organized economic warfare. The period should also reveal to us (3) that monetary policy and trade control are aspects of the same thing and, though usefully separated in theory, are not really separable in practice.

Devaluations, to repeat, are like tariff increases (plus export subsidies). Relative deflation is a form of devaluation, often useful, but likely to degenerate into absolute or general deflation which, like general inflation, is a political and economic disease. In the past decentralization of monetary control and lack of international organization for concerted fiscal action, as well as misunderstanding of the monetary responsibilities of the state, left the world a rather helpless victim of deflations. England ran the gold or sterling standard creditably, to be sure, when one considers her small monetary power—much as she kept the world at peace with small military power. Acquiring financial hegemony after the last war, we administered it abominably, in spite of our abundant power.

There will be no excuse for our failing so miserably again. Our monetary power will be overwhelming. In this respect, we face none of England's old difficulties as the world's banker. We need only stabilize our dollar domestically and make it freely convertible into goods by unsubsidized exportation and unrestricted or unmanipulated importation—and, incidentally, by maintaining free internal markets, and decent commercial policies among our own functional minorities or producer, pressure-group "states," for which purposes free foreign trade is the best simple means.[8]

American conservatives and libertarians still hold all the cards. They could easily win the peace if only they had any sense. But they displayed little sense when unopposed and act like hysterical fools now that some threat to their world has arisen. Their whole institutional complex—private property, private enterprise, an unobtrusive, instrumental state, and systematic dispersion of power—rests primarily upon free trade and a stable currency. But they reflexively oppose lower tariffs and antitrust prosecutions. They demand smaller deficits during deflations and larger ones during wars. They applaud governmental regulation or control of business in all their worst manifestations (e.g., in foreign trade, in coal-mining, in resale price maintenance) and loudly deplore it where it is indispensable, desirable, or innocuous (e.g., in fiscal-monetary stabilization, in crude-oil extraction, in public utilities). This is no way to resist a collectivist danger. If free enterprise is destroyed, it will be because its would-be guardians have stupidly cut away its foundations.

Given a long peace, this destruction might have proceeded so long and so far that it could not have been undone. If collectivism had not prematurely precipitated global war, it might have triumphed everywhere by sheer default, that is, by the unwitting co-operation of misguided enemies.

A mistaken military calculation now gives Anglo-American democracy a chance to clean its house and to re-establish its potentiality and promise as an ecumenical movement or faith. This is an exciting and challenging opportunity which we should cherish because it was nearly lost and might soon be lost again. To capture and hold it will require wise action on many policy fronts. One may properly be skeptical of any grand scheme for short-cutting the necessarily slow growth of international political organization. But, to repeat, one should not be skeptical or cynical about the democratic, societal process of doing the big things, if the obvious little things of proximate, deliberate action are not grossly misplanned or miscarried.

What is exciting about postwar economic policy is its inordinate potentialities for good, along with the large freedom of action which the occasion offers. The usual solicitude about small vested interests should not now be inhibiting. They have been buffeted unmercifully in the industrial transition to war, and, inevitably, will be buffeted again in the transition to peace. Industrial investment must be reallocated wholesale in any case. It may be adjusted almost as easily to one policy framework as another. Besides, having been rough about wartime conversion, we might well be a little rough about winning the peace. A few producer groups too weak to survive under free exchange should not be allowed to thwart a sound national and international reconstruction.

One hopeful circumstance is that monetary reconstruction must be so thoroughgoing. The landmarks and traditional relations are gone or obscured. All that remains is the American gold price, itself a recent innovation. We must decide where to stabilize our price level, as must many other nations, where their currencies still exist. A whole structure of exchange rates must be reconstituted, tried out, and then, at least by gradual readjustments, reconstituted again. We may revalue the dollar upward internationally by lowering the gold price, or by leveling our tariff, or by both devices. The prices of sterling and other foreign currencies, in terms of dollars, may then be fixed at higher levels if we revalue radically, at lower levels if we do not. If we retain protection, other nations must obtain lower dollar prices of the currencies when parities are determined; if we abolish protection, we may demand higher exchange rates against the dollar, for example, a higher dollar price of sterling, which would "protect" us against excessive imports and stimulate our exports.[9] So regarded, the issue is not protection versus no protection for our trade but simply the uniform, undiscriminating protection of a proper exchange rate versus a mixture of this with artibary, discriminating protection of politically selected domestic producer groups. If we continue to protect some industries by tariffs or subsidies, we must, in the adjustment of exchange rates, accept less protection for others and less favorable parities for our exporters.[10]

Moreover, in this flexible framework of action and negotiation, and with our huge gold stock, neither gold-price reduction nor tariff reduction need embarrass or restrict us in domestic monetary-fiscal policy. The notion that freer trade would interfere in this country with a proper fiscal policy aimed at large domestic employment is simply an anachronism —a kind of intellectual tropism which now often misguides thought. We can stabilize our price level almost anywhere we please, if our pleasure is not insane, and expect other nations to accept reasonable exchange-rate adjustments to it. Even if the adjustments left the dollar relatively weak (an unlikely contingency indeed), the worst that could happen would be exchange of our redundant gold for something useful or yieldful; and that process itself would probably serve only to raise price levels elsewhere, to conform with exchange rates and our level, and not require any reduction here to prevent excessive drain on our gold—if one can imagine or define excessive drain.

The practical program of responsible American action in commercial policy is fairly clear: (1) We should leave the gold price where it is, at least until alternatives to its reduction have been exhausted. (2) We should reverse our action of 1933, not by lowering the gold price, but by lowering our tariffs and abolishing tariff protection—substituting explicit subsidies in those cases (if any) where only the lesser evil is an alternative to protection. (3) We should generously help to implement some simple version of the Keynes Plan for oiling the new monetary machinery and for facilitating such orderly alteration of initial, experimental parities as experience may dictate. (4) We should seek extensive collaboration from other nations in the fiscal task of price-level stabilization, with the purpose of securing reasonable stability in the commodity values of the major currencies. Finally, and perhaps as a basis for all relevant negotiations, we should determine where we hope or intend to stabilize our domestic price level after the war, or after reconversion, and then communicate this decision to other nations.

Along these lines we could contribute both a better world order and a better America, avoiding grave dangers to individualism at home and avoiding hopeless isolation in an otherwise collectivist or statist world.

XIII

The Beveridge Program: An Unsympathetic Interpretation*

BEVERIDGE'S *Full Employment in a Free Society*[1] is a powerful tract. Written by a nominal Liberal, radical-reactionary in its substantive proposals, libertarian in its rhetoric, this second Beveridge Report may forecast or largely determine the course of British postwar policy. It is a highly convenient marriage of the first Report[2] and *The Economics of Full Employment*.[3] Seeking a national economic-financial program which would accommodate his expensive Plan, Sir William found it whole at the Oxford Institute, in a hyper-Keynesian scheme of tightly regimented economy and extreme economic nationalism. The six studies (by Burchardt, Kalecki, Schumacher, Worswick, Balogh, and Mandelbaum) evidently were prepared specifically for Beveridge—as was the beautiful Kaldor memorandum, which, incorporated as an Appendix, affords the quantitative framework of his tract. The larger book, in what is new for Beveridge, seems to be written out of Kaldor and the six studies, especially those of Kalecki and Balogh.

Sir William again calls Englishmen to a crusade against Want, Disease, Squalor, and Ignorance. He promises an early end of these evils, with no sacrifice of *essential* liberties and with little or no increase of pre-war taxes. He also promises England prosperity and power, without dependence on her benighted ally across the sea.

The immediate program is summarized as follows (pp. 272–73):

* Reprinted by permission from the *Journal of Political Economy*, LIII, No. 3 (September, 1945), 212–33.

277

Abolition of Want by Social Security and Children's Allowances increasing and stabilizing consumption.

Collective Outlay to secure good houses, good food, fuel and other necessaries at stable prices for all, and a National Health Service without a charge on treatment.

Encouragement and Regulation of Private Investment by a National Investment Board, to rejuvenate and expand the mechanical equipment of the country while stabilizing the process of doing so.

Extension of the Public Sector of Industry so as to increase the scope of direct stabilization of investment and to bring monopolies under public control.

A National Budget based on the datum of man-power and designed to ensure year by year total outlay sufficient to set up demand for the whole productive resources of the country.

Control of the Location of Industry with full powers, including transport, on a national plan.

Organized Mobility of Labour to prevent aimless movement, the hawking of labour and mis-direction of juveniles, while facilitating movement when it is desirable.

Controlled Marketing of Primary Products, so as to stabilize overseas demand to the utmost.

International Trading Arrangements based on acceptance of the three fundamental conditions of multilateral trade: full employment, balancing of international accounts, and stability of economic policy.

It is indeed a bold scheme. Domestically, England will finance a welfare program which seemed beyond her pre-war means. Internationally, she will go her own way regardless, if not defiant, of the United States.

What is wrong with the prescription? Well—very little, if one likes the pre-war German scheme as a national way of life, and if England is tough and powerful enough to get away with it. Evidently the German authorities erred only in aiming at war instead of at welfare. So a sporting old Englishman urges England to take over the German game, not diffidently as in the thirties but zealously, and to show the world how it should be played. England's commercial power is to be mobilized and concentrated, to improve her terms of trade, to recruit satellites for a tight sterling bloc, and to insulate herself and them from unstable, unplanned economies, that is, from the United States.

Beveridge affects indifference to issues of collectivism versus individualism. The program is declared to be equally compatible with socialism and with private enterprise—which seems disingenuous. Any intelligent planning or broad policy prescription must aim at a kind of system as well as at particularist ends. One must plan for free-market controls just as carefully as (indeed, more so than) for socialization. One may (must) sensibly plan for socialization, national, provincial, or local, in particular economic areas—liquidity creation, insurance and annuities, public utilities, health, education, etc.— and for free markets and free enterprise in others. Sir William's planning, in all substantive aspects, is collectivist; his neutrality is exhibited only in his rhetoric, and in willingness to tolerate private enterprise if and while it can survive anomalously or vestigially, in spite of policy.

He would delegate vast discretionary powers to central authorities. He would create control machinery which, in economic matters, would adequately serve the most authoritarian regime. On the other hand, nothing is to be done to enforce competition,[4] to facilitate new enterprise, or to diminish the artificial (i.e., merely private) economies of monopolistic size. The cartel system is to be preserved and strengthened. Freedom in the management of private income is nominally preserved, but only within a framework of, first, heavy penalties (excises) and large premiums (subsidies) on the major items of consumption and, second, price ceilings and rationing. There would also be nominal freedom of enterprise and investment within this uncongenial framework, but subject also to discretionary rationing of essential materials, to arbitrary pricing of block imports, to subsidized, directed export, and to licensing by a National Investment Board with broad powers to restrict investment in particular industries or localities. Price ceilings and (subsidized) governmental enterprise are recommended, not only to curtail profits in otherwise profitable industries but also to force "deeper investment" or cost reduction in unprosperous, decadent (export?) industries. Cartels, to be sure, must be reasonable and co-operative; otherwise their industries must be socialized. Trade-unions must not strike for unduly rapid increase in wage rates; otherwise wages must be fixed by the state.[5] It is that simple.

Sir William seems tolerant of private enterprise if it is not (save in minor industries) competitive, that is, of syndicates which serve as instruments of the central authorities. The "chaotic" dispersion of power implicit in free enterprise evidently must be "corrected," if only to avoid "the tendency to competitive overinvestment, that will persist so long as any important industry is not under unified control." The English enterpriser, if not already moribund, is evidently to be accorded a quicker euthanasia than the rentier—which is a sad denouement for the worthy liberal program of making a risk-taker and equity-investor out of the rentier.

MONETARY-FISCAL POLICY

Beveridge implicitly identifies monetary stabilization with planning—thus concealing and confusing the important, controversial issue about planning. The "unplanned economy" of his aspersions is a free-market economy without any sensible monetary system, that is, an economy exposed to indefinite, cumulative deflation and institutionally unprotected against it. He thus appropriates, as a virtue of planning, a kind of reform which is indispensable to tolerable functioning of a libertarian, free-market system—and which, unlike his program, requires no departure from the rule of law. Monetary stabilization can and should be achieved under definite, legislative-constitutional rules of fiscal policy and without substantial reliance on discretionary authorities.

This distinction—rules or laws versus authorities—is the nub of the real planning issue. It is obscured by the fact that both libertarian and collectivist programs call for radical financial reform, the former more clearly and more specifically than the latter. Planners would control the price level by promiscuous intervention, innocent or plausible in detail and revolutionary in total. Libertarians would radically alter the private financial structure, economizing kinds of intervention and purging the old system of anomalies in crucial particulars. Those who would extend and consolidate the rule of law thus may appear more radical than those who would abandon it; recourse to discretionary authorities revolutionizes our political-economic system without seeming to change it at all.

The old monetary-fiscal-banking system involved provision of indispensable liquidity by devices which minimal standards of permissible corporation finance would have precluded. Moreover, it involved reliance on precisely the kind of discretionary authorities (central banks) which Beveridge and other planners would now multiply and more generously empower. Gradual but radical reform in fiscal practice, in banking, and in corporate finance is, properly conceived, an anticollectivist program. It should seek (1) to concentrate issue powers and borrowing powers where they belong (i.e., in the government or the Treasury, which alone can create genuine liquidity) and to focus sharply the responsibility for their exercise; (2) to assure monetary stability under definite, coherent rules of fiscal practice that will minimize delegation of authority, minimize detailed intervention, and minimize the monetary uncertainty afflicting private, competitive business; (3) to confine private financial enterprises to their proper business of mobilizing and canalizing equity investment; and thus (4) to maximize free-market control of relative prices and, through prices, of relative production and consumption.

Beveridge is not interested in altering the financial structure or in focusing political responsibility in the use of fiscal powers; neither does he propose any rules for their exercise—save the rhetorical rule of full employment, which, properly, is not an instrumental end at all. Full employment is a worthy purpose which, *among others*, instrumental ends, policy rules, and laws should be designed to serve. To propose it as a rule is to by-pass the democratic process and to propose government by authorities, which, instead of legislation, will implement the purpose. Beveridge is wisely and eloquently opposed to inflation as well as to deflation (p. 202); but stable money comes in only by the back door, not as a guide or proximate goal but as a wishful afterthought—or, perhaps, as an excuse for direct controls.

Monetary stability, says Beveridge, is inadequate; this is also a distinctive article of a libertarian faith. What he means, however, is that fiscal policy must afford, not over-all stability but persistent inflation pressure, in order that control *by* relative prices may be displaced with direct, discretionary control *of* relative prices and of consumption, production, and investment. The English economy is to be subjected, by deficit finance, to a continuous inflation pressure, which, in turn, will be frustrated by nonfiscal means. Liberal procedure would use fiscal devices to get monetary stability, and then deal with other problems within that framework. Beveridge would use them, along with an overvalued pound, to enlarge the scope for detailed intervention by authorities or, as he puts it, for the imposition of social priorities. This is standard collectivist technique, making a peacetime virtue of wartime (alleged) necessity, that is, of foreign-trade monopoly and domestic rationing, for consumer goods, industrial materials, and investment permits. The cause of large employment is thus made to serve other ends—better terms of foreign trade (national monopoly-monopsony exploitation), economic imperialism, severe sumptuary controls, and governmental direction of new investment.

The whole monetary argument is deeply confused by the typical Keynesian blurring of the difference between currency issue and governmental borrowing, that is, by a preoccupation with flows that disregards stocks. The banking process is simply taken for granted. The government, however, must absolutely determine the rate of interest, fixing it against increase and, indeed, reducing it gradually by one-twentieth of 1 per cent each year—to zero in about sixty years (p. 341).

All this, and the suggested techniques,[6] may puzzle the reader until he apprehends the real trick: *the English debt is to be wholly monetized*. Bonds are to be kept perfectly liquid at par, that is, guaranteed against even momentary depreciation. They will have the substantial attributes of currency, plus some interest plus policy assurance of interim appreciation. *The interest rate thus becomes a pure hoarding premium*—and the scheme, purporting to promote private investment, is admirably contrived to restrict it, by offering investors in government securities a liquidity which private enterprise cannot offer, or pretend to offer, without suicidal risk. I have never liked the Gesell-Fisher-Dahlberg schemes; if we must tax hoarding, steady increase in the price level, while dangerous, is the only elegant means. As between taxing hoarding and subsidizing it, however, the latter certainly has no merit save that it can more easily (and more foolishly) be done. Its only virtue is that of checking private investment (and consumption?) and thus creating an apparent necessity of vast public outlay.

Governmental borrowing, I submit, is always wrong—a fiscal error or heritage of error. It may be pardonable in great war emergencies, when democracies seem morally incapable of taxing adequately to their spending. Given such indulgence, however, debt should afterward be rapidly retired; borrowing-powers should be conserved for emergencies and, in wartime, against contingently long war. Otherwise, we impair our last line of defense against inflation and, incidentally, invite awkward leakage during depressions. Furthermore, bonds should be kept as illiquid as possible, by use of the consol or perpetuity form, in order to afford the maximum gain-and-loss leverage for open-market operations. Instead of supplying additional bonds during depressions, the government should take them away as fast as possible, maximizing at such times the rate at which debt is retired, that is, monetized. For boom periods the Keynesians are perhaps right: interest-rate (open-market) measures should be minimized; increased taxation and reduced spending should carry the load.[7]

Beveridge and his Oxford colleagues would evade the whole question of bonds versus currency by making them identical and by converting open-market operations into permanent bid-and-offer at par. If bonds are undersubscribed, then Ways-and-Means advances are recommended, thus to provide redundant reserves which will generate the additional subscriptions; if bonds are oversubscribed, then the interest rate should be reduced! No need to worry about the debt, for the interest rate can be reduced faster than the debt increases, and before long to zero!

One's first reaction is a picture of Englishmen rushing into assets like Germans in 1923—if one overlooks what the author and his friends have learned from the Germany of the thirties. Flight into foreign currencies or securities would be prevented by comprehensive exchange control. Flight into domestic equities or industrial properties, if not wholly discouraged by the trade-unions, would be inhibited by product-price ceilings and rationing, by materials allocation, etc. Flight into new real investment may similarly be frustrated, with the help of the Investment Board. This leaves only consumption and consumer capital, where rationing would check the flight. The debt policy thus amply supplements budgetary policy, creating inflation pressure via money stocks, as well as via flows, and further enlarging the scope for "social priorities." Flight into assets ceases to be a freedom and becomes a crime.

Since the government can so easily fix "the interest rate" when it asks lenders to sacrifice nothing in liquidity, Beveridge is at pains to explain why it should not promptly reduce it to zero. The minor reason is that it might cause windfall gains to holders of old securities and real assets; the major reason, as with Hansen, is that private banks and insurance companies might thereby be unduly disturbed. Thus Beveridge would proceed gradually, in order to preserve the two forms of private business which are least essential to, if not incompatible with, a free-enterprise, free-market system. On the other hand, it may be noted that his debt policy really means 100 per cent reserve banking, with a diminishing transitional subsidy, which, if not extended to other bondholders, would make fairly good sense[8]—also that his debt policy is the one now followed in the United States!

KALDOR'S ROUTES

The best part of the book is Kaldor's analysis and forecast of national income and outlay (Appen. C). I cannot pretend to judge his statistical estimates for 1948; but they seem useful and plausible—especially if translated into guesses about the secular monetary expansion necessary to stabilize price levels in the face of rising real income and increasing demand for liquidity.

Kaldor examines three main "routes" to full employment in 1948: (I) 1938 taxes with enlarged public outlay; (II) a balanced budget with (fabulous) increase of both revenues and expenditures; (III) 1938 "real" expenditures with uniform reduction of all 1938 taxes, that is, with tax-induced increase in private outlay. To accommodate wartime increase in labor costs, the price level is assumed to be higher by 33 per cent in 1948 than in 1938.

Route I is estimated to require a deficit of £230 million; Route III, a deficit of £340 million; Route II, an increase of about £1,000 million in both revenues and expenditures (Tables 18 and 46). These estimates involve an adverse foreign balance of £130 million; with imports restricted and (or) exports expanded to eliminate this adverse balance, the requisite deficits are estimated at £100 (instead of £230) million for Route I and at £160 (instead of £340) million for Route III (Table 47)—thus highlighting the foreign-trade problem. Estimates are also offered for a Route IIa (tax increases confined to direct taxes) and for a Route IIIa (tax reductions confined to indirect taxes). I suspect that Kaldor exaggerates the long-term deficit difference between Routes I and III (£230–£340 million) and understates that difference between Routes III and IIIa (£340–£285 million); also that he overestimates corporate earnings and the long-term increase in savings resulting from secular increase in national income.[9] A non-

Keynesian would like to know how much smaller the requisite deficits would be if financed by issues carrying no hoarding premium; also, how different the whole picture would be if the government debt were largely in a consol form and thus available for expansionist retirement, that is, for extra-budgetary conversion from a poor money substitute into the real thing.

Some readers will be amazed, if not exasperated, by the estimates under Route II, which seem merely to satirize the pay-as-you-go rule. An effort at interpretation may be in order, for we are likely to see much of such statistical extravagances in this country. What they really estimate (I think) is how to maintain the price level, as real income rises, without any increase in the quantity of money (or in the "moneyness" of debt)—a fabulous undertaking which few budget-balancers would contemplate and which past practice never involved. Governments, balancing their budgets in the old days, simply left to the banking system the task of expanding secularly the money supply, first, as bank notes, later mainly as bank deposits. This responsibility of providing additional liquidity as real income rose, the banking system, as a matter of historical accident and timely proliferation, did meet after a fashion, by fits and starts and with occasional collapses. It was a spurious liquidity or money that the banks provided; it was highly perverse in its short-term fluctuations; and it served long-term needs poorly or accidentally.

Some of us believe that the whole development of private banking reflects a fundamental error in governmental policy and was institutionally anomalous from the start. The anomaly, however, becomes less glaring as the banks come to hold mainly government bonds and as their cash reserves are supplemented by obligations little different from cash. The old rules of sound commercial banking called for a credit currency resting upon assets of minimal liquidity (for the system) and peculiarly subject to sudden and cumulative deflation. Now, however, even in this country, the credit currency rests mainly on government bonds, whose prices normally would rise in the face of depression and increased demand for liquidity. Always dependent on the Treasury (or on central banks as virtual sub-treasuries) for liquidity which only governments can genuinely supply, banks are now essentially Treasury branches, by the nature of their assets as well as their liabilities.

To those who like or take for granted the banking anomaly, the issue of currency by the government seems itself anomalous, if not evidence of fiscal depravity. The government, they imply, should supply deflation-preventing liquidity only by loan expenditure, that is, by expanding its debt sufficiently to induce absorption of bonds by the banks.

The Keynesian arguments really presuppose that new issues of government bonds will so be absorbed and that liquidity may be increased only in this way. There is thus some devious correctness in their upside-down rule that governments should borrow in depressions and should not borrow during booms. Business is, to be sure, no longer starved for capital and need not incur the suicidal risks involved in continuous financing through banks; and banks, in turn, are disinclined to provide business capital on terms which preclude their liquidating before other and prior claimants can enforce their claims. The old devices for expanding liquidity are, fortunately, a thing of the past. So, if one must rely on fractional-reserve bank expansion to provide our effective money, there is apparently no way to prevent deflation but to pour bonds into banks—into central banks to augment reserves and into private banks to augment deposits.[10]

If government bonds sold to banks were ineligible for purchase by others, the system might be intelligible, as simply one of subsidizing the services of warehousing and transferring funds. Actually, bonds are used both to increase liquidity and to decrease it. They are sold to banks for injecting new money and, often simultaneously, to others for withdrawing money. Such inherently confusing practice facilitates the financial argument of books like these.

Kaldor does not get himself much involved with the dubious

analysis of his colleagues or with extravagant policy proposals. One exception is noteworthy:

"In general, if considerable changes in the structure of income distribution were desired, it is better to tackle the problem directly—by forcing producers to sell at lower prices relatively to costs—than indirectly through changes in taxation or some combined scheme of taxation and subsidies. The main reason for this is that it is extremely difficult to devise a scheme where the consequential higher taxation on profits would not in itself have adverse effects on incentives and hence on employment" (p. 348). It is indeed a strange notion that direct, discretionary control is less injurious to incentives than is (income) taxation.

Kaldor's estimates will seem less surprising (to repeat) if interpreted as showing the expansion of bank currency necessary to finance secularly rising production at a stable price level— and, for Route II, as showing the fabulous increase in both taxes and spending that would be necessary, with rising real income, to stabilize the price level without increasing the quantity of money. It surely seems natural that people should try to become absolutely more liquid as they become more prosperous; to prevent their trying, the state would have to take away most of their incomes. There should be no quarrel about the need for increasing liquidity in a progressive economy. I should like to see it effected straightforwardly, by governmental currency issue and without multiple bank expansion. But one need not be distressed about it in any case. It is *compatible* with very modest total budgets and need proceed little or no faster than it has during the past century. Such is the modicum of sense implicit in loose talk about the virtues of a rising public debt: increase in real debt (consols) is always ominous and unfortunate; increase in currency or liquidity, as necessary to implement rules of monetary stabilization, is not only innocuous but quite salutary.

Kaldor also sketches a Route IV, combining Routes II*a* and III*a*, whereby some authority, presumably Kaldor, would be

empowered to manipulate an elaborate structure of subsidies
and excises, with the purpose of reducing the requisite deficit
(i.e., monetary expansion) under Route III*a*. His interest in
this route is, one hopes, merely academic; amid so much good
work, he may easily be pardoned this relapse into the irresponsible cleverness of his colleagues. Beveridge dismisses
Route IV—perhaps as a too candid description of his own
proposals.

THE BEVERIDGE ROUTE

Sir William likes the objective in Route II (possibly because
he misunderstands it) but not the magnitudes. He rejects
Routes III and III*a* for the obvious reason that they will not
accommodate his Plan and plumps for Route I. His objection
to Routes III and III*a* is that they would leave people too
much freedom and preclude adequate imposition of social priorities. This may be a defensible position as regards much of his
Plan, especially its scheme of medical and health services.

Throughout the book it is asserted that any prospective deficiency in aggregate outlay should be made good by additional public outlay, that is, that expenditures rather than revenues should be the variable factor in fiscal stabilization.[11] The
argument, however, relates entirely to the choice among starting budgets (i.e., to the level of spending in 1948). Surely, one
might accept Sir William's initial spending program and still
argue that the annual adjustments should be in revenues, not
in spending. Discussing public works and the White Paper, he
comes close to this choice but evades the issue. On his own arguments, however, one might plump for varying revenue, for
example, by varying the income-tax exemptions, and for stable
spending.

That Beveridge is more interventionist than egalitarian is
suggested by his categorical rejection of Route III*a*. One must
indeed value highly the transfer expenditures of his Plan to
demand them all and severally at the price of the pre-war
English excises, which he would retain intact—not to mention

the "employer contribution." My preferences would accord high priority to reduction of duties on tea, tobacco, beer, etc., which make heavy inroads on the smallest incomes, and to avoidance of a tax penalty on private employment. Much of what Beveridge would accomplish by food and fuel subsidies, moreover, could be accomplished simply by removing inordinate mass excises and educating consumers on dietary requirements, that is, by enlarging consumer freedom instead of extending interference and manipulation. Temporary subsidies for critical nutrients, during an intensive program of nutrition education, may be defended as a kind of infant-industry investment in better dietary habits; but that is not a Beveridge proposal. Central control must be a great good, if two largely offsetting kinds of intervention are better than neither.

Like most projects for a welfare state, Sir William's proposals reflect high moral purpose and, in detail, seem eminently reasonable. Only by adding them up and apprehending the total does one see what a radical-reactionary revolution is involved. Nor is this apparent if one accepts with each proposed intervention the author's wishfully low estimate of the probable amount. In each case a worthy end is aimed at, and only "fringe" intervention implied. The authorities may all be as popular as Lord Woolton; and co-operation may dissipate the conflicts of interest among organized groups. But Beveridge, I think, deceives his reader, if not himself. Every direct control will increase the need for other controls; and the aggregate of intervention is meagerly indicated by his particularist approach. Beveridge seems to promise that rationing will be largely or usually unnecessary and that the Investment Board will only deflect slightly the flow of private investment. Such reassurances seem unrealistic. If free-market controls through competition are devitalized or destroyed, there is nothing left to sustain economic order except governmental intervention, which must then become ubiquitous.

The Investment Board is proposed as a moderate extension

of eminently sound urban planning and zoning. It seems a plausible means for dealing with the military-strategic problem of metropolitan London and the cancerous affliction of inordinate population density. Less persuasive is the argument for diverting private investment according to the location of unemployment or according to governmental notions of over-invested and underinvested industries. Still more questionable is the proposed protection of sunk public investment in local improvements, especially when one apprehends how closely this objective will coincide with that of protecting past industrial investment and that, in turn, with protecting workers in established centers against potential competition elsewhere. Besides, there are the possibilities of preventing inflationary private investment in order that inflationary public outlay may proceed. Such a board, I submit, cannot really function without more power than any discretionary authority should have.

Beveridge would plan for 97 per cent employment, allowing a smaller margin for frictional or migrational unemployment than has, to my knowledge, ever been responsibly proposed. He demands a sellers' market for labor—a continuous excess of vacant jobs over idle hands—which obviously invites flight into assets via the labor market. Since it would mean an inflationary spiral of wage-rate increase even in the absence of any labor organization, Beveridge is naturally solicitous lest the trade-unions make demands which would frustrate efforts to sustain the value of money.

"Particular wage demands which exceed what employers are able to pay with their existing prices and which force a raising of prices, may bring gains to the workers of the industry concerned, but they will do so at the expense of all other workers, whose real wages fall owing to the rise in prices. The other workers will naturally try to restore the position, by putting forward demands of their own. There is a real danger that sectional wage bargaining, pursued without regard to its effects upon prices, may lead to a vicious spiral of inflation, with money wages chasing prices and without any gain in real wages for the working class as a whole" (p. 199).

To expect labor monopolies not to demand monopolistic wages is, under any circumstances, unrealistic. To ask, with Sir William, that they use their power to keep wage rates below competitive levels is quixotic. The practical suggestions are: (1) preaching; (2) that "the central organizations of labour . . . . should devote their attention to the problem of achieving a unified wage policy which ensures that the demands of individual unions will be judged with reference to the economic situation as a whole" (pp. 199–200); and (3) the fixing of wages by the state (p. 207). The second suggestion implies that the Trades Union Congress General Council might grant or withhold licenses to demand wage increases—which would make suggestions 2 and 3 identical, since an agency with such power would either become part of the state or conversely.

Hostile critics will chide Sir William about his abolishing "free collective bargaining." National trade-unions are obviously incompatible with stable prices under his scheme, unless they serve as passive instruments of the governmental authorities. Libertarians, however, are ill advised to press this point against a planner who, in these matters, is rarely candid and sensible. For what he diffidently concedes to be incompatible with his scheme is certainly incompatible with the tolerable functioning of a free-enterprise system. Relative wages must be determined either by competition among workers (and among employers) or by central authorities.

FOREIGN TRADE POLICY

Beveridge reserves the crucial subject of commercial policy for his penultimate chapter. Up to this point, one may suspect that this old Liberal is deliberately contriving a nightmarish scheme to show what England may or must do if America repudiates its minimal responsibilities for economic-financial co-operation. The whole program, one hopes, is merely a policy-construct for bargaining with the United States. Indeed, it does reasonably describe what is likely to happen unless we radically reduce our tariff and firmly undertake, with the consultation and co-operation of our friends, to provide the world with the stable currency necessary to orderly, peaceful trade.

Chapter vi ("International Implications . . . .") disappoints such hope. The Keynesian rejuvenation yields only apostasy—a "Baloghism" more zealous than Sir William's old free-trade internationalism. When one puts together the foreign-trade proposals, filling in eloquent omissions, only then does one apprehend the full collectivist import of the whole scheme. Shorn of euphemisms, it calls for pure state trading abroad, that is, for governmental monopoly of foreign trade.

During the interwar period, the English economy, weakened by overvaluation of the pound, became rapidly uncompetitive and syndicalist, by virtue especially of the commercial policies of the thirties. To restore free enterprise and competitive controls within England, substantially free foreign trade—trade controlled by proper exchange rates—would appear indispensable. To collectivize foreign trade in England or to subject it largely to the manipulation of discretionary authorities is to consolidate English syndicalism and, in turn, to socialize industry. Private enterprise, even some new enterprise, may persist for a time but, in substance, simply as a beneficiary of state orders. Lacking the autonomous discipline of competition and facing mainly political uncertainties, private business would be largely a contracting-out by governmental authorities, as it is in wartime. Whether industries are socialized or continued under private enterprise, in this sense, is of interest only to Socialists and is indeed, as Beveridge asserts, a matter of mere detail and expediency.

What I have said so far is admittedly an extreme interpretation of the Beveridge program. It may seem cavalierly to reject his own interpretation at many points and to impute meanings which he disavows. Sir William argues his case largely in terms of the same considerations I would invoke to support very different measures; having been carried along quite a way, I may now misrepresent the substantive scheme as much in opposition as does Sir William in his skilful advocacy. At all events, my case rests largely on interpretation of the proposed commercial policy.

The introductory argument of chapter vi, while sound enough as economics, gives little attention to the political dangers of discriminatory practices or to the economic effects of retaliation. The following passage will indicate the general tone: "The virtue of international trade is that it saves labour; the virtue of a full employment policy is that it uses labour. It would be senseless to save labour through international trade only in order to waste labour in unemployment" (p. 211). The general conclusions are put as follows:

"General multilateral trading . . . . is possible only if three conditions, or assumptions, are fulfilled: first, each of the participating nations must aim at full employment within its borders and must do so without relying on export surpluses as the principal means to full employment. Second, each of the participating nations must be prepared to balance its accounts with the rest of the world; for that purpose any nation which, for any reason, systematically sells abroad in goods or services more than it buys from abroad, and so has an export surplus, must be prepared to grant long-term loans sufficient to enable the rest of the world to pay for those exports, without losing gold or other reserves essential for international liquidity. Third, each of the participating nations must aim at a certain stability of economic behavior—continuity in tariff, subsidy, foreign exchange and other economic policies—and must refrain from introducing important changes in these policies without prior consultation with the other participants" (p. 218).

"International trade can be arranged in one way if all important industrial countries have policies of full employment;

it must be arranged in another way if any important industrial country does not have such a policy" (p. 225).

One may sympathize with the fear of another American deflation—although it seems politically too improbable for serious concern. That our deflation of 1929–33 was a tragic failure to discharge minimal governmental responsibilities, domestic and international, is beyond dispute. Along with tariff legislation and, worst of all, our devaluation, it was the cause of world economic disaster and perhaps of the ensuing war. For the devaluation, no plausible apology can be offered save blind ignorance among responsible leaders. One should distinguish, however, between sins of omission and of commission. Only a dictator, able to lower wage rates at will, could well be accused of imposing general deflation for national advantage. It is one thing to stress the urgent world need for a stable dollar—indeed, for stability in all the major currencies. It is another to recommend discriminatory measures against national deflation, which, however deplorable, is simply an error of ignorant inaction. Discrimination, whatever the excuses, must always seem a hostile or unfriendly act. To use national sanctions against nations for their failure to maintain British standards of wise finance is to multiply the occasions for international schism and ill-will.

Conceding the worst that can be said of our role in the thirties, one may also question the British record. They devalued, to be sure, out of necessity. There was no necessity, however, about the earlier quixotic overvaluation of the pound or about their persisting in error to the end, that is, until it had to be corrected at, for the world, the worst possible time. Until these things are forgotten and until England is prepared to eschew overvaluation, her spokesmen might more humbly pursue international monetary co-operation and not assume that English finance, past and future, affords a norm by which other nations may be judged as eligible for, or exempt from, quarantine.

The policy choice, says Beveridge, is between (1) general

multilateral trading, (2) regional multilateral trading, and (3) bilateralism (p. 239). In spite of much talk about the virtues of No. 1, it soon appears that he is counting on Nos. 2 and 3. Moreover, unless I misread him, he refuses to consider nondiscrimination or equality of treatment on any terms.

"The second of the three alternatives for international trade is regionalism. This means multilateral trading not throughout the world but between a group of countries, sufficiently complementary to one another, and sufficiently alike in their economic policies, including the pursuit of full employment, to make it easy for them to work together. . . . . Britain might become the financial centre, of a sterling full employment area, as before the first World War she was the financial centre of the world. This would not, of course, prevent trade between countries in different regions, but such trade would take place subject to special controls.

"A policy of regionalism applied in Europe or in the British Commonwealth or both together should not be regarded as in any way unfriendly to the United States or to Soviet Russia. Room must be kept in the world for a variety of economic policies in different countries. Soviet Russia will certainly continue to have a completely managed economy; the United States is likely to return, at any rate for some time to come, to a large measure of freedom from Government action. It should be open to Britain, and countries which like her desire to follow the middle course of full employment in a free society, to do so, without being charged with pursuing selfish or national aims.

"It is difficult to believe—in truth it is incredible—that, if a general multilateral system could not be established throughout the world, Britain would fail to find other countries, sufficient with her to make up a region of stable prosperity, ensuring to her the essential imports in return for her exports, ensuring to them markets and capital. But if for any reason this could not or could not immediately be secured, there remains the last certain recourse of bilateralism. This for Britain would mean the making of specific bargains with individual countries to ensure the supply of imports of food and of raw materials indispensable for British industry, including in such bargains provisions as to means of payment and the exchange between their respective currencies.

"The first of the three alternatives is, as has been emphasized before, the most desirable in itself and most in accord with Britain's role and traditions in the past. To realize it Britain should do everything possible, except [sic] surrender the right to fall back on the other alternatives, if the first one could not be attained in full and satisfactory measure. It is better to secure multilateral trading in a limited region where it has good prospects of success and can be made the basis of wider trading later, than to aim at multilateral trading in the world at large, without effective agreement on its fundamental conditions.

"That it would be possible either under the second or under the third alternative to ensure the imports required for our prosperity, if we are prepared to take the necessary steps, is not open to reasonable doubt. Nor is it doubtful that strong central planning of Britain's internal affairs will make her more, not less, useful as a partner in world affairs. *International trade, both for imports and for exports, will on the whole have to come under public management, in place of being left to market forces either competitive or monopolistic.* The organs which serve for planning at home will serve also for planning in a wider sphere" (pp. 239–41). (My italics.)

". . . . while hoping for the best, that is success in our efforts for world-wide economic order, we must be prepared for failure and must retain for that event all necessary powers to ensure the second or third best" (p. 241).

Is he not here urging England to seek at once the best of every possible world and to risk no commitments on behalf of better or best?

Most significant is Sir William's conception of the best arrangement—what he means by general multilateral trading for Britain and what he would offer in return for our fullest co-operation.

"On the assumption of the Atlantic Charter, that all the larger countries will announce and adopt a policy for maintaining employment at home, international trade can be based on the most desirable of the three alternatives. That is to say, the first aim should be a world-wide trading and clearing system, with international arrangements providing adequate lasting liquidity for multilateral trading, without requiring individual countries to subordinate domestic economic policy to international exigencies. Subject to the adoption by all countries of suitable economic policies, such a system could have been developed out of the first British proposals for international clearing by adding thereto machinery for directed international investment. It could be developed out of the recent joint proposals for an International Monetary Fund. But, even under such a system, Britain, with other countries, must retain and exercise powers not used before the first World War, including:

a) Control of capital movements. This appears to involve control of all exchanges.
b) Making of long-term contracts for the purchase of essential raw materials and food.
c) Making of long-term contracts for the planned supply of exports to develop backward areas" (p. 239).

The remark under point a is at least candid, by contrast with most current talk about "limited" exchange control. That Sir William means every word of it is indicated by his approving quotation from the British Treasury Memorandum of April, 1943:

"There is no country which can, in future, safely allow the flight of funds for political reasons or to evade domestic taxation or in anticipation of the owner turning refugee. Equally, there is no country that can safely receive fugitive funds, which constitute an unwanted import of capital, yet cannot safely be used for fixed investment. For these reasons it is widely held that control of capital movements, both inward and outward, should be a permanent feature of the post-war system" (p. 237).

Note the word "permanent." Exclusive governmental lending abroad is not an unreasonable inference and, like governmental trading, is certainly not calculated to minimize friction among the powers! Capital flight in the thirties, with its unprecedented demands on liquidity, was largely an incident of Nazi persecution and aggression. What prospective cause of wild property migration calls for permanent restrictions in post-transition England? Is such restriction appropriate to an orderly world or compatible with the desired large international flow of investment funds? Does Beveridge want exchange control merely to prevent capital flight or for other purposes too?

It is implied under point *b*, and elsewhere assumed, that "an increasing proportion of British imports, mainly food and raw materials, will come under collective management" (p. 235)—in other words, block purchasing and government import monopoly. To ask us and others to co-operate, on these terms, toward freer and more stable trade, is disingenuous. Englishmen may expect the central purchasing authority to eschew monopsony practices, to avoid ancillary bargain, to purchase always in the cheapest market, and never to use purchasing for political-diplomatic purposes. Other nations, however, will surely discount or ignore promises of such administration; England could expect no one abroad to acknowledge the fact if, miraculously, such promises were carried out. Block purchase, by a great trading nation, must be regarded as inherently discriminatory. Freer trade and reasonable equality of treatment are, for England, not compatible with the prohibition of private trade.

If one combines points *b* and *c*—and separation is fanciful—one gets pure bilateralism. Here, perhaps, is the meaning of "retain all necessary powers." Beveridge's terms for eschewing bilateralism are, it seems, carte blanche to practice it. "General multilateral trading" thus appears to mean only that the British trading authority would entertain bids and offers from many countries!

The author's restrictionist predilection is evident at many points:

"If, further, Britain seeks full employment in the first instance less by increasing free purchasing power, which consumers might use for imports, than by physical improvements at home, she may avoid much of the rise of imports that would follow otherwise through full employment itself" (p. 214).

". . . . the White Paper concentrates too much on increasing exports and not sufficiently on stabilizing them. 'To avoid an unfavourable foreign balance, we must export much more than we did before the war.' Is this certain? There is the alternative of cutting down imports and becoming more independent; the figures given recently by the Minister of Production show how great are the possibilities of self-dependence, even for Britain" (p. 267).

Sir William is also adamant against living off capital abroad, that is, against borrowing or further repatriation of English investments. Kaldor contemplates, with at least statistical equanimity, an adverse foreign balance of £130 million—which seems not extravagant for a time, if one shares their concern about the technical condition of British industry, especially in the export trades. It is not clear whether the opposition to capital import reflects mainly imperialist zeal or reluctance to risk borrowing from America or recognition that the total scheme would preclude either borrowing or voluntary capital repatriation. Incidentally, the quantitative discussion appears to assume that the vast blocked balances now due to other countries will be funded into low-rate sterling bonds—which is unlikely to produce highly satisfied creditors or willing adherents to a sterling bloc.

That Beveridge would offer little for American co-operation is clear from his remarks about cartels:

"In the fourth place, a problem arises from the fact that the course of international trade in a number of articles is now determined or influenced by international cartel agreements. Such cartels may serve a good purpose in stabilizing trade and production. The whole trend of the argument of this Part of the Report is towards a management of international trade, in place of leaving it to unregulated competition. That is to say, it is towards that for which the cartels stand. To attempt to destroy or stop cartellization would, therefore, be a contradiction of policy. . . . . What is wanted is that those who have the responsibility of conducting great and highly organized industries should come to regard themselves as the agents of a wider policy than that of their business. Just under what forms and by what institutions this can best be accomplished can probably be learned only by experience" (p. 238).

Unlike many American economists, Beveridge is at least consistent in his attitude toward cartels and commodity agreements. The case for points *b* and *c* is argued in terms of the need for stabilizing overseas demand—admittedly a presumptuous enterprise for Britain, to be pursued on behalf of favored areas. Here the author reveals a preoccupation with fluctuations in raw-materials prices as causal prices in "the cycle"—a thesis stressed at many points. This notion of causality is perhaps an unavoidable incident of long study of time series. The argument makes some sense as support of a commodity-reserve currency but is, I think, simply spurious as exculpation of cartels or as commendation of output-restricting, relative-price-raising schemes.[12]

The most ominous feature of the Beveridge program is an omission. The postwar dollar-sterling rate is, I believe, not once mentioned in the book! It may be unfair to put the worst construction on ambiguities and on a chapter which, while pleading for American co-operation, lays down impossible British terms. In any case, one may be pardoned for filling in an exchange-rate policy as best one can—and for resting one's case against the program largely on so crucial an omission.

Given a not overvalued pound, the Beveridge program, if not simply inoperable, might belie my interpretations. It might involve only moderate intervention at home and only provisional, temporary departure from decent commercial policy. However, everything in the program implies determination to keep the pound at its present dollar price or as high as may be necessary to afford large scope for discriminating controls. This is the obvious means to better terms of trade—and for propping up real income. And it is the natural inference from discussion which is everywhere preoccupied with leakages and only vague and wishful about the volume of exports.

Given a radically overvalued pound, block exporting is specified by implication. Importation would be nominally very profitable—for the government; export would be nominally unprofitable—and thus dependent on subsidy. Whether Sir William intends it so is not clear. He mentions the possible necessity of governmental enterprise in export production[13] and of subsidies for cost-reducing investment in the export trades. One of his arguments against Route III is that it might unduly increase consumption at the expense of necessary investment—which, unless he means governmental investment, sounds strange in a Keynesian context. However, if my interpretations are ungenerous, it would be more ungenerous to suppose that Beveridge did not understand his own scheme or could not, if he chose to do so, fill in the omissions.

England, to be sure, will find it hard to maintain her standard of living or her position as a great power. Collectivist trading abroad may permit betterment of her terms of trade—in the absence of effective retaliation. But it invites a kind of economic warfare which England can initiate only at grave risk to her own security and to peace for the world. What alarms me, as an ardent Anglophile, is that such English policy is incompatible with Anglo-American solidarity; indeed, it promises sharply to divide those solidly democratic nations whose close collaboration seems indispensable to a good peace. Espousing governmental trading, England may force such trading on neighboring countries whom we also cherish as close friends and allies. She may create an awful problem for the Dominions —and perhaps a struggle for their economic allegiance. Besides, she may aggravate indefinitely the international problem of colonies and mandates—disqualifying herself, at least in our eyes, for the wide trusteeship which an open-door policy commended and justified.

Does Beveridge intend to propose that we establish federal monopoly of foreign trade as a condition of English collaboration, and, alternatively, that the two nations divide the Western world into separate and rivalrous trading systems, one moving close to Russia, the other thereby pushed farther away? This I can hardly believe. So I am driven back to my first hunch: it is all a nightmarish construct, designed to overcome our lethargy and intransigence. But is it? I simply do not know. It is either a devilish fine piece of English diplomacy or a brilliant plan for a free society to end free societies.

Trying to interpret and criticize the Beveridge program, I have certainly not done justice to the book. It is excellently organized, well written, abundantly informative, and rich in statistical data. The style and pace reveal the hand of an experienced journalist. Few major policy problems are left aside; a fine balance in relative emphasis is achieved; and the policy prescriptions, like the discussion, are comprehensive and integrated.

The best of the text, of course, is the section on the "Facts of Unemployment" (pp. 40–90), an admirable summary of the author's earlier work. Few will question his argument for organized mobility of labor, that is, for an integrated system of employment exchanges, toward which England has made only some headway and the United States really none.

On many important issues, the policy judgments and supporting arguments are unsurpassed, for example, on the case for a stable price level.

". . . . adoption by the State of a definite policy in regard to prices, becomes an almost inevitable accompaniment of a policy of maintaining employment, in a progressive society. This is an issue which, though certainly not absent from J. M. Keynes' mind, is not treated by him at any length" (p. 101).

"In the prospective circumstances of Britain, the ingenious

arguments which have been advanced in the past, on the one hand for a policy of gently falling prices and on the other hand for a policy of gently rising prices, lose their validity. A falling price level increases the share of the total income going to rentiers. This, in view of the inevitably large national debt, is a grave disadvantage. But it does not justify the opposite suggestion that the right policy is one of rising prices, so that the claims of rentiers are cut down automatically. In future, with the vastly increased proportion of aged persons in the total population, the numerically most important class of rentiers will be old-age pensioners. If it is desired to cut down the gains of rentiers, or any particular class of them, that should be done directly through taxation—by death duties, by differentiation between earned and unearned incomes, and in other ways. Letting the price level rise is a clumsy form of taxation" (p. 202).

With these persuasions, Beveridge might have advocated, as a monetary-fiscal program, the most expansive budgetary arrangements consistent with price-level stability—which would open, instead of close, the way to international (Anglo-American) co-operation.

He is wisely critical of schemes (the Lever Brothers pamphlet and the White Paper) for stabilizing either total investment or total outlay by variable outlay for public works (pp. 180–84, 261–63). He firmly rejects the use of variable social insurance contributions with, among others, one argument which should settle that issue for good: "If it is good for social insurance contributions it is even better for general taxation" (p. 264). Even those who will have none of his centralized, discretionary control (Investment Board) will like the discussion of industry location, as a problem of urban and regional planning, and feel obliged to study other control devices less incompatible with the rule of law. Account must be taken of his (and Worswick's) point that labor is far more mobile among industries or occupations than among localities.

In short, this second Beveridge Report, like the first, richly rewards the reading, especially for those who dislike its program.

Systematic comment on the Oxford studies is not appropriate here, for the central ideas and proposals are incorporated in the Beveridge book. Several of the essays, moreover, are very repetitious. The most exasperating is Schumacher's. But those of Kalecki and Balogh are more stimulating and analytical and deserve attention.

Kalecki presents an admirable, concise statement of hyper-Keynesian doctrines. His general position is familiar. It rests partly on a capital theory for the firm (increasing risk) which strikes me as merely misleading—implying or assuming that new investment must come from old firms, that prosperous firms will find it increasingly hard to attract new capital as they prosper, and that large firms can acquire new capital only on less favorable terms (including higher flotation costs!) than small ones. (Being distressed about merely private economies of monopolistic size, I wish the latter implications were realistic.) I can likewise find little sense in his discussion of the widening and deepening of capital—although the argument that deepening requires direct governmental action may accurately reflect the degree of competition and enterprise recently prevalent in England. Kalecki proposes to measure rise in labor productivity as though it were independent of capital increase and then to determine how much additional capital is needed to equip for sustained full employment. Evidently the capital-labor proportions are fixed, save for technical innovations; deepening depends exclusively on such innovations; and they, in turn, are rare or discontinuous if not revolutionary. If this is the new capital theory, *The Nature and Necessity of Interest* is indeed a great book. Incidentally, Kalecki's general argument, like that of his colleagues (save Kaldor) implicitly does violence to the facts of life, especially as regards the quantitative possibilities of raising consumption by leveling the income distribution.

Kalecki is more engaging and more academic in his practical proposals than in his general theory. His interest-rate, debt-policy scheme, adopted by Beveridge, is mentioned above (pp. 280 ff.). He is less worried than Beveridge about too rapid increase of wage rates; for it need not, he says, cause increase of prices; it can be offset by subsidies, financed by additional taxes on the upper incomes! Moreover, this would reduce deficits; for the taxes, coming partly from savings, would have to yield far more than the subsidy outlays. Some of Kaldor's arithmetic would be useful at this point! Incidentally, this scheme, starting with a general excise on all employment ("employers' contribution"), would add a general subsidy for all consumer-goods production—all summing up to a differential penalty on capital-goods production or real investment!

The increase of income tax, he admits, might impair incentives to invest. But that is easy. Just "modify" the income tax, so that the added rate would apply to income calculated before depreciation but with deduction for new real investment! The base for the added rate would thus be consumption plus hoarding. His colleagues (but not Beveridge) take this scheme very seriously—as will, perhaps, Professor Fisher and as anyone familiar with tax procedure or accounting will not. A new enterprise, with large current investment and little current revenue, would certainly come off badly. If carry-forward is contemplated, then the scheme merely denies depreciation on past investment, while permitting it for investment postdating the "modification"—and with minimum instead of maximum rates of charge!

Kalecki may have more misgivings about this "modified income tax" than do his colleagues. He proposes an alternative: finance the subsidies out of an annual capital levy, that is, with a heavy, flat-rate general property tax—which in theory, to be sure, avoids relative penalty on investment by an equal tax on hoards. American economists are unlikely to applaud this fiscal discovery! But, to repeat, the essay as a whole deserves attention as a brilliant summary statement which reveals clearly the virtues and the faults of the new economics.

Balogh presents a sophisticated attack on classical doctrines, showing what the new economics contributes to foreign-trade theory. His central propositions may perhaps be stated as follows: (1) direct, discriminating controls permit a nation, after disturbance of its international position, to readjust with better results all around than would be possible by adherence to classical, over-all devices (deflation or devaluation); (2) stable trade within a discriminating bloc of nations co-operating in full-employment programs (monetary stabilization?) may be more advantageous for all members than unstable, undiscriminating trade on a wider or global scale; (2a) backward nations may be more prosperous and progressive, without capital imports, as members of such a sterling bloc than they would be, with American loans, as participants in a larger, unstable system of free or undiscriminating trade.

Under governmental trading, as under collectivism in general, the most improbable results are conceivable; under free trade, enough monetary instability can be disastrous. So I see little reason to question Balogh's formal position—save when he transcribes the "possibly may be" of his argument as "probably will be" in his conclusion.

The classical devices work well only with "highly inelastic expectations" in the whole trading system—or, as I prefer to say, only with an accepted, implemented policy of monetary stabilization, in the dominant nation and/or as a matter of organized co-operation among the financial powers. The old regime was good only as regards relative prices, relative price and wage levels, and, save for the gold standard, exchange rates. Under the gold standard, each national financial structure was like a single bank in a system of banks with negligible reserves, no central fisc, and (hence) no central bank. Almost any national arrangements *might* work better than participation in such a collapsible banking system. Even so, Balogh's propositions have only the dubious virtue of being formally unassailable, like the infant-industry case for protection.

Conventional price theory presupposes a fisc that sustains over-all monetary stability; and it points implicitly to such an institution as indispensable for good functioning of a free-market economy. The old foreign-trade doctrines implicitly involved some corresponding assumption—anomalously, to be sure, since a powerful international fisc is almost inconceivable. In this way, however, they, too, indicated sound policy objectives, that is, co-operative stabilization of a dominant currency and/or internal stabilization of particular currencies with flexible, free-market exchange rates.

The old economics is commended by its normative implications, by its definite first-approximations of policy goals. It stands or falls less as an analysis of an institutional system than as a device for diagnosing its faults and for describing, in important aspects, a good system which the actual one approximates and, with proper measures, can approximate more closely. Its strength is in its implied political philosophy. Its wisdom is that of seeking solutions which are within the rule of law, compatible with great dispersion or deconcentration of power, and conducive to extensive supranational organization on a basis that facilitates indefinite peaceful extension.

Certainly another kind of system, ruled by authorities, *might be* more efficient and more progressive—if one excludes liberty as an aspect of efficiency and capacity for freedom and responsibility, among individuals and among nations, as a measure of progress. Discretionary authorities, omniscient and benevolent, surely could in some sense do better than any scheme involving democratic, legislative rules and competitive dispersion of power. After any disturbing change they could promptly effect the same arrangements which competition would achieve slowly or with "unnecessary" oscillations. Indeed, they could probably avoid all real disturbances by anticipating them! But some of us dislike government by authorities, partly because we think they would not be wise and good and partly because we would still dislike it if they were.

The case for a libertarian system within advanced nations is, I think, very strong: competitive dispersion of power is preferable to syndicalist civil war and to collectivist power concentration. Even stronger is the case for libertarian trading among all the more democratic nations. If some nations or blocs might gain by governmental trading, it offers no promising basis for international organization—only prospect of organized rivalry, which would divide the democracies into mutually hostile camps and thus create disorder, insecurity, and aggression throughout the world.

The old monetary-commercial system, with all its faults, did involve a substantial measure of real international organization. This organization was implicit in subtle restraints or self-denying ordinances as to national foreign-trade practices. How substantial and precious it was became apparent only as it was lost during the thirties. The loss may be charged mainly to America. But a first step toward a good peace is the rebuilding of what was so recently destroyed, that is, restoring minimal standards of international decency in national commercial practices. We must, of course, go much further, not only with positive monetary collaboration but also in translating the formality of nondiscrimination into greater reality and substance—not to mention "level of treatment" and freer trade. But it is reckless to dismiss as unimportant the old formal equality of treatment—as it is to impugn "merely" formal equality of persons before the law.

Realistic policy will seek to recapture what little international organization we had achieved, as a step toward the much more that is requisite for peace. Formal equality, under a multitude of tariff rates frequently altered, may seem only nominally different from discriminating control—and, of course, might be more harmful all around. In fact, however, if not inherently less discriminatory and less restrictive (as I believe), it is less likely to induce hostile retaliation or cumulative counterrestriction. Moreover, while it may, as with us, involve awful legislative abuse and corruption, it is still legislative—another formal matter not to be lightly dismissed.

If what Balogh really means is that, as international traders in the thirties, European nations behaved as well as or better than the United States, let him have it so. He makes a strong case for bilateralism as a European reaction to our awful behavior—and for our talking softly about foreign evils in commercial policy. His prescriptions for the future, however, are made of recriminations about the past. There is no world order ahead on his policy road. That European bilateralism is defensible as a reaction to American deflation certainly does not commend either as an element in an international postwar program—and the same must, of course, be said of our bilateral foreign lending, that is, of "tied" loans.

Balogh's essay, properly construed, is an argument for Anglo-American co-operation in monetary-fiscal stabilization. The argument is a closely reasoned amalgam of Keynesian and classical economics and is perhaps meticulously correct. The conclusions, however, are extremist and belligerent, calling his adopted country, her friends, and all available recruits to economic organization against the United States. Their general tone may be indicated by two sections of his summary.

"Small and poor countries are likely to lose most from a restoration of the uncontrolled action of international market forces. The highly imperfect character of the international markets for manufactured goods, the high risk and the automatic acquisition of selling power in the lands of large economic areas will tend to stabilize their existent inferiority. Their internal investment, and hence their economic progress, would be restricted, and their employment policy imperilled . . . ." (*Oxford Studies*, p. 179).

"The advantages which a poorer country joining such a regional block would derive, in security of employment, high productivity and rapid economic progress through planned redistribution of industrial resources and skill, should secure the adherence of most countries, even against the blandishments of foreign loans from possibly adversely affected export surplus countries" (*ibid.*, p. 180).

Balogh and Beveridge would complete a destruction of international political-economic organization which the thirties began—perhaps because it is a kind of organization that requires American leadership or participation. This might be a proper penalty for our past sins. It might, as a long-odds venture, increase England's relative power and eventuate in a powerful sterling empire. It certainly is not compatible with much liberty within nations or with much peace among them. Moreover, it would leave us in much the kind of world that we American interventionists and Anglophiles portrayed as the likely outcome of irresponsible isolationism, that is, of a German victory.

The important criticisms of the Beveridge-Oxford program have to do with political philosophy more than with economics. A libertarian indictment of the program might run somewhat as follows: It largely ignores all the hard problems of "freedom versus organization"; it would single-mindedly pursue certain narrowly economic ends at frightful cost or risk in terms of other values; it contemplates a kind of national economy that precludes effective international organization or minimal solidarity among the Western democracies; it repudiates the democratic process of rule-making in favor of "democratic" empowering of authorities, that is, in favor of "plebicitary democracy"; it rejects democratic dispersion of power, decentralization and federalism in government, and the instrumental state, in favor of dominant central-government authority; it cuts away economic freedom as a bulwark of other liberties and makes an end of the modern separation of the economic and the political; trustful of government and authorities, it is distrustful of society and of responsibly free citizens; it would end the rule of law by the delegation of powers. Some such distortion or disordering of values is perhaps an inescapable consequence of the great depression and the war. The craving for proximate security, national and individual, has become a dangerous obsession—dangerous not only to other values but especially, if one sees beyond tomorrow, to security itself. Real security requires organization for progressive dispersion of power, within nations and among them. The planning of Beveridge and his colleagues offers only extreme national concentration —which at best can only impose peace within nations while precluding peace among them.

These two books afford eloquent testimony on one obvious point: there will be no good peace unless the United States boldly leads the way toward freer trade and monetary stability in the Western world.

BIBLIOGRAPHY[1]

"The Tax Exemption Question," *Journal of Business* (State University of Iowa), I, No. 4 (March, 1923), 9–12, 24.

Review: Harry Gunnison Brown, *The Economics of Taxation, Journal of Political Economy*, XXXIV, No. 1 (February, 1926), 134–36.

Review: Harrison B. Spaulding, *The Income Tax in Great Britain and the United States, Journal of Political Economy*, XXXVII, No. 3 (June, 1929), 373–75.

Review: James W. Angell, *The Recovery of Germany, Journal of Political Economy*, XXXIX, No. 2 (April, 1931), 263–66.

"Syllabus Materials for Economics 201." Chicago: University of Chicago Bookstore, 1933 and revised. Pp. 62. (Mimeographed.)

Review: T. E. Gregory, *The Gold Standard and Its Future, Journal of Political Economy*, XLI, No. 1 (February, 1933), 137.

"Inflation" (bibliographical note), *Book List*, April, 1933, pp. 221–24.

"Mercantilism as Liberalism," a review article on Charles A. Beard (ed.), *America Faces the Future, Journal of Political Economy*, XLI, No. 4 (August, 1933), 548–51.

"Banking and Currency Reform," "Banking and Business Cycles," and "Long-Time Objectives of Monetary Management." Three memoranda, November, 1933. (Mimeographed.)

A Positive Program for Laissez Faire: Some Proposals for a Liberal Economic Policy. "Public Policy Pamphlet," No. 15. Chicago: University of Chicago Press, 1934. Pp. iv+40.

"Currency Systems and Commercial Policy," a memorandum published in *International Economic Relations*, pp. 344–49. Minneapolis: University of Minnesota Press, 1934.

"The Commodity Dollar." A review of George F. Warren and Frank A. Pearson's *Prices, New Republic*, January 31, 1934, pp. 341–42.

"Money and the New Deal," a review of Leo Pasvolsky's *Current Monetary Issues, New Republic*, February 21, 1934, pp. 53–54.

"The Gold Cure," a review of Lionel Edie's *Dollars;* Edwin Walter Kemmerer's *Kemmerer on Money;* O. M. W. Sprague's *Recovery and Common Sense;* Eleanor Lansing Dulles's *The Dollar, the Franc and Inflation;* Willard E. Atkins' *Gold and Your Money;* and Francis W. Hirst's *Money, Gold, Silver and Paper, New Republic*, June 6, 1934, pp. 106–7.

Review: Sir Josiah Stamp, *Taxation during the War, Journal of Political Economy*, XLII, No. 5 (October, 1934), 716–17.

1. Essays marked with an asterisk (*) appear in this volume.

313

"Economic Reconstruction: The Columbia Report," a review article on *Economic Reconstruction: Report of the Columbia University Commission, Journal of Political Economy,* XLII, No. 6 (December, 1934), 795–99.

Review: Bhalchandra P. Adarkar, *The Principles and Problems of Federal Finance, Journal of Political Economy,* XLIII, No. 2 (April, 1935), 267–69.

Review: Lauchlin Currie, *The Supply and Control of Money in the United States, Journal of Political Economy,* XLIII, No. 4 (August, 1935), 555–58.

"The President's Inheritance Tax Policy," *Polity,* III, Nos. 7 and 8 (July and August, 1935), 124–27.

"Depression Economics," a review of Sir Charles Morgan-Webb's *The Money Depression;* Frederick Soddy's *The Role of Money;* and Anonymous, *Moneyless Government, Christian Century,* November 6, 1935, p. 1421.

*"Rules versus Authorities in Monetary Policy," *Journal of Political Economy,* XLIV, No. 1 (February, 1936), 1–30. Also published in Findlay MacKenzie (ed.), *Planned Society.* New York: Prentice-Hall, 1937.

*"The Requisites of Free Competition," *American Economic Review, Supplement,* XXVI, No. 1 (March, 1936), 68–76.

Review: John Maynard Keynes, *The General Theory of Employment, Interest and Money, Christian Century,* July 22, 1936, pp. 1016–17.

Review: C. O. Hardy, *Is There Enough Gold? Journal of Farm Economics,* XIX, No. 1 (February, 1937), 371–73.

Review: Committee on Taxation of the Twentieth Century Fund, Inc., *Facing the Tax Problem: A Survey of Taxation in the United States and a Program for the Future, Journal of Political Economy,* XLV, No. 4 (August, 1937), 532–35.

Review: Antonio de Viti de Marco, *First Principles of Public Finance,* and *Grundlehren der Finanzwirtschaft, Journal of Political Economy,* XLV, No. 5 (October, 1937), 712–17.

Personal Income Taxation: The Definition of Income as a Problem of Fiscal Policy. Chicago: University of Chicago Press, 1938. Pp. xi+238.

"Capital Gains," a discussion in the Conference on Research in National Income and Wealth, *Studies in Income and Wealth,* II, 255–59. New York: National Bureau of Economic Research, 1938.

Review: A. S. J. Baster, *The Twilight of American Capitalism, Journal of Political Economy,* XLVI, No. 5 (October, 1938), 728–29.

Review: Alvin Harvey Hansen, *Full Recovery or Stagnation? Journal of Political Economy,* XLVII, No. 2 (April, 1939), 272–76.

"Problems of Policy in Federal Taxation," *Law School Conferences on Public Law* (University of Chicago Law School), 1940, pp. 1–11.

"Incidence Theory and Fiscal Policy" (summary of discussion), *American Economic Review, Supplement,* XXX, Part II, No. 1 (March, 1940), 242–44.

*"For a Free-Market Liberalism," a review article on Thurman Arnold's

The Bottlenecks of Business, University of Chicago Law Review, VIII, No. 2 (February, 1941), 202–14.

Review: Gardner C. Means, D. E. Montgomery, J. M. Clark, Alvin H. Hansen, and Mordecai Ezekiel, *The Structure of the American Economy,* Part II: *Toward Full Use of Resources. A Symposium,* Review of Economic Statistics, XXIV, No. 1 (February, 1942), 44–47.

Review: Albert G. Hart and Edward D. Allen, in collaboration with nine other members of the Economics Staff of Iowa State College, *Paying for Defense,* Harvard Law Review, LV, No. 5 (March, 1942), 888–92.

*"Hansen on Fiscal Policy," a review article on Alvin H. Hansen's *Fiscal Policy and Business Cycles,* Journal of Political Economy, L, No. 2 (April, 1942), 161–96.

Review: Lewis Corey, *The Unfinished Task: Economic Reconstruction for Democracy,* American Economic Review, XXXII, No. 3, Part 1 (September, 1942), 616–21.

"Trade and the Peace," in Seymour Harris (ed.), *Postwar Economic Problems,* pp. 141–55. New York: McGraw-Hill Book Co., 1943.

*"Postwar Economic Policy: Some Traditional Liberal Proposals," *American Economic Review, Supplement,* XXXIII, No. 1 (March, 1943), 431–45.

Review: Roswell Magill, *The Impact of Federal Taxes,* University of Chicago Law Review, X, No. 4 (July, 1943), 502–4.

"Postwar Federal Tax Reform." Chicago, 1944. Pp. 140. (Mimeographed.)

*"Some Reflections on Syndicalism," *Journal of Political Economy,* LII, No. 1 (March, 1944), 1–25.

*"Economic Stability and Antitrust Policy," *University of Chicago Law Review,* XI, No. 4 (June, 1944), 338–48.

*"The U.S. Holds the Cards," *Fortune,* September, 1944, pp. 156–59, 196–200. [The original version of this essay was written in May, 1944, and appear as chapter xii in this volume.]

*"On Debt Policy," *Journal of Political Economy,* LII, No. 4 (December, 1944), 356–61.

*"A Political Credo" (not previously published).

"International Monetary and Credit Arrangements" (discussion), *American Economic Review,* XXXV, No. 2 (May, 1945), 294–96.

"Should the Capital-Gains Tax Be Repealed?" *Modern Industry,* August 15, 1945, pp. 117–30.

*"The Beveridge Program: An Unsympathetic Interpretation," a review article on William H. Beveridge, *Full Employment in a Free Society,* and *The Economics of Full Employment: Six Studies Prepared at the Oxford Institute of Statistics,* Journal of Political Economy, LIII, No. 3 (September, 1945), 212–33.

Review: Benjamin Graham, *World Commodities and World Currency,* Journal of Political Economy, LIII, No. 3 (September, 1945), 279–81.

Review: William Diamond, *The Economic Thought of Woodrow Wilson, Journal of Political Economy*, LIII, No. 4 (December, 1945), 365–67.

"Federal Tax Reform," *International Postwar Problems*, III, No. 1 (January, 1946), 19–30.

*"Debt Policy and Banking Policy," *Review of Economic Statistics*, XXVIII, No. 2 (May, 1946), 85–9.

"Income Tax," *Encyclopaedia Britannica* (1946), XII, 135–36.

"Federal Tax Reform," *University of Chicago Law Review*, XIV, No. 1 (December, 1946), 20–65. [Extracts from an unpublished manuscript on "Postwar Federal Tax Reform."]

NOTES

NOTES TO CHAPTER I

1. This, of course, is a minimal prescription; redistribution afterward presents hard tasks of devising measures that will mitigate inequality without inordinately adverse effects, especially on production; and the best means must be applied with caution and restraint.

2. There is, to repeat, a problem of avoiding inordinate and consolidated concentration of property among families; but it is relatively trivial and, with almost every revenue act, becomes more so.

3. Besides, bad local government is largely a phenomenon of the great, high-density metropolis and thus an argument against centralization. The giant metropolis is itself centralization gone mad; it has no place in the good society and is largely a heritage of policy errors, e.g., in freight classification.

4. There is, to be sure, too much very small government—and too much very small business enterprise. In both respects there is too much bigness, too much smallness, and a dearth of moderate-sized units. Moreover, there are surely special kinds of centralization which will more than repay their costs, e.g., in research, in formulating standards, in "policing" very bad communities (like criminals or temporary defectives), and in revenue collection, provided centrally imposed taxes can be shared without much control of local expenditure. To condemn all centralization is to condemn organization and order—which makes no sense. The problem is not one of avoiding centralization but of economizing it and discriminating wisely among kinds. Centralization paradoxically is a necessary means of decentralization, just as concentration of power is a means to its dispersion.

5. Some will regard freedom of migration as an essential feature of a federation. Surely it will usually be desirable, but it should not be regarded as co-ordinate with free trade or as indispensable to strong supranational federation.

6. The corruption of American democracy in its pension legislation and rivers-and-harbors appropriations is notorious. Such things, along with silver legislation, however, are trivial by comparison with tariff subsidies, in terms either of the dollar amounts involved or of the moral perversion of representative government. As with municipal "machines," the small corruption we smell and recognize as such is less alarming than is our incapacity to smell the malodors of gross departure from the rule of law or our complacency about such departures. The future may see radical reduction in tariff subsidies. It may also witness a new flowering of old evils in vast federal programs of public works. What principle has been suggested for allocating such grand dispensations, save that of proximate political expediency, i.e., of concentrating them in areas which promise to be marginal at the next presidential election? Public works, financed responsibly within the "bene-

317

fit area" (possibly very large), are one thing; federal public works are another.

7. Which implies freedom *from* overlarge organizations either of firms or of workers.

8. Liberals, however, must quit arguing, carelessly and hysterically, that centralization or socialization is inherently a one-way process; such argument is rhetorical suicide, if not apostasy. Like it or not, there will be many such experiments. It is for the collectivist to deny that they are experimental and may commonly be temporary or transitional.

We shall always be getting into messes, in both government and private industry; and central-government control will often seem, and frequently be, the best available expedient. Indeed, it may offer the only promising route back to satisfactory organization under decentralized government or competitive-voluntary associations. Such doubtless is now the situation in several nations of Europe and, to a lesser extent, in England. It well may be the case in our own aluminum industry. But alienation is at least as easy as socialization and is likely to come about either from very bad or, as already suggested, from very good governmental operation.

Much federal initiative and control in highway construction was desirable in its time; it has perhaps served its purpose and soon may largely be abandoned. Our metropolitan governments possibly should now acquire much or most of the land in their areas, if only to alienate it again with proper control of its private use. Perhaps our federal government should now undertake major housing projects, if it can thereby break the way to modern, efficient construction and eliminate the cost-increasing impositions of trade-unions and "protectionist" building codes. Urgent welfare activities, e.g., in public health and mass medical service, may require at the start an extreme federal centralization that may rapidly be cut away after the activities are established and their main problems solved.

There will be and should be no arrest or reversal of centralization on all fronts. In the possible good future, power and responsibility will be both concentrated and dispersed simultaneously in different areas of governmental (and of private-corporate) activity—and in the same area at different times. Liberals cannot wisely or hopefully oppose all "socialistic" experimentation; they should not fear its possible successes. They may urge that it proceed continuously in both directions and with deliberate economy of both concentration and delegation of power. In the long view (which libertarians must calmly stress) there is no obvious bias in such experimentation, save that arising from war and international disorganization. Libertarian prophecies of impending doom, save from global war, are as romantic as adolescent-radical notions of how all social problems can be solved. The development of political-economic institutions, if not altogether like that of language, is not altogether different either. Hysteria is unbecoming to liberals; they must have faith in social process and in the durability of liberty; for their kind of society simply cannot be promoted by revolutions or by counterrevolutions. A liberal screams (or despairs) only as an apostate.

9. Subject, of course, to taxation which, if reasonably stable, may be

highly progressive and effectively restrictive as to inequality. To design highly progressive taxes that will not involve serious social diseconomies is not a simple matter; but it can be done, though it certainly has not been well done by any legislature to date.

10. And, probably more important, differential protection against infringement litigation. The extreme vulnerability of small firms to such litigation and the great advantages of combination and vast size on this score suggest perhaps the most serious indictment of our patent law.

11. Even the latter kind of fighting probably costs the public far more than it costs the participants, who, indeed, may commonly gain more from stoppages than they lose.

NOTES TO CHAPTER II

1. The reference here, of course, is merely to that kind of planning which, like mercantilism, implies elaborate regulation of trade, both foreign and domestic, and extensive political control of relative prices, relative wages, and investment.

2. It is, perhaps, easy, from this general viewpoint, to see both advantages and serious practical difficulties in the development of labor organization along industrial, as against occupational, lines.

3. For the disillusioned economist-liberal, a certain bitter satisfaction may be found in the spectacle of capitalism, and the whole institution of property, collapsing under the feet of distinguished propertied gentlemen addressing their brethren on the remarkable virtues of the sales tax.

4. The essential practice of modern banking is that of maintaining obligations payable on demand, or on short notice, while holding "cash" amounting to only *a small fraction* of those obligations.

5. It will be necessary to revise notions commonly accepted (especially by courts) as to the maximum size of firm compatible with effective competition. The general rule and ultimate objective should be that of fixing in each industry a maximum size of firm such that the results of perfect competition would be approximated even if all firms attained the maximum size. One may suggest, tentatively, that in major industries no ownership unit should produce or control more than 5 per cent of the total output. Any such rule, of course, raises the difficult question of what is "a commodity"—of how industries or significant classes of commodities should be defined. A period of several years should be allowed for orderly readjustment, the full restrictions coming into effect only gradually. Special arrangements would be necessary, of course, in the case of new industries and new products.

6. It should be clear that *the measures here proposed have no affinity whatever with schemes for socialization or nationalization of banking.* Indeed, they contemplate a financial system under which there would be the least danger and the least occasion for government control over the lending function, i.e., over the allocation of investment funds. One of the great faults of the present banking system is that it is peculiarly exposed to socialization, merely because of its instability. If we could isolate the lending and investment business from

deposit banking, we might eliminate a real danger of government control or socialization in an area where it is most important to avoid it.

7. Any treatment of the problem of monetary and banking reform, within space limits appropriate to this tract, must suffer from serious omissions and oversimplification. Correction of these faults would require extended discussion of the following considerations, among others:

a) There is likely to be extreme economic instability under any financial system where *the same funds* are made to serve at once *as investment funds for industry and trade* and *as the liquid cash reserves of individuals*. Our financial structure has been built largely on the illusion that funds can at the same time be both available and invested—and this observation applies to our savings banks (and in lesser degree to many other financial institutions) as well as commercial, demand-deposit banking. Thus, any reform which dealt merely with demand deposits and checking accounts might largely fail to accomplish the results intended—might lead, indeed, to a merely nominal transformation of demand deposits into the savings account form.

b) A major source of instability is also to be found in the widespread practice of borrowing at short term. Most of the capital requirements which are met by such borrowing are of a permanent, continuing character. Indeed, under modern conditions there are few types of enterprise where funds, once invested, are or can be promptly disinvested again, in the ordinary course of business. The existence of a large volume of short-term commercial debt is thus peculiarly inimical to stability, since any general demand for repayment forces industry into an effort at liquidation which cannot succeed and cannot fail to produce serious disorder. Short-term debts, moreover, are, like time deposits, closely akin to money and demand deposits, since they provide in normal times an attractive and effective substitute medium in which the liquid "cash" reserves of individuals may be held.

In the interest of economic stability it would be desirable to bring about conversion of all investment (property) into the residual-equity form. A large volume of contractual obligations, with maturities, is inherently dangerous in an economy where orderly liquidation on a large scale is simply impossible. But the problem of long-term debt is less serious. Adequate reform of our monetary and financial system does call, however, for the sharpest separation between money and money substitutes, on the one hand, and investments, on the other—between debts which are regarded as convertible into money by demand upon the debtor (or by refusal of renewal), and debts which may be realized upon only by sale to third parties. It is the role of banking, and of the Federal Reserve System especially, to obscure this distinction.

c) Effective administration, through a monetary authority, of any sound rule of monetary policy would be impossible apart from the closest cooperation, on the part of the Treasury and Congress, with respect to fiscal practices. Ultimate control of the currency (and the banks) lies in the management of government expenditure, taxation, and borrowing; and the establishment of a separate monetary authority implies a division of powers which would be workable only with thoroughgoing co-ordination and co-operation. Every change in the relation between taxation and expenditure, in either the amount or the form of the public debt, and even in the character of tax levies, has monetary effects of first magnitude. Thus, specifications for sound monetary and banking reform cannot be drawn without reformulation of the whole problem of government finance. Monetary policy must ultimately be implemented through fiscal arrangements.

8. Some students would justify the reduction of inequality on the ground that it is essential to the political stability of the system; others, on the ground that it is important for the reduction of unemployment and for the mitigation of industrial fluctuations. The former position, while tenable, involves an unhappy confusion of means and ends. The latter, in my opinion, is open to the same objection and also to the characterization of completely spurious economics. Moreover, the methods proposed by exponents of this now widely accepted position (widespread unionization, reduction of hours, and increase of wage rates *in a depression*) are the immediate occasion for the assertion that progressive taxation is the only effective means for improving the distribution of income.

9. Considerations of equity clearly demand provision for further rebates in the more extreme cases, especially where persons pay large income taxes and later lose practically all their income and property.

10. The adoption of this proposal (*loc. cit.*, p. 66) should be accompanied by appropriate changes in the now inadequate and anomalous provisions regarding transfers of property by gift. Every transfer of property should be treated as a "realization" by the former owner; where property is given away, such transfer should be made the occasion for calculation of taxable gain or loss to the donor (as to the decedent's estate) for purposes of income tax. When property acquired by gift is disposed of by the donee, his gain or loss should be calculated on the basis of value at the time of acquisition.

Suppose that Jones, in 1935, buys 100 shares of common stock at $100 per share; that he transfers these 100 shares by gift to a relative named Smith in 1940, at which time the market price of the stock is $200; and that, in 1942, Smith sells the 100 shares at a price of $150. Now, under the arrangements here proposed, these transfers would give rise to the following reportings for personal income tax: by Jones, in 1940, a gain of $10,000 (value of stock when disposed of by gift *minus* original cost); by Smith, in 1940, $20,000 as income obtained by gift (see proposal 2, p. 67); and by Smith, in 1942, a loss of $5,000 (value of stock when received by gift *minus* amount realized from sale).

Under an income tax which employs the "realization criterion," property should never be allowed to pass out of the possession of an individual without a final reconciliation—without a final calculation of gain or loss to him (or to his estate). However, since the practical problem is that of preventing wholesale and deliberate tax avoidance, a good case can be made, on grounds of administrative simplification, for not allowing deduction of "paper losses" on property disposed of by gift, even though the corresponding "paper profits" are included in taxable income.

It should be noted that the adoption of the measures here proposed, regarding transfers of property by gift, inheritance, and bequest, would solve rather completely the problem of undistributed corporate earnings as a problem of personal income taxation—and would eliminate the need for the kind of measures suggested in the text (p. 66, last paragraph).

11. It is worth noting that the recent sharp reduction in the gold value of the dollar is likely to create the ideal conditions for (and, internationally, the necessity of) gradual, continued tariff reduction—and, thereby, for raising the prices of export products, notably cotton and wheat, *relative* to other prices.

12. The recent phenomenal rise in building costs, with almost no building going on at all, is a case in point.

13. There remains one point which has not been properly emphasized, namely, that genuinely liberal reform must aim primarily at explicit changes in the rules of the economic game and must minimize reliance on control or regulation through nominally administrative bodies with large discretionary, policy-determining powers. The point has already been noted with respect to monetary and banking reform; but it is of decisive importance in many other fields. There is now profound significance in the distinction between a government of men and a government of rules; and, to the extent that we move toward the former, we are accepting or inviting fascism. One high-road to dictatorship lies in the creation of a large number of petty, specialized authorities in particular fields. For an old-fashioned liberal it is terrifying to reflect on the amount of arbitrary power which has recently been delegated to the President, the Secretary of the Treasury, the N.R.A., the A.A.A., the R.F.C., the S.E.C., etc. However reasonable this expedient in an acute emergency, we must face the fact that emergency measures are unlikely to prove entirely temporary and also the fact that we were making substantial strides in this direction long before the emergency arose.

A substantial measure of administrative discretion is obviously essential to good government, but it must be economized. If large latitude must often be allowed in the administration of new reform measures, we should seek afterward to reduce the powers of the administrative authorities as rapidly as experience provides the basis for more definitive legislative rules.

NOTES TO CHAPTER IV

1. *The Bottlenecks of Business.* By Thurman Arnold. New York: Reynal & Hitchcock, 1940. Pp. ix+335. $2.50.

2. *Schechter* v. *United States,* 295 U.S. 495 (1935).

3. *The Symbols of Government* (1935); *The Folklore of Capitalism* (1937).

4. It may forestall misunderstanding to explain that I intend here no reference to theological truth or to "first principles" derived from God, popes, or formal logic.

5. This is not the place to spell out details of my own tentative schemes for such reform. Indeed, I must confess that my thinking along these lines has not advanced much since I made some rash proposals a few years ago in a "Public Policy Pamphlet," *A Positive Program for Laissez Faire: Some Proposals*

for a Liberal Economic Policy (1934) [chap. ii of this collection]. I am certain
that any competent specialist following the same general ideas, could formulate better concrete suggestions; I wish that some of them would make
the effort.

NOTES TO CHAPTER VI

1. The manuscript of this article was prepared in 1941. It was designed,
not for publication, but as an exercise in formulating privately some persuasions or prejudices which kept creeping into discussions of other subjects
or problems. Later, several friends looked at the manuscript. Some of them,
though not all, questioned the presumption against publication. So the
matter was referred to the editors. After they decided to publish, one insert
and a few footnotes were added to the original draft.

2. Quoted in A. C. Pigou, *Economics in Practice* (London, 1935), pp. 10–11.

3. An essential difference between federal and local corruption (aside
from orders of magnitude, in which state and local bodies are simply out of
the running) is that the latter generally stinks, while the former is generally
practiced by seemingly honest people and effected in impeccably legal ways.
The kind that stinks has, on balance, much to commend it relatively to
democrats.

4. Several economist-publicists have recently proposed an antimonopoly
program based merely on adult education and exhortation. Tycoons, it
seems, need only be made to see the monopoly advantages of lower prices
and larger volume (i.e., the "error" of orthodox marginal analysis). Labor
leaders need only be taught to regard themselves as merchandisers or
marketers of labor. On my view, everything depends on whether the pupils
are monopolists or not. If not, they may usefully be instructed in the arts of
marketing things competitively. Among monopolists, however, economic
illiteracy should be carefully fostered and conserved. Any larger understanding of how best to exercise or to argument their powers would be a national and international calamity. And I wholly distrust a scheme for misleading them (and everyone else) by wholesale dissemination of ingenuous
economic fallacies and upside-down price theories.

5. It has seemed best in this essay simply to recognize that unions perform many useful functions and render many valuable services besides those
having to do with wage rates, labor costs, restrictive practices, and monopoly
or bargaining power—without attempting to detail or to appraise the
salutary activities or aspects of activities. This deliberate omission implies no
inclination to question or to minimize the good things of unionism, but merely a disposition to emphasize considerations and aspects which are the proper
and special business of economists as such. To stress those things which are
especially amenable to quantitative or abstract analysis is not to imply that
others are unimportant.

Two other apologies may also be offered. First, any passing appraisal of
the things here neglected would be inadequate and would imply claims to a
hearing in areas of inquiry where the claims could not be sustained. Second,
I wish to avoid the cheap rhetoric of weaselers who "believe in collective

bargaining *but*. . . . ." This category runs all the way from "but really don't, save as among employers" to "but not in the closed shop." The latter "but" calls for comment. To my mind, it almost says that strong unions should not be shorn of any power but that weak ones should be slowed down in acquiring power. The closed shop, like overt violence, is an invaluable device for acquiring power and yet, as an explicit privilege or contract provision, is of almost no importance for the exercise of power once acquired and strongly held. The notion that labor monopolies can be frustrated or mitigated merely by forbidding the closed shop is, I submit, almost wholly ingenuous and mistaken.

I wish I could honestly and tactfully propose that large unions be protected and fostered in their good functions and deprived of their socially bad ones (monopoly power). Like others, I can *wish* for this solution, but, also like others, I cannot honestly propose it, for I have no notion *how* it could be done. Politicians may go on advocating schemes defined merely in terms of everyone's ends, without any reference to means or implementation —and fearlessly opposing sin in general. Professors, after a prodigious spree, should now eschew such rhetorical intoxicants and go back to work. However, it is perhaps not merely wishful to suggest that many of the good festures of unionism *could* be preserved, and monopoly powers perhaps kept within reason, by limiting the size of unions and proscribing collusion among them. Having said this, one must pause for riotous heckling about "company unions" and then try calmly to assert that the case against company unions is strongest when asserted only against bad ones and, like the case against means tests, is not impressive when stated categorically or when supported only by bad (i.e., historical) evidence.

6. It is difficult to focus attention upon the potentially greater problem of labor monopoly without seeming to underestimate the corresponding and complementary problem of enterprise monopoly. My best defense against this charge may be found elsewhere, e.g., in "Postwar Economic Policy: Some Traditional-Liberal Proposals," *American Economic Review, Supplement,* March, 1943, pp. 431–45 [chap. xi of this collection].

7. One finds here a source of both economies and diseconomies in large as against small firms. The former can afford more elaborate methods of selecting and grading, while the latter can tolerate wider quality dispersion and more differentiation in remuneration. Smallness has much to commend it socially, since it promises better utilization of exceptionally good workers and employment rather than unemployment for substandard workers.

8. This persuasion will explain my diffidence about problems of labor monopsony, i.e., about the one or only argument from pure economic theory which condones labor monopolies. There are, I believe, no important cases in fact where employers face, and act in terms of, wide discrepancy between average cost (wage) and marginal cost of labor. In any event, such phenomena are short-run and short-lived; and the remedies proposed (save those suggested below, n. 11) are worse than the affliction. Moreover, the usual rational analysis in terms of short-run marginal costs of monopsonists, like corresponding analysis in terms of marginal revenues under monopolistic

competition, is fundamentally irrational; no sane enterpriser would ever behave in accordance with the Robinson-Chamberlin prescriptions for maximizing profits—and, on their premises, would lose his shirt if he did.

Incidentally, I am wholly intolerant of the apology usually made, for labor monopolies and for almost every particular racket, that "everyone is doing it." A prominent educator is alleged recently to have said, also by way of apology: "There is no *public* interest any more; there are only *interests*." If such statements are true, moral, or realistic, we should all make careers in the army and assert that military dictatorship is the only feasible foreign policy and the only means to internal peace or prosperity! Another implication is that nothing should be done about anything until everything has been done about everything else.

9. There is, I presume, little question that strong unions do commonly deliver really high-quality labor.

10. Given genuine solicitude about small businesses (and mainly misguided proposals for financing them), repeal of the Walsh-Healy Act merits consideration.

11. Perhaps the best investment by government in better labor standards is improvement of labor exchanges and public employment agencies, facilitation of labor mobility and migration, and systematic informing of enterprisers about areas of labor redundancy, actual and prospective. Labor markets can and should be made more competitive as among firms, industries, and localities and more flexible, as well as less monopolistic, on the supply side. All this is proper and urgent public business.

12. One may recognize the possibility that, with wide or universal organization of workers, federations of unions might enforce some moderation of wage demands and of exclusive, restrictive practices among the labor aristocracies. Such internal discipline among and between unions is a real contingency in small, homogeneous nations like Sweden (especially if complemented by a strong free-trade tradition). In a vast nation or a culturally heterogeneous population, the possibility may be dismissed as utterly unsubstantial. Moreover, the development of such effective "regulation" would involve radical constitutional change in the political system, i.e., reduction of the Congress or national legislature to a status not unlike that of the British crown.

It is interesting to note that Swedish co-operatives have at times discharged functions of our Antitrust Division—which is not a decisive reason for abolishing that agency here!

13. Dr. Gerhard Meyer reminds me that all this is admirably stated in Dicey, *Law and Opinion in England* (2d ed.), esp. pp. 150 ff., 190 ff., and 467 ff. Dicey in turn reminds me that perhaps everything I have tried to say was better said by Bentham and the Benthamites.

NOTES TO CHAPTER VII

1. These views have been presented more fully by the writer in a tract entitled *A Positive Program for Laissez Faire: Some Proposals for a Liberal Eco-*

nomic Policy ("Public Policy Pamphlet," No. 15 [Chicago: University of Chicago Press, 1934]) [chap. ii of this collection].

2. See mimeographed memorandum on "Banking and Currency Reform" (with Supplement and Appendix), prepared and circulated by several Chicago economists in November, 1933. See also the pamphlet mentioned above, n. 1.

3. The two features of the scheme are clearly separable, each calling for appraisal on its merits. The banking proposals might be adopted along with many different monetary arrangements, including the international gold standard.

4. All reform proposals which depend on or imply a categorical distinction between circulating media (say, demand deposits) and noncirculating near-moneys (time deposits, savings accounts, treasury bills, commercial paper of large corporations) are exposed to serious criticism on that account. Moreover, those who argue that the 100 per cent reserve system need not be a seriously disturbing innovation, because of the opportunities for expansion of savings-deposit banking, are in effect proposing that we undertake radical institutional changes for utterly trivial gains. Indeed, they are really arguing for drastic reform on the grounds that its intended effects would never be realized.

5. If one finds this question unclear and the following discussion confusing for lack of definite assumptions regarding currency, one may assume, for the moment, any monetary system which does not provide for the deliberate offsetting of velocity changes by wholesale changes of quantity. The intention, however, is to focus attention on monetary factors outside the central field of currency and to inquire as to the conditions in the field of private finance which would be most (and least) conducive to stability under any particular set of rules as to the currency.

6. It might be argued that the emphasis here is misplaced and that what may be called "voluntary liquidation" is quantitatively more important than liquidation forced by creditors. Undoubtedly, there have been enormous accumulations of cash and near-moneys, and wholesale reductions of debts which might easily have been renewed or refunded, by firms which could anticipate no threat of bankruptcy in the significant future. Whatever the facts, however, the observation is hardly in point, as the following comments may indicate:

a) We are concerned in this paper with monetary factors—with the financial structure as a source of aggravation in booms and depressions. Voluntary liquidation (as evidenced by voluntary reduction of debts and by the augmenting of reserves of cash and near-moneys) must be regarded, on the other hand, as induced essentially by relative-price maladjustments, i.e., as attributable to monopoly and other sources of price rigidity. The distinction between monetary and nonmonetary factors seems indispensable analytically; and, from the viewpoint of practical policy, it is certainly useful to separate the factors which have to do with currency, banking, fiscal practice, and business finance from those which have to do with industrial monopoly, the labor market, and public regulation of utility charges. To suggest that monetary factors be conceived and defined very broadly, as relating to other phases of private finance as well as to banking, is not to question the importance of nonmonetary factors.

b) Given monopoly and limited flexibility of prices, the efforts of even a small percentage of firms to meet unrenewable and unrefundable obligations of early maturity, or to guard against prospective difficulties, may create or greatly aggravate the maladjustments which dictate liquidation (suspension of investment, hoarding) by firms whose debts represent no threat whatever to continued solvency. It may be appropriate to ask how much voluntary liquidation has been "caused" by involuntary liquidation elsewhere, whatever the difficulties of answering the question quantitatively.

7. Even with such a simple financial structure, decentralization of security markets would be further conducive to stability. The concentration of security trading in a few large centers greatly facilitates hysterical mob movements of bullishness and bearishness; and it is dangerous, indeed, to have such sensitive and conspicuous barometers of speculative temper in a system where they easily create the conditions which they predict. The maintenance of ready markets (liquidity) for investment assets is possible only with great risks and costs; we have probably gone much too far in facilitating gambling in property rights and in fostering the dangerous illusion of general liquidity of investments.

8. To some critics it may seem a mistake to emphasize the possibilities of depression aggravation from bond maturities without mentioning the possible aggravation of booms through new issues. Here, however, an appearance of elegant symmetry would conceal a real distortion. Obligations of distant maturity (as already implied) are subject to substantial changes of selling prices, even apart from changing prospects of their discharge. At the time of issue, bonds are little nearer to money, and hardly more acceptable as media for use in hoards, than are other property rights generally. They come close to the money category, or become significant as money substitutes, only as they approach maturity—i.e., only as they become short-term debts. (These distinctions obviously relate merely to differences of degree along a continuous scale, as is inevitable with reference to any realistic and useful conception of money and money functions.) At all events, the possible inflationary effect of bond flotation is simply not of the same order of magnitude as the possible deflationary effect of their retirement. The issue of long-term bonds during a boom is unlikely, in itself, to alter much the velocity of circulating media; but the discharge of such obligations in a depression may induce the former holders to increase their cash reserves by something like the amount of the funds so received, i.e., to hoard on a scale which otherwise would have been difficult or impossible. Bond issues might be concentrated heavily in periods of speculative optimism, and they might be absorbed largely by inflationary dishoarding; but the form of issue (whether of bonds or stocks or partnership equities) could hardly be regarded as an important independent factor.

Under the existing financial organization, of course, bond flotations of large magnitude are likely to be coincident with general credit expansion and dishoarding; and thus, whatever the qualitative control of banking and whatever the actual content of bank portfolios, the increase of deposit currency will serve to absorb such issues. Moreover, a merely empirical study of industrial fluctuations (especially of the so-called "long cycles") may easily lead to unfortunate inferences as to causation or (evading a slippery conception) to gross underestimate of the importance of banking and of the results attainable by reform in that area.

9. If banks were to confine their investments to long-term obligations, several benefits would accrue. Business would be less exposed to paralyzing withdrawals of working capital; and the banks would largely lose the power, dangerous to themselves as well as to the community, of precipitating chaotic liquidation. Bankers, freed from the illusion of liquidity, would have to face more squarely the necessity of meeting demands for cash by transferring (selling) their investments; thus, their own judgment, if not the demands of depositors, would probably lead them to maintain more nearly appropriate cushions of stockholder equities. There might be significant gains, moreover, in better allocation of investment funds, for investment in long-term securities would probably mean more fundamental and more thorough analysis of the debtor enterprises. Certainly there are disadvantages in a system under which large volumes of funds are allocated primarily with respect to the borrower's immediate outlook and the opportunities for liquidation ahead of other creditors.

Of course, there would also be some disadvantages for the banks. Thorough analysis of prospective investments would be expensive. Moreover, short-term paper has one attractive feature, namely, that one can seldom be expected to tell what it is worth. Thus owners, depositors, and examiners are frequently spared for considerable periods the awareness that banks are insolvent—usually, indeed, until that distressing condition has passed. With portfolios of securities, on the other hand, the magnitude of stockholder equities would be seriously exposed to the bitter test of prices on the security exchanges.

It seems, at all events, that desirable changes in the content of bank portfolios might be defined roughly in terms of transfer from earlier to later kinds of assets in the following list: (1) short-term commercial paper; (2) long-term private obligations; (3) federal securities; (4) legal-tender currency.

10. This is not the place to argue the matter in any detail. See the writer's memorandum to the Commission of Inquiry into National Policy in International Economic Relations (Hutchins Commission), published in its report, *International Economic Relations* (Minneapolis: University of Minnesota Press, 1934), pp. 344–49.

It may be noted that the gold-standard arrangement simply does not define a monetary system based on rules in any sense consistent with our usage in this paper. It defines a policy merely in terms of its end or objective, and not in terms of means—not in terms of rules of operation. To be sure, such rules might be established. To illustrate, Congress might establish a monetary authority with large powers and with a definite mandate (1) to buy and sell gold freely at a fixed price and (2) to maintain a fixed, constant proportion between the amount of its gold holdings and the total amount of money (including demand deposits) in circulation. It is doubtful whether much enthusiastic or intelligent support could be recruited for such a scheme—or for any other which would establish real rules for the operation of the gold-standard system.

11. The choice of a particular price index, as the basis of a definitive rule of policy, presents serious difficulties. If monetary uncertainties are to be minimized and the monetary authority limited to a strictly administrative function, the commodities whose prices are included in the index must be (1) commodities which can (with a minimum of difficulty) be sharply defined in terms of physical specifications and (2) commodities which (as so defined) are and probably will continue to be actively traded in highly organized and highly competitive markets. The index must be highly sensitive; otherwise, the administrative authority would be compelled to postpone its actions unduly after significant disturbances or (Heaven forbid!)obliged to use discretion in anticipating changes. All prices subject to deliberate regulation, whether by producers or by governmental agencies, obviously should be excluded—and all prices which are likely to fall into this class in the significant future!

If a reasonably inclusive, representative index could be designed in accordance with these specifications, it would still be very unsatisfactory. Such an index, governed predominantly by the prices of standardized, basic commodities, would give us an excessively "inflationary" rule, for the production of these commodities is likely to be affected most markedly by the progress of technical efficiency; with such an index we should depart far indeed from the ideal of a neutral money. Moreover, an index of this kind would be peculiarly sensitive to changes and disturbances originating abroad; thus, it might often dictate monetary measures which would be undesirable and merely disturbing domestically. It would seem best to employ an index made up primarily of prices of "domestic," rather than of internationally traded, goods; but it would probably not be possible to construct an index of this kind which would be at all satisfactory in terms of the other considerations which we have noted.

The writer's notion as to how these conflicting considerations should be weighed, for a judicious, practical decision, may be inferred roughly from the order in which they are mentioned above.

12. The literature of money, however, seems on the whole greatly to overstress this consideration and to minimize the prospects of automatic adjustment through anticipations, under a definite and stable monetary constitution. This may be the result of the widespread practice of discussing the question of what monetary policy should be, in terms of an implied assumption that knowledge of that policy is to be the exclusive possession of an inscrutable monetary authority. The outcome, at all events, is a critical appraisal of possible rules of policy which relates mainly to difficulties of the transition period rather than to the operation of these rules as established bases of anticipations.

This criticism is conspicuously applicable to the usual discussions of "justice" as between debtors and creditors. It is clear that, given a minimum of uncertainty as to money, differences in the monetary rules would tend to be compensated by differences in interest yields. The same point is relevant, moreover, if less obvious and decisive, with respect to "forced saving" and induced maladjustments generally. If the monetary constitution called for a rising, instead of a stable or a declining, price level, economic behavior would be modified considerably in every sphere—in the labor market, among employers and labor leaders as well; in the determination of the "administered" prices, by both public and private agencies; and, of course, in the money markets.

Generally speaking, it is very difficult to judge the merits of any precise rule of monetary policy on the basis of experience in an economy where no such rule has obtained and where economic behavior has been profoundly influenced by the extreme monetary uncertainty. (The common criticism of price-level stabilization, on the basis of our experience during—and after—the twenties, is thus without much force.) The primary objective of reform should be that of minimizing this kind of uncertainty for the future. From the point of view of ultimate operation, it seems likely that many different rules would serve about equally well. Thus, it is appropriate to focus attention on the difficulties of transition—explicitly.

13. The alternative position would hold that sheer temporizing is less dangerous than definite commitment to any precise, inflexible monetary rule. Given stabilization of a price index, organized groups might establish the "administered" prices and wage rates at a level which would prohibit tolerable functioning of the economy as a whole. To guard against this contingency, the monetary authority might be set up as a kind of agency of monopoly control, with an implied policy of countering every general increase of monopoly prices and wages with deliberate inflation of the whole price level.

Such therapy would alleviate the patient's distress by eliminating possibility of his recovery. We cannot long preserve existing political and economic institutions by countering the infection of monopoly with the opiates of monetary dictators. The uncertainties of business as to, notably, wage rates and freight rates may be as serious as those relating to money; but it would seem sheer folly deliberately to create monetary uncertainties in the hope of salutary counteraction or offsetting effects. Especially alarming, along these lines, is the possibility of a long-continued struggle between the monetary authority, raising the price level to diminish unemployment, and labor organizations seeking, with able assistance from the Department of Labor, to advance wage rates ahead of price-level changes—and even, avowedly, to assist the monetary authority by increasing purchasing power! At all events, under such a monetary scheme, the controlled parts of the price structure would probably be manipulated in such manner as to require an indefinite, revolution-creating inflation; indeed, this seems to define the real threat of fascism in this country and the likely route toward it. If monopoly proves fatal to capitalism, inflation will be the announced cause of death.

14. As evidence of the grave moral dangers of present policies, one need

mention only two superlative contributions of our legislature and executive to the degradation of representative government: the silver legislation and the Guffey-Snyder Bill.

15. These other grounds, of course, have to do mainly with the monopoly problem. For the writer's views, see the pamphlet mentioned in n. 1.

16. That the fixed-quantity policy would go too far in this direction, however, is a contention to conjure with. Speculative movements with respect to money will always be somewhat cumulative and self-aggravating, even given the most drastic reforms in the field of private finance. Thus, conceding the merits of long-run fixity in the quantity of money, one may argue that provision should be made for temporary changes to offset changes in velocity. But this view, however commendable in principle, has not been, and probably cannot be, translated into significant practical proposals. The difficulties of drafting satisfactory rules based on elaborate statistical measures of velocity seem decisive. On the other hand, if one wants a system based on rule, it would be folly to enact legislation calling for secular constancy in the quantity of money but leaving the administrative authority free to make "temporary" changes at its own discretion.

These considerations emphasize one great advantage of a price-index rule, namely, that it defines, within a definite long-term rule, appropriate measures for dealing with velocity changes. However, it is possible that, with a more flexible price structure and a narrowly limited amount of short-term financing, the anchor of a fixed quantity of circulating media might suffice to induce prompt reversal of hoarding and dishoarding movements. And moderate cyclical fluctuations might wisely be accepted as the price paid for the conspicuous superiority of the fixed-quantity rule in terms of other considerations. Substantial sacrifice might well be made to obtain greater simplicity and definiteness; to avoid the inherent limitations of index numbers, especially as elements in permanent legislation; to escape the continuing disturbance of positive monetary action; and to dispense with powerful administrative authorities. On the other hand, the price-index rule is eminently preferable for the immediate future—and certainly will remain the more expedient solution unless and until a highly competitive economy is realized and the structure of private money contracts drastically modified.

17. The so-called "100 per cent" scheme of banking reform can easily be defended only as the proper first step toward reconstruction of our whole financial organization. Standing by itself, as an isolated measure, it would promise little but evasion—small effects at the price of serious disturbance—and would deserve classification as merely another crank scheme.

18. Indeed, the time seems fully ripe for a declaration by Congress and the Administration against further increase in the American price level. This does not imply that early and rapid recovery is now assured or that the federal budget should promptly be balanced; but it does mean that the gravest dangers are involved in relying upon further reduction in the commodity value of the dollar for correction of the relative-price maladjustments which still impede recovery. A sound program must now undertake to bring about reduction of those controlled prices and wage rates which remain high rela-

tive to other prices. The problem of relative-price maladjustments must be worked out along the line of the present general level, if reasonable precautions are to be taken against a chaotic boom, wholesale dishoarding, and uncontrollable inflation.

There may now be little agreement on the merits of price-index stabilization as a permanent rule of monetary (fiscal) policy; but there would probably be a surprising unanimity among reputable economists on the proposition that fiscal and banking policy henceforth should not permit any further rise of prices generally. At all events, announcement by the Administration (with supporting congressional resolutions) of its intention to use all its powers to prevent a further rise in the level of prices is the first important step which can be taken to reduce uncertainty as to monetary conditions in the near future. With such an important beginning, we might move on afterward to more and more definitive rules, as political and economic developments permit.

To appreciate the danger of our present position, a moment's reflection should suffice: simply contemplate the political fate of any leader who, in the midst of the credit inflation now imminent, would try to stand in the way or to impose real checks. As a mob, we have probably learned much less than nothing since 1929; the long depression has only put us in the mood to draw and quarter anyone who would deny us the release of an exciting prosperity. And, incidentally, those political leaders who talk most about balanced budgets and sound currency would, by virtue of the magnificent simplicity of these nostrums, probably do least to check wholesale dishoarding and expansion of private credit. But a reasonable rule of policy, erected now, might save us where nothing else would.

19. In the writer's opinion, the same issue is, or rather ought to be, fundamental in the current controversy as to qualitative versus quantitative control of credit. Qualitative control not only implies avoidance of all definite, meaningful rules; but, while espoused by persons peculiarly hostile to government interference with private business, it also implies a much broader range of political interference and a less specialized conception of appropriate governmental function. Indeed, qualitative control of credit essentially amounts to political control over the *direction* of private investment. Control over the quantity of media, on the other hand, is consistent with the narrowest conception of the proper role of political control—with the narrowest definition of control of the currency. Those who argue for greater and more direct control of quantity by political agencies would argue quite as vigorously that the *allocation* of investment funds should be directed only by the freest competition—that this allocation should be entirely freed from the influence of Congress, the Treasury, any monetary authority, or any organization of bankers in the form of bankers' banks.

The so-called 100 per cent scheme was suggested, at least by its Chicago proponents, largely, if not primarily, with the notion that reform along such lines would serve to minimize the danger of increasing political control over the direction of investment, i.e., the danger, both of socialization of banking in its present form and of "financial planning" administered by organizations of private banks. From this viewpoint one may deplore the mass of legislation which has given special status to banking corporations and the development of many kinds of supervision and regulation (qualitative control) which has served to differentiate the obligations of banks from other private obligations and to facilitate their use as money. If a rigid separation could be achieved between the business of warehousing and transferring funds and that of mobilizing funds for lending and investment, the state might properly limit its regulation of the latter type of business to the provision of ordinary safeguards against fraud and the maintenance of competitive conditions in the investment markets.

The 100 per cent banking scheme has been characterized as socialistic, and advocates of quantitative control have been charged with the intention of turning the banking business over to politicians. While both observations are intellectually beneath notice, they might be countered, for purposes of vulgar debate, with the remark that most defenders of qualitative control are impliedly espousing syndicalist ideas and, for their own purposes, a corporative state. At all events, the task for serious students, here as elsewhere, is that of defining carefully the proper spheres for competitive and political controls and of discovering how each may best be implemented in its own sphere. If the 100 per cent scheme has any merit, it is largely that of directing attention to this problem in connection with the reform of a financial system which has acquired a functional complexity that renders useful analysis as difficult as it is important.

20. Congress would really be the administrative agency in any event. It could always revoke the powers of the monetary authority or nullify that agency's efforts to execute the price-index rule. Observance of the rule would require appropriate budgetary practice and thus would depend basically upon revenue and appropriation measures. The administrative function of the monetary authority might therefore be conceived mainly in terms of temporary devices for checking or ironing out small aberrations of the index. Its main responsibility, properly, would be that of giving advice and making recommendations to the executive and to the legislature with respect to the budget.

It may be interesting, if gratuitous, to note some features of fiscal practice under a properly executed price-index policy. The old perversity of fiscal changes would, of course, disappear. We should have to get accustomed—assuming continued increase in "physical production"—to the novel phenomenon of chronic budget deficits accompanied by declining interest charges or, at least, not accompanied by corresponding growth of the interest-bearing debt. (That this experience might induce widespread financial insanity is perhaps an argument in favor of a quantity rule.) The Treasury would systematically borrow when interest rates were high and reduce its interest-bearing debt when rates were lowest; in other words, it would consistently make open-market purchases of its obligations when their prices were highest and sell them when their prices were abnormally low.

Under either a price-index or a quantity rule, by the way, there would presumably be no justification for a complex structure of federal debt.

Treasury obligations might properly be confined to two simple forms, lawful money and consols or perpetuities (which would facilitate deletion of the usual textbook observations about benefits to future generations and probable service-life of public improvements).

21. It may be interesting to note that the whole argument of this paper might properly be developed with primary emphasis upon problems of government finance. With the growth of deposit currency and central banking, not only has monetary policy been left without substantial foundation in legislative rule and without adequate implementation but fiscal policy also has lost its appropriate orientation. Nominally, of course, it has been ordered in terms of the requirements of the gold standard—and it may be conceded that the prestige of gold has occasionally enforced some discipline in government finance. But the rule of maintaining convertibility or redemption has the obvious limitation of any legislative policy which is defined merely in terms of its end. There was no assurance that budgetary arrangements (or the behavior of the banking authorities) would actually be consistent with continued adherence to the rule—and even little prospect that blame for its violation would fall upon those really responsible. Whatever the other limitations of the gold-standard system (see n. 10), its administration, at all events, was left largely to the banking authorities, with only vague recognition that reckless accumulation of federal indebtedness might give rise to difficulties.

One consequence is the conspicuous absence, in both popular and academic discussion, of anything that might seriously be called principles of sound fiscal practice. (For eloquent testimony on this point, see the textbooks on public finance.) There are no accepted criteria for criticism; there is no real basis for intelligent public opinion and, thus, little opportunity for effective democratic control. Moreover, within the uncertain limits set by the requirements of the gold standard, there are indefinitely large opportunities for doing things backward in the field of government finance (as well as in banking)—and political pressures assure that these opportunities will be fairly well exhausted.

Just as the financial system is conducive to utterly perverse changes in the quantity of credit, so likewise does it lead almost inevitably to extreme perversity in fiscal changes. During periods of expanding profits and credit inflation, tax rates are reduced, expenditures increased, and long-term obligations retired (instead of being refunded and increased to permit the impounding of currency). In the face of declining production and employment, taxes are increased (especially the critical excises), expenditures are usually curtailed, and money is obtained by borrowing (instead of being created by the Treasury or released from previously accumulated balances). Moreover, little real comfort can be found in recent recognition of this perversity, for it promises only temporary, one-sided correction in the case of expenditures and, thus, perhaps greater ultimate confusion.

It may seem a counsel of sheer cynicism or of utter despair to suggest that all our established fiscal practices should be entirely reversed—and, as regards the possibilities of reform within our present financial organization, it is so intended. Sound fiscal policies are impossible (cannot even be defined) without precise and firmly established rules of monetary policy; but the early adoption of, or rapid movement toward, such rules is entirely feasible.

22. To assure popular approval, strong moral support, and thus political stability, it would be desirable, under a price-index rule, to employ an index whose changes would correspond roughly to changes in living costs for families of modal income. Some weight certainly should be given to this consideration; but, adding it to those mentioned in n. 11, one sees that the best attainable index must fall far short of what is desirable on this, or on any other, particular criterion.

23. *International Economic Relations*, pp. 96–98.

NOTES TO CHAPTER VIII

1. Alvin H. Hansen, *Fiscal Policy and Business Cycles*. New York: W. W. Norton & Co., Inc., 1941. Pp. ix+462. $3.75.

2. *Business Cycles* (New York, 1939), esp. pp. 1032–50.

3. The argument may throw some light on the origins of recoveries historically; but it seems trivial even on that score, as against the fact that deflation, beyond some extreme, must involve "negative elasticity of expectations" via political repercussions in monetary and fiscal policy.

4. At another point (p. 325) he says: "It is equally to be doubted that a realistic solution can be found in price reduction designed to bring about expansion of output in various separate industries. The individual industry could, indeed, afford to reduce the prices of its commodities if it could reasonably assume that it is confronted by an elastic demand situation. This, in point of fact, however, is usually not the case. . . . . This means that a price reduction will bring no increase in the dollar volume of sales, while at the same time the expanded output clearly results in some increase in the total money cost."

What is true here for industries taken one at a time may be (is?) very untrue for all or for a considerable number. Certainly, no group in position to control its own wages or prices can ordinarily advantage itself by price or wage concessions; they will usually find themselves far short of the ideal pure-monopoly situation. This, indeed, is the glaring problem of syndicalist organization. Given a pattern of fiscal compensation, all such groups (not to mention the rest of the community) might be better off if all made concessions. Competition would compel them, as a group of groups, to forgo the privilege of biting off their own noses; but without competition there apparently is no means of getting action in the common interest or even in the common interest of the monopolists themselves.

5. One perhaps should not begrudge Hansen the rhetorical device of criticizing theories instead of theorists; but his critical sallies are too largely directed at straw men. Rarely is it possible to identify any important economist with the views under attack. Thus advocates of relative-price adjustment are usually vigorous advocates of monetary and fiscal measures as well.

Few, if any, would pretend that lowering of rigid prices is a sufficient or, by itself, helpful means for stopping deflation. In any case, Hansen's difficulties here may perhaps be explained by his own penchant for overly simple explanation, which leads him to contrast his position with other views, falsely reduced to similar simplicity.

6. See my review of Hansen, *Full Recovery or Stagnation?* in *Journal of Political Economy*, XLVII (April, 1939), 272–76.

7. Chap. iii on "Monetary Policy in the Depression" makes no mention of devaluation. Following it is a chapter entitled "Fiscal Policy in the Recovery."

8. Where I refer to currency issue, many readers will prefer to read "borrowing from banks" and, where I refer to borrowing, to read "borrowing from the public," i.e., from individuals and nonbanking enterprises. The issue here does not mainly concern the merits of Hansen's proposals as against my own suggestions for banking reform and financial reconstruction (see my "Rules versus Authorities in Monetary Policy," *Journal of Political Economy*, XLIV [February, 1936], 1–30) [chap. vii in this collection]. For present purposes, currency issue is a clearer conception than borrowing from banks, since additional currency is rather certain to remain in banks, while bonds may not stay put, either physically or as net additions to banking assets.

9. G. Cassel, *The Nature and Necessity of Interest* (London, 1903).

10. See my "Rules versus Authorities in Monetary Policy," *op. cit.*, and *A Positive Program for Laissez Faire* (Chicago, 1934).

11. Hansen never tires of asserting that spending is not inflationary if there is involuntary unemployment. This fashionable dogmatism, while roughly valid under assumption of constant labor cost or rigid wage rates (waiving questions of "laws of return"), is untrue of a world where labor "categories" contain enormous qualitative dispersion and is grossly untrue in a world of one-way rigidity where rates are, in fact, highly responsive to upward changes of income, business earnings, and employment, from whatever level.

12. Zealous collectivists may welcome the atrophy and decay which this scheme promises for private enterprise; but they should be appalled by the wage-rate (minorities) problems which such demise of capitalism would bequeath to the new order. For conservatives, some bitter satisfaction may be found in contemplating the attitude of intelligent, responsible socialists toward powerful labor organizations in a society otherwise constructed to their taste.

13. It might be difficult to sustain always this maximum of monetary expansion under a stable-index rule—and easy to fall short of it if authorities were careful not to go beyond. Thus a practical argument can be made for accepting the rule of a negligibly rising index, rising at a minimum significant rate of, say, 1 per cent per annum. This would avoid the "dead-center" problem of the stable index, assuring the maximum of expansion under that rule by requiring just perceptibly more. I regret this apparent concession to the proposal to tax hoards; but the scheme at worst involves the only elegant

application of that proposal and thus promises good implementation of bad policy if political pressures force us to it.

14. This suggests a fatal weakness of schemes for supranational currencies or world currencies.

15. I am amazed that a person of Hansen's sophistication should assert (p. 125) that "even property taxes—and this applies particularly to rented residences—are, in large part, shifted by property owners to the general public." It would be interesting to see how novelties of capital theory and cycle theory might be employed to validate Seligman on this point!

16. It is rarely recognized that sales taxes and pay-roll taxes are probably far less regressive than are the important federal excises, levied as specific taxes (uniform over wide ranges of price and quality) and upon commodities of extremely low income elasticity.

17. Permit my recording here my irritation at Hansen's seemingly approving reference (p. 442) to the food-stamp plan. This scheme, possibly defensible as a temporary measure, represents, I think, utterly immoral political merchandising, whereby federal subsidy to producers (ultimately to landowners) is packaged and sold politically as poor relief, with indefinite possibilities of administrative patronage in the relative dispensations to different agricultural interests and sections.

NOTES TO CHAPTER IX

1. The proper tax form, as I shall argue elsewhere, is a holeproof personal income tax, with a high and stable basic rate, with a variable exemption level, and, of course, with extensive source collection.

It is interesting to speculate, in this connection, on how the democratic process would work if currency, instead of debt, were the residual element in fiscal policy or practice. Normally, of course, Congress makes appropriations and levies taxes, leaving the Treasury to cover deficits by borrowing, under generous, elastic, and routine authorizations, or to utilize any surplus for debt reduction. Suppose this practice were reversed, i.e., that all legislation regarding sale or purchase of debt (consols) were mandatory, like tax legislation, and that all deficits or surpluses were handled automatically, under broad, permissive, continuing authorizations, by issuing or retiring currency. It is arguable that, if issue powers were really confined to the government (i.e., with 100 per cent or ceiling reserves), this scheme would produce more responsible fiscal policy than the prevailing one.

What we are really proposing, of course, lies in between. There would be no borrowing authorizations save for consols; i.e., the Treasury would have no freedom or discretionary power with respect to maturities, and possibly none as to nominal interest rates. Subject to that limitation, however, and a mandate to stabilize a price index, the Treasury would have generous or unconfining authorizations for both currency issue and borrowing. Revenue surpluses or deficits would then determine the decrease or increase in the aggregate of currency and consols; while the necessities of price-level stabilization would determine changes in the relative amounts of currency and consols. Excessive expenditure relative to taxes would then reflect itself in the i ncrease of consols or, with an inordinate amount outstanding, in failure of a proper debt-reduction program. A mass electorate may be expected to understand the virtues of price-level stabilization and the need for conserving borrowing powers against the contingency of war or, during wars, against the contingency of very long war. It might, with a simple debt structure, recognize practices which jeopardized or sacrificed these objectives and effectively threaten the political future of leaders who indulged or espoused such practices.

2. These references to "maximizing," and others which follow, are perhaps polemic extravagances, for the "conditions" alone imply determinate amounts.

3. For merely monetary purposes, of course, open-market operations should be conducted with equities, not with money contracts at all. Only a collectivist, however, may intelligently offer this counsel of monetary perfection. With ultimate control lying in revenues and expenditures, the strong case for any open-market measures lies where there is an interest-bearing debt requiring some management in any case. There is little reason, in an economy where government is already surfeited with (misused) monetary powers, for admiring the collectivist state for its still larger powers.

4. It does not follow that debt should never be retired during prosperous years, though it certainly should be retired more slowly at such times, and not at all unless inflation is otherwise fully under control. If tax rates are properly sustained and increased during prosperous years, open-market operations may properly show a balance of purchases even at such times. In depression or deflation, debt retirement should reach its maximal rate, as part of a deliberate program of monetizing bonds. For the good future, retirement of our huge war and pre-war debt will be a continuous process at varying rates, not a matter of alternate forward and backward steps. There will be no more sense in sustaining the aggregate amount than there was in acquiring it in the first place. If our democracy again becomes responsible financially, our bonded debt will fall at least as rapidly after this war as it did during the twenties. Borrowing power must be carefully conserved, if only against the inflation contingencies of our next (first) total war. Unused borrowing power and a record of fiscal good faith (which it is still our opportunity to initiate) are now grossly undervalued relative to an army and navy; but I will lay my bets for the future on an America which protects internal unity and morale by real fiscal prudence.

5. The losses, of course, may properly be minimized by avoiding instability, i.e., by making stabilization measures really effective.

6. The captious critic will note here an exception to my general rule about maximizing interest rates!

NOTES TO CHAPTER X

1. See my note, "On Debt Policy," *Journal of Political Economy*, LII (1944), 356–61 [chap. ix of this collection].

2. To argue that price-index stabilization is a proper guiding rule of monetary-fiscal policy is *not* to recommend that an existing price level be

sustained or consolidated after radical, recent change. Indeed, the strongest case can now (1945) be made for gradual, controlled deflation and for a firm, political commitment to stabilize (after recent quality deterioration is undone, after direct controls are abandoned, and after monetary-fiscal policy has again made contact with the market) at or near our 1941–42 price level. A similar recommendation evidently has been made for Sweden by the "Myrdal Commission," which proposes that "those groups in the community which have suffered a reduction in real income during the war, owing to prices having risen more than incomes, will recover their former real standard, *not by an increase in the nominal money incomes, but by a lowering of the price level.*" (As reported in *Index*, September, 1945, p. 32.)

One virtue of the 1941–42 level is that, as an announced, accepted goal, it might enable us to sustain the present value of our money! Merely holding the line, now as in 1931–32, is a nearly impossible task. Besides, we should somewhat reverse the recent expropriation of bondholders, annuitants, and wartime money-hoarders, if only to minimize perversity in monetary expectations during future inflation dangers or wars. This achievement would be worth some cost in larger transitional unemployment; but no such cost is likely to be incurred—unless one assumes (absurdly) that strategic wage rates will go their own way regardless of monetary policy or monetary expectations. If our commodity-price level now is high relative to wage rates, adjustment should be made largely in the price level; and labor should be encouraged to demand and expect increases in real wages rather than in money wage rates during the next years. Monetary stabilization will probably remain a forlorn hope unless and until we are prepared not only to accept it firmly as a rule or principle of policy but also to establish in fiscal practice a basis for expectations that inflationary (and deflationary) aberrations, if not prevented, will afterward be reversed. The wise beginning would be deliberate, gradual reversal of our recent wartime inflation. At the least, we should make now an advance commitment to reverse any further decline in the value of money if such decline does occur.

3. Whether the increase involved in conversion to longer maturities and reduction of liquidity features should be regarded as more than nominal change of interest rates is a neglected question of definition. In any case, to raise yields on federal obligations, by making them less nearly equivalent to currency, is not, in any significant sense or measure, to raise the cost of capital for long-term private investment—save possibly for great corporations which, within narrow limits, may rival governments in the liquidity they can offer. Most current talk about fixing or controlling interest rates has, for me, simply no meaning, save as talk about varying the "moneyness" of governmental obligations. Surely our government could reduce its interest *payments* to zero, by monetizing its whole debt. Does anyone hold that such action now would lower the cost of capital funds for private firms? Low rates deriving from liquidity that only government with issue powers can give to securities may stimulate *governmental* investment, by making it seem irresistibly cheap in terms of quite misleading interest-burden calculations. How they promote private investment, save by creating expectations of in-

flation, I cannot see. Incidentally, one virtue of leaving a large amount of unsupported consols outstanding is that we might then discover empirically whether, panics apart, their yields could be lowered by increasing liquidity. In the financial good society, open-market purchase of consols would, by announcement effects, tend to lower their prices rather than to raise them.

4. Empirical evidence as to secular increase in the demand for money or liquidity is, however, a precarious basis for long-term policy. Trends in such demands cannot confidently be extrapolated from periods of extreme monetary instability and uncertainty into a long future of (proposed) highly stable money value. Rising mass incomes should increase somewhat demands for liquid reserves; but monetary stabilization, if achieved and sustained, would tend steadily to reduce such demands. The prospect of monetizing gradually our whole federal debt over a generation may thus be illusory, or anomalously dependent on the sustaining of much monetary instability and uncertainty. If so, the greater tax cost of bond retirement will be handsomely compensated by the greater monetary security that a smaller (increase in) money quantity will involve. The long-term possibility of monetizing bonds is, if real, a mixed blessing: it mitigates tax problems while aggravating monetary problems. The smaller the amount of money required in the future for monetary stabilization, the more adequate and powerful will be the proper, simple devices of fiscal stabilization. Certainly it is desirable that small changes in mass income taxes should suffice to produce large and prompt monetary effects. Indeed, the desirable public confidence in monetary stabilization is ultimately the prime instrument of stabilization; and every increase in such confidence would, *ceteris paribus*, be reflected in a lower demand for liquidity. On balance, therefore, one may hope that monetary stabilization and debt retirement will require a secular excess of revenues over expenditures.

5. Besides an average expectancy of "real" return (net real productivity), assets and equities, by contrast with consols, offer an inflation hedge which, in view of the asymmetry of political inflation-deflation expectations, people must be paid to forgo—unless property in assets and equities, and especially in "sunk" investment, is in turn becoming so differentially insecure and exploitable as to render our institutional system unworkable. This latter proviso perhaps suggests the distinctive reason for the recently low levels both of private investment and of interest rates.

6. One reason for the persistence of banking is our lamentable failure to develop proper institutions for mobilizing the savings of middle-income families. If legislatures and economists were more concerned about giving us good, small investment trusts and less concerned about making bank accounts and life insurance safe and salable, we might get a better structure of financial organization.

NOTES TO CHAPTER XII

1. I mean here not that the specialists have not been influenced, often inordinately, by recent attacks on monetary orthodoxy but that, even when

emancipated from narrow orthodoxy, they tend to think and plan like metallists and to stress inordinately the banking, as against the fiscal, process.

2. Granted eventual respite from political leadership, which, in both parties, preaches and practices the doctrine that (given the maximum amount of made-work in O.P.A. and in the other agencies of "direct" control) inflation is the best form of taxation!

3. Since the value of gold is so obviously a matter of fiat, it is amusing that "fiat currency" should remain an aspersive phrase.

4. The presumption against subsidies is properly a major article of the libertarian, democratic faith.

5. Much as one may deplore their joint apostrophes to "commodity agreements," which concession, if not designed merely to appease special interests, is a defeatist admission that powerful minorities should plan their particularist monopoly stabilizations against the likely failure of general monetary stabilization!

6. If the *Economist* latterly reflects responsible British opinion about postwar commercial policy and is not merely exhibiting a policy-construct designed for bargaining with us, the peace is already lost!

7. Historians will ridicule such simplistic notions about the "causes" of epochal events. They may sometime explain our monetary mistakes as merely a superficial aspect of profound historical or cultural trends. The long view of distant pasts is inevitably rather determinist, if only because the human mind insists upon imposing its own constructs upon reality. The short view of the piecemeal reformer may miss the forest in the trees, but it also avoids some delusions of misplaced concreteness; and, at least, it avoids that deadly sense of the unimportance of particulars which makes for cynicism and irresponsibility in matters where democratic discussion can operate. Indeed, the historian is in much the same intellectual mess as the total planner or revolutionary, i.e., he cannot conceivably know enough, even with hindsight, to justify his pretensions. The intellectual's total conception of what the past was is not much more credible than the radical's tale of what the future would be if his total scheme were imposed.

Learned readers will detect, here and elsewhere, that I have just reread Professor Hayek's "Scientism and the Study of Society" (*Economica*, IX, 267–91, X, 34–63, XI, 27–39—August, 1942, February, 1943, February, 1944); also that I have been reading Ernest Barker's *Reflections on Government* (London, 1942). I cannot forbear recommending these two works to anyone who sympathizes at all with ideas this essay seeks to popularize—but with warning that Barker, in a few passages, seems unwittingly to repudiate economic ideas which are indispensable to his general political position and, particularly, to mistake syndicalism for economic democracy.

8. One may here disrespectfully pay respect to a prevailing heresy, namely, that we may solve internal problems by merely fiscal tricks, without bothering about restraints upon internal trade. Monetary stabilization is a powerful and necessary means for facilitating individualist, competitive trading, among functional groups within nations as well as among nations themselves. It cannot bring order or peace into the contest of national

foreign-trade monopolies or into the affairs of a domestic society of syndi-cates. It cannot assure adequate or stable employment save in a nation of substantially free markets for goods and services—or of total collectivism.

9. For simplicity, it is assumed above that the internal price levels or in-come structures of other nations may be treated as given or as independently determined.

10. This point perhaps deserves further exposition for the lay reader. Assume that we know what price levels and wage levels will be in the vari-ous countries, as expressed in their respective currencies—dollars, pounds sterling, francs, marks, krona, lira, etc. The problem, let us say, is to fix ex-change rates (dollar prices of other currencies) in such a way as roughly to balance international payments, including payments for securities and debts which represent long-term capital movements. For simplicity, i.e., to avoid discussing relations among a multitude of currencies, let us use the pound sterling or English money as typical or representative of all foreign currencies.

Suppose now that an exchange rate of $4.00 per pound would afford balanced payments between America and all other nations if there were to be no American protective tariff. Clearly, then, payments would be far out of balance, i.e., our exports would exceed our imports (including long-term securities) at a $4.00 rate, if there were protective tariffs here. The $4.00 rate would be too high with our tariff system if it were appropriate without that barrier. Retaining protective duties, we should have to fix a lower exchange rate, say $3.00 per pound. At this rate of $3.00, it would be profitable to im-port many nondutiable or moderately dutiable commodities which it would have been unprofitable to import under free trade and a $4.00 exchange rate. Thus, other domestic industries would lose the "protection" of the higher exchange rate because some were inordinately protected by heavy import duties. Moreover, production for export would also be very adversely affect-ed. American goods which can be sold abroad, in particular quantities, at £1 will yield the American producers $3.00 per unit, instead of the $4.00 per unit they would have yielded without our tariff.

Thus, if we favor some industries with heavy import duties, we must in-jure other domestic industries, both many which produce in competition with other imports and all those which produce for export. Furthermore, the uniform protection of a proper exchange rate is conducive both to larger to-tal trade and to more efficient use of our national resources. And, viewed internationally, such protection is less exposed to arbitrary and inoppor-tune manipulation than is a miscellany of duties on particular imports—which duties are continuously exposed to political logrolling and pressure-group demands.

NOTES TO CHAPTER XIII

1 By William H. Beveridge. New York: W. W. Norton & Co., Inc., 1945. Pp. 429. $3.75.

2. *Social Insurance and Allied Services: Report by Sir William Beveridge.* Lon-don: His Majesty's Stationery Office; New York, 1942.

3. *The Economics of Full Employment: Six Studies in Applied Economics Pre-pared at the Oxford University Institute of Statistics.* Oxford: Basil Blackwell, 1944. Pp. vii+213. 12s. 6d.

4. "As a general principle it may be laid down that business competition must be free, not forced. If in any industry a strong tendency develops towards collaboration between independent units or towards their amalgamation, the part of the State should be, not to try vainly to stop that tendency but to bring it under control" (p. 204).

5. "If trade unions under full employment press wage claims unreasonably, maintenance of a stable price level will become impossible; wage determination will perforce become a function of the State. If the private owners of business undertakings under full employment set out to exploit consumers by organizing monopolies and price rings, or abuse their economic power for political purposes, or fail, with all the help of the State and in an expanding economy, to stabilize the process of investment, the private owners cannot for long be left in their ownership" (p. 207).

6. "It may be asked, what happens if the Government wishes to borrow and spend £100 millions and the public is not prepared to subscribe more than (say) £60 millions to the long-term or short-term issues 'on tap'? The answer, again, is simple. A deficit expenditure of £100 millions having been decided upon in the light of the general economic situation, the Government raises the balance of £40 millions through 'Ways and Means Advances' from the Bank of England. As it proceeds to spend the £100 millions, it increases the stock of the community's savings by £100 millions. These new savings will again have to be held in some form—in cash, deposits, bills, or bonds. Having spent £40 millions out of 'Ways and Means Advances' from the Bank of England, the cash basis of the banking system has been increased by that amount. The banks will not want to hold more than their customary ratio of cash against deposits. Thus they will, during the next period, again subscribe to the 'tap' issues. The public will not wish to hold all their new savings in the form of cash or bank deposits (these being determined by business turnover) and will also subscribe to 'tap' issues. The banks can subscribe to these issues only to the extent that the public are prepared to hold more bank deposits. If the public refuse to hold any of their current new savings in additional bank deposits, because their demand for cash is satiated, all the subscription to the 'tap' issues will come from the public and none from the banks. Bank deposits and bank assets will cease to expand.

"The essence of what has been said above is this: maintaining a stable rate of interest means, first, deciding what the rate of interest should be and, second, offering the citizens exactly what, in view of the thus determined rate, they are anxious to have. In practical terms, this means keeping long-term bonds and short-term paper on 'tap' and 'creating' additional cash or Central Bank money by borrowing from the Bank of England whenever 'tap' subscriptions are insufficient to cover the budget deficit. This does not mean inflation, because the very size of the deficit is decided upon as an antidote to the 'deflationary gap' which would exist in the absence of deficit. If, as may well happen, 'tap' subscriptions exceed the amount required by the government, this shows that the rate of interest offered is higher than is necessary, and should lead the government to lower the rate" (pp. 339–40).

7. For argument along these lines, see my "On Debt Policy," *Journal of Political Economy*, LII (1944), 356–61 [chap. ix in this collection]. One great

virtue of the consol form, by the way, is that it affords an excellent inflation barometer; its price changes reflect prevailing expectations as to the price level.

8. Alternatively, it may be regarded as a device for "proving" that interest-rate policy is inherently impotent, by contriving arrangements under which it has no meaning, i.e., arrangements whereby open-market operations would have only the negligible leverage of a call-loan rate.

It may be noted in passing that, in the United States, as an incidental virtue of generally bad debt policy, we are moving toward 100 per cent reserve banking, by making certain bond issues ineligible for bank ownership. Shortly, we may see special bonds carrying, with low interest rates and high liquidity, a "deposit-issue" privilege.

9. American extrapolators, however, should read Kaldor, especially par. 41, p. 385: "The available evidence points to the conclusion that with the long run rise in incomes, consumption rises more or less proportionately (cf. Clark, *National Income and Outlay*, ch. viii); the disproportionate rise in savings following upon an increase in incomes . . . . is a typically short-run phenomenon." [However, he goes on to say:]

"The most reasonable hypothesis for estimating savings out of available income in 1948 appeared to be to assume that for that part of the rise in real incomes which is due to long-run factors (i.e. the rise in productivity) savings rise in the same proportion as real income . . . . ; while for that part which is due to the elimination of unemployment, savings increase in a higher proportion. . . . . This assumption implies that in the long run the proportion of income saved varies, not with the amount of real income, but with the level of employment."

This is a clever restatement of a vulnerable Keynesian assumption about the facts of life; but I see less reason for accepting it than for accepting the cruder assumption. If it avoids danger of empirical attack, it is equally immune to verification.

10. If this is what is meant by "mature economy," namely, that business will no longer put its liquidity increasingly under call by banks, praise God for the attainment of adult discretion.

11. "The Minister introducing the Budget, after estimating how much private citizens may be expected to spend on consumption and on investment together under a condition of full employment, must propose public outlay sufficient, with the estimated private outlay, to bring about that condition, that is to say to employ the whole man-power of the country" (p. 31).

12. See, for argument on these points, my "Economic Stability and Antitrust Policy," *University of Chicago Law Review*, XI (1944), 338–48 [chap. v in this collection]; also a review of Benjamin Graham, *World Commodities and World Currency*, in *Journal of Political Economy*, LIII (September, 1945), 279–81.

13. "If buoyancy of the home market should cause British industrialists to neglect the foreign market, it would be necessary for the Government either to create sufficient inducements for private traders to export or itself to take a hand in the export business" (p. 211).

Index[1]

1 This Index was prepared by Mr. Raymond H. McEvoy.

345